D1388975

NEWTON RIGG COLLEGE
109572

THE  BOOK OF

TREE PLANTING AND *MANAGEMENT*

THE  BOOK OF

TREE PLANTING AND *MANAGEMENT*

KEITH RUSHFORTH

DAVID & CHARLES
Newton Abbot London North Pomfret (Vt)

British Library Cataloguing in Publication Data

Rushforth, Keith
The Hillier book of tree planting and management.
1. Tree planting 2. Trees, Care of
I. Title
634.9'5 SB435

ISBN 0-7153-8589-5

Typeset by Typesetters (Birmingham) Limited, Smethwick, West Midlands
and printed in Great Britain
by Butler & Tanner Limited, Frome and London
for David & Charles Publishers plc
Brunel House Newton Abbot Devon

Published in the United States of America
by David & Charles Inc
North Pomfret Vermont 05053 USA

Contents

The Hillier Gardens and Arboretum

The Arboretum was begun in 1953 when Sir Harold Hillier and his family moved to Jermyns from Winchester. Since its early beginnings the Arboretum has continually expanded both in its size and plant collections. Keen to secure both his life's work and the long-term future of the Arboretum, Sir Harold established a charitable trust in the mid-1970's and gifted the Arboretum to Hampshire County Council in 1977.

Since becoming responsible for the Arboretum, the County Council has always been keen to fulfil Sir Harold's objective of growing the widest range of hardy trees and shrubs in the temperate world. This has involved not just the purchase of further land to grow the plants, but also the creation of the necessary 'infrastructure' for running a 160 acre garden and arboretum which is open to the general public for most of the year.

To this end, substantial improvements have been made. Additional land has been purchased to accommodate the expanding plant collections, which today number some 36,000 plants covering 10,000 different types. This diversity is unique, as an equal blend of both species and cultivars can be found. Records of plants and their locations have been dramatically improved with the introduction of a computerised plant record system. This has not only benefitted the staff, but also professional horticulturalists, botanists and those visitors who should like to know what plants are growing at the Arboretum and where.

Situated between the Hampshire villages of Ampfield and Braishfield, 3 miles east of Romsey and 9 miles west of Winchester, the Gardens and Arboretum are open to the public from 10am to 5pm, Monday to Friday, throughout the year, and from 1pm to 6pm on weekends and bank holidays from March to mid-November. For further details telephone (0794) 68787.

Introduction

TREES include some of the most beautiful and useful of plants and it is the objective of this book to enhance the enjoyment of their beauty. The book is intended to provide pertinent information on the enjoyment, management, planting and replacement of trees, to assist people whether they are responsible for a single tree or thousands – from small gardens to parks to amenity societies.

Much time, effort and money is spent on the planting, tending and maintenance of trees, a lot is well-spent yet too high a proportion is misdirected. The trees may fail due to inadequate planting or lack of simple attention in the early stages, or the choice of species may not be appropriate to the site. In urban areas especially, too many butchered trees speak of species inappropriate to the location being planted or allowed to grow, or of right decisions not being taken when needed.

Chapter 1 is headed 'Why Plant Trees?' and discusses many positive aspects and attributes of trees in answering this question. **Chapter 2** investigates the factors which make the soils and the climate, and how these should affect the choice of species and management of the site. **Chapter 3** is concerned with getting the design of the planting correct from the beginning, with detailed discussion of aspects of planting design for woodland, parkland, parks and gardens, housing estates, factories, offices, hospitals, schools and the provision of shelter. **Chapter 4** is concerned with planting and establishing trees, to ensure that money spent is wisely and effectively used to achieve its purpose.

Chapter 5 looks at the care of existing and ageing trees, including effective and sympathetic tree surgery. **Chapter 6** considers the creative management of the trees, when and how to replace existing trees so that both present and future generations can enjoy trees on the site.

Chapter 7 discusses pests, diseases and disorders which may affect trees, how they can be recognised and what action should be taken. **Chapter 8** gives an indication of the cost of tree surgery and planting and relates to the aspects discussed in earlier chapters. **Chapter 9** contains a brief outline of English Common and Statutory law relating to trees and looks at problems which trees may cause, or be accused of causing, including subsidence.

The **Gazetteer** gives information on all the principal species, and many minor ones, grown in Britain. This includes an assessment of their value as amenity trees, the soils and conditions for which they are suited and any limitations or special advantages. The gazetteer provides flesh to the earlier chapters and will assist in the management of existing trees and the choice of new ones. This latter task is made easier by the provision at the rear of the book of twenty-four **lists** which give suggestions of suitable trees for many different site types or uses. A **bibliography** and **index** provide further details.

Acknowledgements
The text is based on a first draft prepared by Rodney Helliwell, and I would like to record my appreciation of this and gratitude for the many positive comments he has made on the text and also for the photographs he has provided. I would also like to thank John Davis for the excellent line drawings he has contributed.

1
WHY PLANT TREES

TREES contain some of the most majestic of all natural living beings. They can put us in awe with their sheer size and beauty, with the startling colours of their flowers or the brilliance of their autumn foliage. They provide homes for a host of animals and insects and are without parallel in the plant kingdom. They make the major feature in any amenity planting of substance and have a permanence which can span the centuries. The Psalmist used the illustration of a tree growing beside water to give the impression of richness, serenity and security, aspects which trees can provide in our lives today. Yet they are vulnerable to our whims and fancies. To give the full richness, beauty and joy to our lives, they need careful managing.

Trees are fundamental to many aspects of our lives. Without trees, life would be very different; timber would not be available for house construction or for the manufacture of paper, the landscape would be changed, with less scale, variation and shelter, even our diet would be more constrained! The reasons for planting trees will alter from site to site but the different attributes of trees can be discussed under a number of headings; obviously, in any given situation, only one or two reasons may be of paramount significance.

Amenity

Amenity considerations include all places where beauty rather than some practical product is the prime consideration in the planting. It therefore encompasses most planting in parks and gardens and some screening and forestry plantings. Amenity can be at two levels, viz. in the leaf shape, colour, texture and seasonal pattern of variation which are characters of individual plants and in the broad brush approach of landscape design. The two are not incompatible, but relate to the distance and perspective from which they are enjoyed. The features of a plant will influence its appearance and amenity worth.

Leaf Shapes and Sizes

The size of the leaves will affect the degree of shade produced, and therefore be useful in different situations. Very often large leaves, such as

possessed by plane trees (*Platanus*), tend to make for denser shade, giving a cool spot in a hot summer and creating a dense barrier of foliage, whilst small or pinnate leaves, e.g. birch (*Betula*) and rowan (*Sorbus*), produce a lighter, more dappled shade or make a screen which does not totally separate the two areas. However, some trees, especially beech (*Fagus sylvatica*) and conifers like yew (*Taxus baccata*) have small and very dense leaves. Leaf size also alters the appreciation of distance; a long narrow vista can be shortened by using a large leafed plant at the far end, whilst small leaves will give the appearance of the trees being more distant, and therefore make a space appear larger.

Leaves are normally green due to the chlorophyll they contain. Green is a very restful colour to the eye and should be the basic and commonest colour in any planting. Trees vary in the greenness of their foliage, ranging from very dark, almost black, greens, as produced by several evergreens, such as Portuguese laurel (*Prunus lusitanica*) or Monterey pine (*Pinus radiata*), to light and bright greens, particularly in the new foliage of most trees, like beech (*Fagus sylvatica*) or larch (*Larix decidua*).

Red, yellow and purple leaf colours come from carotine or carotinoids which are found in small quantities in most leaves. Selected plants or forms may have much higher percentages of these pigments and therefore have yellow foliage, as in *Robinia pseudacacia* 'Frisia' or golden forms of Lawson cypress (*Chamaecyparis lawsoniana* cultivars). Purple foliage, such as shown by copper beech (*Fagus sylvatica* forma *purpurea*) or some Japanese maples (*Acer palmatum* forma *atropurpureum*), originates in the same way, but from other pigments.

These foliage variants may be extremely useful in giving variety to a planting or vista; they can be used to ring the changes to prevent the scenery appearing just a mass of dull greens by introducing an element of change or surprise. However, like any surprise, they must not be used too frequently, else their very attribute becomes a hindrance. In a landscape setting, it is fair to say that purple is often grossly over-used, but in a garden arrangement, a greater element of purple can be justified. Purple foliage, like other leaf colours, tends to darken with age and few purple plants retain a bright colour during the summer months. One valuable exception is *Cercis canadensis* 'Forest Pansy', which retains a good foliage into August and then again when in autumn colour. Golds and yellows are more restful to the eye and can be tolerated to a greater extent. List 15 gives details of genera containing plants with purple foliage and list 16 those with gold or yellow foliage.

Blue foliage is caused by a waxy covering to the leaves. Most frequently planted in this group are some of the conifers, such as Atlas cedar (*Cedrus atlantica* forma *glauca*) or blue spruce (*Picea pungens* forma *glauca*), or some of the eucalypts (*Eucalyptus*); in each of these examples, the colour

1 Pleasant mature park with many trees

is most strongly developed on the young foliage, i.e. the foliage which has not had time to develop a tough protective layer of tissue and therefore is more likely to lose moisture. A similar effect is obtained from some very hairy plants, in which the thick coat of hairs appear silver, such as the underside of leaves of shrubs like *Senecio* 'Sunshine' or certain of the tree rhododendrons such as *Rhododendron sinogrande*. These colours, therefore, come from the covering of the leaves, not by any change in the leaves themselves. List 17 summarises the genera with grey, silver or blue foliaged species or forms.

Variegated foliage occurs when parts of the plant do not produce any green chlorophyll pigment or where parts have more of the yellow or gold pigments. Sometimes the cause is a virus interfering with the plant's metabolism, as is the situation with the spotted aucuba (*Aucuba japonica* 'Variegata') or variegated cherry laurel (*Prunus laurocerasus* 'Marbled White'); in other plants, it is genetic or physiological in origin. Similar effects can also result from the mis-use of herbicides! Generally, variegation caused by virus infections should be avoided, as most plant viruses will thrive on a variety of different plants and, apart from causing economic losses on fruit crops, also reduce the vigour of garden plants. List 14 details genera containing variegated plants.

Leaf colour often changes with the seasons. Most plants flush (i.e. make the new growth from the buds) a much lighter colour than that developed after a few weeks. Beech is one of the most attractive of trees in spring with foliage which opens a delicate light green. Other plants may flush with a purple foliage, e.g. *Acer platanoides* 'Schwedleri' , but soon assume a greener colour. More unusual is *Prunus virginiana* 'Schubert', in which the leaves start off green but become purple as they mature. List 18 gives details of genera with attractive non-green new foliage.

Many plants assume brilliant colours in the autumn season, providing one of the greatest colour displays. The season and soil have a strong influence on autumn colour, although some plants, such as Cappaducian (*Acer cappadocicum*) or paperbark (*A. griseum*) maples, are very reliable. List 13 details genera with outstanding autumn colour.

Different leaf types will also behave differently when they have fallen off the trees. Some such as those of magnolia (*Magnolia*), poplar (*Populus*) or willow (*Salix*) quickly rot down, leaving no more than the trace of the leaf veins by next spring, but others, such as beech (*Fagus sylvatica*), plane (*Platanus* × *hispanica*) and *Sorbus thibetica* 'John Mitchell', are very slow to decompose.

Flower Effect

Flowers come in a variety of sizes, shapes and colours. For a number of trees they represent the principal reason for planting, e.g. the Japanese cherry 'Kanzan' is spectacular in blossom but can scarcely be accused of outstanding beauty for the remainder of the year. Other flowers are more subtle, or create their impact not by their size or colour but by the fragrance offered, such as that produced by many limes (*Tilia*) or the blossom of may (*Crataegus monogyna*). Fragrance, like colour, is partly a question of personal taste and preference. Some smells only register with a proportion of the population, or sometimes what is sweet to one person can be unpleasant to another, especially if received as too strong a dose. List 6 gives tree genera with good flowers and list 20 those with fragrant flowers.

Fruit Effect

Fruit provides a further season of display. It is most prominent in the autumn, before or after leaf fall. Cherries (*Prunus*), however, ripen in June or July, whilst Hubei rowan (*Sorbus hupehensis*) or *Cotoneaster glaucophyllus* do not colour the fruits until late autumn. Fruit is sometimes a drawback in an amenity tree. Children throwing sticks or stones to dislodge conkers from a horse chestnut (*Aesculus hippocastanum*) can be a nuisance, as well as causing damage, or the fruits may make a squashy mess on the pavement. The location and likely form of the fruit should always be considered in regard to the location of the tree! List 7 gives trees with attractive fruits.

Habit and Bark

Bark becomes much more noticeable when the tree is leafless in winter, although some barks, such as the ruggedness of oak bark or the smoothness of beech, are apparent throughout the year. The silvery bark of some birches can be used to brighten the winter scene, whilst the flaking bark of planes or strawberry trees (*Arbutus*) gives quite a different effect. List 12 gives genera with attractive barks or winter twigs.

Habit is a very prominent aspect of most trees. The gracefully pendulous twigs of silver birch (*Betula pendula*) create a very different impression from the strict formality of a Lombardy poplar (*Populus nigra* 'Italica'), or the billowing crown of a mature sycamore (*Acer pseudoplatanus*). Habit also changes with the age and development of the tree. Two commonly planted examples are the 'Fastigiata' clone of hornbeam (*Carpinus betulus*) and *Prunus* 'Kanzan'. 'Kanzan' as a young tree has a stiff branch structure composed of a number of crossing shoots all pointed roughly at 45 degrees to the horizontal, but as the tree ages, the crown arches out and down, making a semi-pendulous mound. The hornbeam cultivar has a narrow upright crown when young, leading it to be much planted as a street tree; as it reaches the maximum height for the site (with hornbeam often around 15m), the top of the tree ceases making extension growth but the side branches continue, until eventually a rounded dome of radius 15m is formed. The eventual habit of a tree should be considered, although judicious surgery or a finite life for the planting means that over-riding importance need not be attached to what might develop in fifty years' time. List 5 details trees with narrow habits, suitable for confined locations or as street trees.

Landscape Planting

A plant's characters combine to give the beauty of the individual but in the context of a landscape planting the overall design must be considered.

Landscapes which please aesthetically have two basic attributes.

Firstly, they must have an element of unity or coherence in the layout. The various elements must conform to some relatively simple and usually obvious overall pattern, design or idiom. As an example, in mountainous areas the tops of the hills may be covered by rough grass or dwarf shrubs such as heather, the lower slopes with shrubs and trees, and the valley floor with small green fields and farms, where trees and large shrubs are restricted to riverine habits or shelter. This style of landscape has an essential 'rightness'; it fits the perceived pattern of natural vegetation and man's land usage, with dwarf plants and rough pasture on the exposed hill, and the vegetation becoming progressively taller at lower levels on the valley sides but with intensive agriculture on the rich valley bottoms. Such a landscape would be disrupted by the reseeding of the upper slopes with a bright green grass, the planting of trees (or the making of fields!) in geometrically shaped blocks across the hillside or allowing scrub to grow in the low-lying fields. Similarly, the deliberately designed landscapes of 'Capability' Brown or Humphrey Repton have a strong overall coherence; they are not merely a random collection of trees, lakes and lawns. On a smaller scale, a churchyard with mown grass, gravestones and a few yew trees, all relating to the church, has a simplicity of style which is almost invariably more pleasing than the random lines of cypresses, cherries and other formal 'ornamental' trees often found planted in municipal cemeteries.

The second basic attribute of an attractive landscape is that it has sufficient variety or detail to avoid being monotonous. The detail must not be allowed to obscure or contradict the overall design but must be consistent with the other elements in the landscape. In the churchyard example, the ground is likely to be uneven, the turf, although mown, will be rough cut and contain wild flowers, and the gravestones will not all be identical, although they will all be of some similar type of stone and be arranged in some recognisable pattern.

A good landscape scheme must combine these two elements of overall uniformity with an attractive and interesting variety. The temptation to produce a scheme which has a strong unifying element but which is so dismal for lack of detailed interest, flexibility or seasonal change, as often seen in landscape plans made by architects and some landscape architects, must be strenuously resisted, as must the opposite failing, particularly a fault of many horticulturalists, to err on the side of using an excess variety of plants, without achieving any cohesion to the design.

Scale of the Planting

The beauty of any planting scheme must rest upon the scale of the planting and the detail of the plants.

Scale consists of two complementary elements; these are the scale in relation to the totality of the area and scale in relation to features on the site.

The scale of the individual site refers to the way that the other plants or features relate to one another. In one sense, a tall or large tree always dwarfs a smaller one, even if the other tree is the second largest in the vicinity. Trees by their sheer bulk have a scale unmatched by other plants. Often if a large tree is removed for some reason, a smaller one which was previously unnoticed will suddenly dominate the scene. Scale in this sense is the sum of the individual features on the site. It will be created by a mixture of aspects of habit, foliage size, texture and colour and relative spacing or layout.

The scale of planting should, as a general rule, be bold and definite.

Within the limits set by practical constraints, the trees and groups of trees should be as large and as prominent as possible. There are, of course exceptions to this rule, for example where an open windswept effect is required or where there are attractive views to be retained or framed. Elsewhere, trees can normally be used to cover up to 50 or 60 per cent of the ground area without being aesthetically displeasing. If there are more trees than this, some open areas or clearings will be needed to provide light, air, visual change and to let more than just the boles of the trees be seen.

Tree planting in parks and large gardens is often on too small a scale to have the desired effect. Provided, however, that practical considerations concerning light to windows or open areas and physical obstruction are observed, there is comparatively little risk of planting being too dominant, and even if it is, or becomes so, the situation can be remedied relatively easily and quickly by removing some of the trees.

Trees can help to give unity to a landscape in a number of ways. They can provide a common theme in areas containing a wide range of activities or articles, such as buildings, signs, poles, paths, roads, vehicles, play equipment or people. They can fill the gaps between buildings and help to join together the separate elements in a landscape to form a coherent composition. They can also be used to mask or partly obscure unsightly objects, or those which do not fit in with the general character of the area.

In the use of trees in the landscape, those with ordinary green foliage will be found to be most useful, trees such as oak (*Quercus robur*), beech (*Fagus sylvatica*), ash (*Fraxinus excelsior*) or lime (*Tilia*). Trees with unusual or peculiar habit shapes or foliage style or colour will usually be less successful, sometimes even positively detrimental; as noted above, copper beech can be very attractive, but only in small measure.

In many landscapes the role of the planting includes the provision of variety. In some urban settings, such as the historic parts of many ancient towns and cities (and in rather fewer new city centre developments) the buildings contain sufficient variety (or are laid out in such a manner as) to create an interesting landscape on their own. Usually, though, further detail and subtle variation are needed in order to avoid monotony. Trees can be very successful in this function, some more so than others. For example, trees with delicate leaves, such as silver birch (*Betula pendula*) or species like rowan (*Sorbus aucuparia*) with pinnate leaves, and those species with fine slender twigs, e.g. weeping willow (*Salix* × *chrysocoma*), are more likely to be useful in breaking up a dense mass of amorphous buildings than trees with large or dense foliage and widely spaced stout shoots, such as Indian bean tree (*Catalpa bignonioides*) or paulownia (*Paulownia tomentosa*). Deciduous trees often show greater variation through the year than evergreens, although evergreens are often needed as a proportion within a design and usually will show their variations at different times from the deciduous trees. Flowers, fruit or autumn colour provide further detail throughout the year, although avoid creating visual confusion with too great a variety of trees.

In parks and gardens which are sufficiently large and self-contained to form their own landscape, there is more scope for the use of trees of different appearance, such as a group of columnar incense cedars (*Calocedrus decurrens*), a blue spruce (*Picea pungens* forma *glauca* cultivar, such as 'Hoopsii' or 'Koster'), a variegated tree such as *Acer platanoides* 'Drummondii' or variegated box elder (*A. negundo* 'Variegata'), or a weeping beech (*Fagus sylvatica* 'Pendula'). However, if the majority of the trees in the garden are of such unusual shape or colour, the effect will very often be disruptive, not harmonious. 'Normal' trees are essential to act both as a background to the unusual items and as a point of reference; the unusual items are then rightly seen as incidents within an overall design, rather than as a rag-bag of individually interesting trees.

Vegetative Versus Seed-Raised Trees

Vegetatively propagated trees are very valuable for a number of uses, expecially where a high degree of uniformity is required such as in an avenue or hedge, or where the chosen plant is one with larger or special flowers. Examples of trees invariably vegetatively propagated are the poplars (*Populus*), Leyland cypress (× *Cupressocyparis leylandii*) and many 'ornamental' species such as cherries (*Prunus*) or crabs (*Malus*).

However, vegetatively propagated trees can have a dulling effect by being too formal, except perhaps where such formality is a feature of the scheme as in an avenue. When only a single clone is used, there is an increased risk of a pathogen or insect pest causing a problem – with a range of plants the genetic differences which make the variation between individuals will often also show in differing resistance to or tolerance of diseases. If fruit set is an aspect of the plant's garden worth, there will often be a reduced set of fruit if only one clone is grown. In an attempt to overcome these problems with vegetatively propagated trees, Hillier Nurseries have selected half a dozen or so superior individuals of the following species. When they are propagated the budwood from these clones is mixed, so that any individual order is likely to be supplied with more than one clone present. The species involved are: *Acer platanoides*, *A. pseudoplatanus*, *Fraxinus excelsior*, *F. ornus*, *Prunus avium*, *Sorbus aucuparia*, *Tilia cordata* and *T. platyphyllos*.

In a garden context, a high proportion of the plants are likely to be of clonal origin. As the space enlarges, such as in a park or country area, seed raised plants should be more widely used, and vegetatively raised ones kept for any specially formal areas, or for plants selected on the basis of extra tolerance of certain harsh conditions.

Shelter/Screening

Shelter and screening can be major practical benefits of tree planting. The purpose of such planting is either to reduce the wind speed passing over an area or to separate an area from a noise or unsightly object.

Wind is both uncomfortable to humans and animals and damaging to many plants. The difference in feel and temperature between a windy site and a sheltered one is obvious to us. Equally, plants are affected by exposure and this can cause significant losses of yield in some agricultural or horticultural crops; for example, in a windy situation, the provision of suitable shelter may give an increase in yield from potatoes of twenty per cent or more (yet have no impact on the crop from a field of peas).

A solid barrier, such as a wall, will reduce the speed of the wind but the effect is short-term and limited to a few times the height of the wall. The wall deflects the wind, forcing it to go around or over the top of it and this increases its speed and creates eddies or turbulence. At around a distance of eight times the height of a wall, eddies start to bring the wind back towards the wall from the opposite direction, creating a zone of turbulence at a distance of between 4 and 8 times the height of the wall; in very windy conditions, the eddies may extend right back to the wall. Walls are, therefore, only of benefit to the plants growing immediately beside them, such as peach trees trained on a walled garden. They are ineffective at providing shelter on a larger scale.

The most effective form of shelter is not a solid barrier but one which will slow the wind down without making it go faster somewhere else. The ideal is a screen which is fifty per cent porous, i.e. half is solid and half is space in some even arrangement. Such a screen will have a significant effect upon wind speed for a considerable number of times its height, both downwind and upwind without creating back currents. The reduction in wind speed immediately behind a porous shelter belt will be less than that achieved within a metre or so of a wall, but will last for much further both downwind, and also for a distance upwind of the barrier. Species and planting arrangements for shelterbelts are given on pages 63–6.

Reduction of Windspeed with a 50% Porous Shelterbelt

Distance from Windbreak	*Percentage reduction in Windspeed*
5 × height of belt	50
10 × height	25
20 × height	10

Trees are very suitable for a sizeable shelterbelt, as they can make a belt of sufficient height to give useful wind reduction both at a distance and for taller structures. They can make playing fields better for playing on, a garden more attractive and productive, and make buildings easier to keep warm in winter, without having to be so close as to intrude upon the scene. Shelterbelts will also act to filter out dust and fumes, trapping the particles on the foliage. List 22 enumerates genera suitable for use in shelterbelts.

Screening

A screen can be used to separate two areas, or to block off an unsightly building from a vista in a park, or as a backcloth for planting.

When planning a screen, it is sensible to consider the height at which the screening is needed. In many gardens, a satisfactory screen between one property and the houses behind may only need to be 5–8m tall; in this situation, creating the screen out of species which will grow 40m tall is not logical, yet more screens in urban gardens are made with Leyland cypress (× *Cupressocyparis leylandii*) which will oblige by growing at a metre a year for 30+ years than any other tree! However, some other large growing trees can make very effective hedges with only a reasonable amount of maintenance, e.g. beech (*Fagus sylvatica*) or Western red cedar (*Thuja plicata*, especially the clone 'Fastigiata'). Also, it may take too long a time to create a hedge 5–8m tall without using fast, tall growing species.

Another aspect of screening is that a screen does not always need to present a solid wall of foliage to function effectively. A screen which draws the eye away from the unsightly object behind will often prove to be more pleasant than one which obliterates whatever is behind. The screen does not, therefore, necessarily need to be evergreen to achieve its planned function. The winter twigs of deciduous trees may be sufficient in practice to shut out the odious item, particularly if associated with something to the side which leads the eye in that direction.

A screen must be attractive. Very little is gained by the use of dismal bands of cypresses to 'screen' a factory building if the band does not break up the outline but stops at the limits of the factory walls and is in any case no more attractive than the building itself. To screen a large unsightly object the belt of planting must both be interesting in its own right and extend beyond the outline of the object.

Backcloth Planting

Backcloth planting is useful to show off a feature or another plant. The feature can be a modern sculpture, or the requirement may be to give the right lighting conditions for the enjoyable use of the bandstand. If the

2 *Street scene brightened by just a single tree*

backcloth planting is to highlight some seasonal foliage or flower colour, it needs to be chosen with the object to be highlighted in mind. Usually, dull greens are best for backcloth plantings, as they make a good background for most colours, such as the blossom of mock orange (*Philadelphus*) or magnolias (*Magnolia*). Bright and light colours, such as light green foliage, generally do not make good backgrounds. However, there are always exceptions; the golden foliage of many cypresses, such as *Cupressus macrocarpa* 'Goldcrest' or *Chamaecyparis lawsoniana* 'Lane', provide a good foil for purple foliage such as *Prunus cerasifera* 'Pissardii', or is it vice versa!

Noise

Noise is not reduced significantly by the foliage and trunks of trees; the actual amount of noise energy absorbed will cause a reduction of only a few decibels. To achieve a significant lowering of noise, some form of solid barrier is needed, either an earth mound or wall, to absorb or deflect the noise. Trees, however, are very useful on the 'out of sight, out of mind' principle; they will significantly reduce the apparent or perceived noise level. Combined with a solid barrier, such as an earth mound, they can be very useful.

Timber and Other Wood Products

Most trees are planted and felled for the value of their timber. This is not an aspect covered in this book. However, the timber value of parkland and even garden trees should not be ignored, as in the right circumstances the products can make a valuable contribution to costs, even if not a profit.

Most timber in the world is consumed as fuel wood and this will be the major market for garden or parkland timber. This is partly because of the species, shape or quality of the timber, which in many cases is likely to contain nails or other unwanted metal items, and partly because there is little else for which the branches (or cordwood) can be used (and parkland trees are usually very branchy). Also, the impossibility of removing the bole intact in many situations is going to dictate this market. Beware of trying to remove timber lengths if the ground is not firm or the access good, as the cost of repairing any damage to turf and tarmac paths may very easily considerably exceed the potential value of most butts. Species which may be worth removing intact are those with a value as veneer timber or which have very good quality wood, such as oak (*Quercus*) and walnut (*Juglans regia*). It is possible to cut butts on site into rough planks of a size which can be manhandled to a road. The value of the wood may sometimes be less than for the butt intact but in some circumstances the use of this technology may be more profitable.

In some parkland situations, it may be desirable or appropriate to leave the felled timber lying where it is, either sawn or carved to make seats or play items, or to decay naturally, providing a home and food for wildlife. Brushwood and bark can be chipped, rather than be burnt, and the chippings used either as a mulch or for surfacing paths or play areas.

Soil Stabilisation and Improvement

Trees can be very useful for binding soft soils together. Willows (*Salix*) and alders (*Alnus*) are especially useful on wet sites; other species can also be valuable. The presence of trees on a site tends to lead to an increase in the soil stability and, except on certain soil types, an improvement in the soil structure and the recycling of nutrients. The depth of rooting and the annual cycle of leaf fall (even from 'evergreens') provides a regular source of material for earthworms, insects, fungi, bacteria and small mammals to feed upon. In most situations this will lead to a slow build up of the soil fauna and flora, which in turn leads to an improvement in soil structure.

Some evergreens, such as spruce (*Picea*) and hemlock (*Tsuga*), produce leaves which are less palatable to earthworms and these can lead to poor soil structure.

Wildlife

The wildlife value of trees, woodlands, parks and gardens is immense and deserves serious consideration. Wildlife ranges from birds and the picturesque grey squirrel (beloved of the public but the cause of immense damage to trees in certain circumstances) to aphids, caterpillars and other insects, to other plants and fungi. All these living items are worthy of consideration, but not all are welcome in each particular area of a park or garden. They are all mutually dependent to some extent. Blue tits cannot raise their young without a sufficient supply of caterpillars on which to feed them. The squirrels need the nuts and shelter of the trees for food and breeding territory. Woodpeckers need decaying trees to provide nesting sites, anvils on which to open hazel nuts and wood-boring grubs to seek out. Even the honeydew which falls from many broadleaved trees is an important source of food for ants and collected by honey bees.

When considering trees from the aspect of wildlife, it is important to bear in mind the requirements of the wildlife. Planting a single birch is unlikely to influence the number of siskins (which feed on the nutlets during the winter) – to maintain a pair of these one would need an acre of birchwood. However, a single oak or birch may offer a home to sawfly larvae, or fungi, and will serve as a food source for passing siskins or other birds.

Much is made in some quarters of the need to plant native trees; sometimes too much. Certainly in Sites of Special Scientific Interest, to introduce foreign trees would be an act of vandalism. Elsewhere, there are also many places where the quality of the natural wildlife suggests that native trees, or a high proportion of them, should be used, to continue the existing balance of wildlife. In parks, gardens, and many other areas, however, the planting can unashamedly be wider ranging in the choice of species.

By planting exotic trees, the range of possible habitats and food sources is enlarged. Many songbirds are able to breed more safely and earlier in the spring because of the extent to which exotic conifers, such as Lawson (*Chamaecyparis lawsoniana*) and Leyland (× *Cupressocyparis leylandii*) cypresses, are planted, providing evergreen sheltered nesting sites safe from marauding cats. Other trees such as some rowans (*Sorbus*) and cotoneasters (*Cotoneaster*) ripen their fruits at a later date than those of native species, thereby providing a larder which lasts into the winter. Many others are of less value to wildlife, either because they are not as palatable, or else because our native (and exotic) wildlife has not awakened to their potential; often, it is because they are less chewed that exotic plants have a higher amenity potential. List 21 gives a résumé of the genera which can have a significant role to play in provision of food or shelter for wildlife.

Food

Apart from the value to wildlife, trees can also offer a food resource to people. Unlike orchards, parkland trees are scarcely likely to provide a major source of nutrition but can offer an extra freshness and a sense of purpose in woodland walks. The foods which can be obtained from amenity trees include nuts from hazel (*Corylus avellana*), sweet chestnut (*Castanea sativa*) and walnut (*Juglans regia*), fungi such as the choice truffles or mushrooms, and nectar for honey bees from many flowers. The leaves of Chinese mahogany (*Cedrela sinensis*), which is occasionally planted, are eaten as a spring vegetable in China! All of these food items should be treated with caution, as similar items can be very poisonous; this includes the honey from certain plants, such as some rhododendrons.

Educational and Historical

Trees can be very useful in an educational context. The lessons can range from the simple teaching of how plants and animals are mutually dependent, through pure botany to teaching aspects of social history, such as how our predecessors lived. The historical timespan is, perhaps, more easily appreciated when standing beside a tree which was a seedling before William the Conqueror won the battle of Hastings. Ancient trees act as reminders from the past, bridging the gap of passing generations. Trees can also be planted as historical records for future years.

In conclusion, there are many good and varied reasons for planting trees.

2

ASSESSING THE SITE AND THE TREE

THE success of any tree planting will depend upon the correct assessment of the site conditions and on matching the appropriate trees to the situation. The local site conditions will include natural factors of climate, soil and land form, and special features such as salt spray in coastal regions. The site conditions, however, also include the effect of man, his animals and buildings upon the trees. All these aspects need to be considered before embarking on a tree planting scheme. In many ways they interrelate, e.g. the windiness of the climate and the topography combine to make the site exposed.

Climate

Climate is a combination of temperature (including winter cold and frost), sunlight, rainfall, humidity and exposure. As these factors can combine in a number of different ways, the world has a multiplicity of different climates. The coverage of this book is of the temperate regions of the world, with special reference to the British Isles and further discussion will be limited to the impact of the different factors which make up climate within the temperate zones.

This section first discusses the factors which constitute climate and how it affects the growing of trees, and then applies this information to the British scene.

Temperate Climates

Within the temperate regions, two main subdivisions of the climate occur; these are continental and maritime climates.

A *maritime* climate, such as that experienced over most of Britain, is one which is dominated by the proximity of a nearby ocean. As the winds blow off the large body of water, they remain cool, are generally strong, and pick up a large quantity of moisture. When they meet land, the wind is forced to rise to pass the landmass; this causes it to cool (due to the air expanding) and cloud forms, leading to rain. Because the wind blowing off the sea is cool, it does not have to rise very high before it drops below the temperature at which most plants grow. Also, in maritime climates, the winter weather is less severe, due to the sea remaining warmer than the landmass, and therefore heating the air as it passes over it. Air blowing off the ocean can give mild periods, even in winter, and cold ones in midsummer. A maritime climate, therefore, is generally mild, changeable and damp, with long spring and autumn seasons.

Under a *continental* climate the land heats up quickly in summer and cools down rapidly in winter. Great differences between summer and winter temperatures are experienced, with only a very short period of spring and autumn. The wind (which usually is less strong anyway) blows off the landmass and therefore is dry. Plants from continental climates are adjusted to an abrupt change between cold winter and hot summer and are often caught out by the constant switching in a maritime climate such as Britain from winter to spring to winter to summer and so on within the space of a few days.

Temperature often is a limiting factor in the suitability of a tree for a given climate. Temperature controls the rate of all biological processes, of which a tree's metabolism forms a part. Trees function within a fairly limited range of temperatures. At low temperatures, life slows down, eventually stopping if the temperature drops too low. The minimum temperature at which 'growth' is reckoned to occur is 6°C (42°F). Some plants, bulbs in particular, are obviously making growth when they push the new leaves up through the snow. However, the use of a minimum temperature does allow an estimate of the length of the growing season to be made; the growing season is defined as the number of days with a mean temperature above 6°C.

As the temperature falls, the rate of a plant's metabolism will slow down, eventually stopping when the temperature drops below that which the tree can tolerate and it dies. Plants vary in their abilities to tolerate temperatures. One way of expressing the need of a species for warmth is to express its growing season requirement in day-degrees; this is the sum of the number of days when the temperature is above 6°C multiplied by the average temperature above 6°C. A plant which has a high heat requirement will therefore need either a longer growing season in cool conditions, or a short hot one. (Within the temperature range in which trees grow, a 10°C rise in temperature will double the rate of a chemical reaction, and therefore indirectly the rate at which plants metabolise.)

Tolerance of winter cold is partly under genetic control and partly a physiological hardening process.

The presence of an element of genetic control of winter cold tolerance means that individuals in a population, or whole populations within the species, are likely to show different tolerances. These tolerances can only be ascertained by trial and error. For some tender plants, just one or two plants out of a batch of seedlings may prove hardy, or a new seed introduction from a different part of the plant's range may be found to be much hardier (or less hardy) that the previous introductions. This highlights the advantage of raising plants from known sources. Eucalypts raised from home collected seed are likely to be a better bet than those raised from Australian seed, but somebody has to be the first to introduce the hardy strain. Some plants tend to be very precise in the amount of winter cold they can survive, others show much greater variation within populations or across the range of the species. Different species growing together at the same place may vary enormously in their hardiness.

The individual planting scheme will dictate whether there is any room for trying trees of species or origins whose winter hardiness is not well documented. In a park or garden, the room for experimentation is usually greater than when landscaping a housing development or creating a shelterbelt, but in any situation, no more than a small percentage of the trees on a site should be of unknown hardiness.

The physiological hardening of plant tissues appears to be a response either to cooler nights or to shorter daylength in autumn (or a combination of both) which lead to changes in the internal constituents of the cells. Again, plants vary in the rate at which they harden their tissues and their ability to withstand unexpected conditions.

Frost can cause devastating damage to some plants, but only rarely affect others. The effect which a frost has on the plant's tissues will depend upon the plant species, the season of occurrence and severity of the frost and the conditions of the thaw. Some species will show damage at any stage of their growth. For instance, the leaves of a paulownia (*Paulownia tomentosa*) will blacken overnight if subjected to even a fairly light frost, whereas the same frost will leave the leaves of a sycamore (*Acer pseudoplatanus*) unaffected.

Frosts in late spring and early autumn are not predictable. The frequency of such frosts varies from site to site but because the plants are making new growth in the spring, or have not fully hardened the growth in the autumn, the tissues are much softer and the likelihood of damage greater for a given frost.

Susceptibility to spring frost damage is particularly a feature of trees from continental climates. Trees from such climates often are misled into making growth too early in the year during a warm period in winter when planted in a maritime climate. However, spring frosts can affect native species as badly, if not as regularly, as they affect some exotic ones. English oak (*Quercus robur*) is occasionally defoliated by spring frosts (although the first flush of foliage is much more often eaten by one of several insects) and ash (*Fraxinus excelsior*) more regularly; late flushing individuals of ash have been selected (see page 16) to overcome this problem. Species like birch (*Betula*), however, are much less likely to suffer from spring frosts, except for some of the exotic ones.

Sunlight

The amount of sunlight available on a site is partly a factor of the climate of the country and partly of site conditions. The total available sunlight will be a climatic factor, but the amount actually available to the tree will depend upon other factors, such as topography and other plants.

Sunlight is important as it is the primary source of energy for photosynthesis. The strength of the sunlight affects the rate at which moisture is lost from the plant and also the soil; shady conditions are always relatively humid for this reason.

Some plants also need sunlight to effectively ripen the wood; a number of trees from continental climates are not fully hardy in the United Kingdom because the current season's growth does not ripen properly in the prevailing relatively low light levels, although withstanding much colder winters elsewhere; examples include crêpe myrtle (*Lagerstroema indica*) and honey locust (*Gleditsia triacanthos*), which although hardy in southern Britain do less well than might reasonably be expected. Equally, there are some trees which naturally grow in misty regions of the world and which are much hardier in Britain than a comparison of temperature records might imply, e.g. monterey pine (*Pinus radiata*) or *Pinus patula*.

Daylength is a very important aspect of the climate. Many plants use this to regulate their growth cycles. The best common example is the florist's chrysanthemum which will only start to produce flower buds in response to shortening days in the autumn; to produce chrysanthemums all the year round, the plants are subjected to a daily blackout to simulate late summer. Many trees, however, also use this regulatory mechanism; moving some birch species more than a few degrees south can cause them to think autumn is coming at the first sign of the evenings drawing in in July, with a deleterious effect on growth.

Rainfall

Rainfall provides the majority of the water supply used by plants; the exceptions are plants growing in wet flushed soils, such as below springs and at the sides of streams, and those in regions of the world where fogs or haars are a frequent phenonomon. The tallest tree in the world, the coastal redwood (*Sequoia sempervirens*) of California, comes from a region where summer fogs provide a substantial part of the water supply during an otherwise dry season.

Trees rarely flourish in regions where the total annual rainfall is less than 250mm (10inches) and do better where it is four or more times as much. But the season during which the rain falls can be as important as the total. The ideal situation is one where the rain falls relatively evenly throughout the year (with, perhaps, a preponderance in the summer).

The energy in the sunlight falling on a unit area can be equated to the depth of water it would cause to evaporate and this is roughly equivalent to the potential loss through evapo-transpiration from the leaves. In Britain, potential evapo-transpiration is very small during the winter months (when many trees are leafless anyway) but is equivalent to 25mm (1inch) of rain in April and September, 50mm (2inches) in May and August and 75mm (3inches) in June and July. When the rainfall in any summer month does not equal or exceed these quantities, a soil moisture deficit is accumulated. If there is spare moisture in the soil it will be used, but when this is exhausted the plant must start to take steps to conserve moisture, or die. The maximum soil-moisture deficit which can be accumulated in Britain in a rainless summer is equivalent to 300mm (12inches) of rain. This deficit is normally made good during the autumn and winter. However, some soils are too porous or shallow to hold such a large quantity of water within the zone which is used by tree roots.

The potential evapo-transpiration figure is important when considering watering. If a general system is being considered, it should be designed to be capable of applying up to 25mm of water per week over the area to be watered, i.e. replacing the most that can be lost; there is no benefit in the system being able to apply several times this amount per week, as the excess will just be wasted. When watering newly planted trees, a similar amount needs to be applied to the root spread of the tree.

Variation of Effect of Climate Across Britain

On a regional scale, it is climate which dictates which trees can, and cannot, be grown. Great Britain is fortunate in having a climate which, for all its unpredictability, is relatively moderate. This allows plants from countries as diverse as Siberia to South Africa and Algeria to Argentina to grow alongside each other. There are, however, differences across the UK which mean that different plants flourish in the east, or north, than thrive in the west or south.

The west of Britain has a climate which is milder in winter and cooler in summer than the rest of the country. The major influence in the climate here is the moisture laden winds blowing off the Atlantic ocean; they bring cloud and rain, and also give a lower level of incident light. Western Britain, therefore, is well suited to plants which cannot tolerate extremes of hot or cold but can grow in relatively low ambient light levels. The western fringe of Britain also has a lower risk of late spring frosts.

The east of Britain by comparison has a less strongly maritime climate. The amount of rainfall drops off from west to east and in eastern and central Britain there is a deficit of rainfall over evapo-transpiration in

3 Walnut tree shaped by the wind in N Cornwall

summer. The climate of eastern Britain also suffers from far more days of frost, with most of eastern and central Britain having more than fifty consecutive frosty days per annum.

Where the east does benefit, allowing different plants to be grown, is in the incidence of sunlight. The lower rainfall is correlated with less cloud and more sunlight. This allows some trees from a continental climate to flourish, when they are scarcely as thrifty in the west. Examples include species such as velvet ash (*Fraxinus velutina*) and lilac (*Syringa*). Another way in which the east benefits is in the more regular cold periods. The example of some plants using daylength for flower production is given above; others use the number of days below a minimum temperature as part of the regulatory mechanism before opening the flowers. Such a plant is forsythia (*Forsythia*) whose flowers will only open in a massed display after certain cold period requirements are met; these are frequently met in eastern Britain but only rarely in the west, therefore the display from forsythia is comparatively poor in the southwest of Britain.

Although the greatest impact upon the British climate is the west-east trend in rainfall and number of frosty days, there are significant effects on the north-south axis.

Southern Britain has a much warmer growing season, with most of the area south of a line drawn from the River Mersey to the Wash (except where the altitude cools the climate such as in inland Wales or the

Cotswolds) experiencing between 2,500 and 3,000 day-degrees during the summer, compared to an average of around 2,000 over much of the rest of the country. This allows many trees from Mediterranean climates and other warm areas to grow, or grow better than they will further north.

There are some plants, however, for which the growing season in southern Britain is too warm and these flourish better in the cooler north. These include some of the silver firs (*Abies*) and rhododendrons (*Rhododendron*) which need careful siting with regard to moisture and exposure in the south but will thrive in most situations in the north.

These effects across mainland Britain can be illustrated by a few examples.

Sitka spruce (*Picea sitchensis*) is planted in larger numbers than all other species put together (due to its pre-eminent use in forestry). It is native to the coastal areas of Pacific northwest America from Alaska down to northern California. With one small exception, it is only found within fifty miles of the sea in a region where the climate is moist and equable. It grows well in the western parts of Britain, but not at all well in central and southeastern England, where the climate is drier. Trees from the southern part of its natural range tend to get going earlier in the season and can grow rapidly, but they are also very susceptible to late spring and early autumn frosts and so are unsuited to areas where such frosts are likely, although they will grow there. Plants raised from the northern end of Sitka spruce's range, from Alaska, are hardy throughout the British Isles but grow more slowly; they are only comparable in growth rate in areas where frost damage debilitates the more southerly origins. In British forestry, the seed for most plants of Sitka spruce used came originally from the Queen Charlotte Isles, off northern British Columbia, as this provenance is hardy and relatively fast growing, making a practical compromise between rate of growth and hardiness.

Corsican pine (*Pinus nigra* subspecies *laricio* or var *maritima*) mirrors Sitka spruce in the parts of the country in which it will flourish. It will thrive in lowland southern Britain, also in the warm sunny climate at Culbin on the Moray Firth. It will not grow, however, on cooler sites and the best development is on those sites which have a warm growing season with more than 2,750 day-degrees. On the cooler sites, the tree is suceptible to a fungus, *Brunchorstia destruens*, which kills the foliage and causes dieback of shoots, eventually killing the tree.

Sycamore (*Acer pseudoplatanus*) has become ubiquitous throughout the British Isles, from the windswept Orkney islands to Cornwall in the southwest, although it will make a grander tree in the moister northern and western climates. Following hot summers in the south and southeast of England, it is susceptible to sooty bark disease caused by the fungus *Cryptostroma corticale*; this disease is unknown or of very minor significance outside the southeast, and even there only causes damage in and immediately following hot summers.

Tree of Heaven (*Ailanthus altissima*) shows a marked preference for a hot climate; even in southern England, it does not come into leaf until well into June. It does not thrive in northern or northwestern parts of the country, although growing very happily in places such as New York or Beijing (Peking) with much colder winters than in Britain.

Soil

The soil is the medium which supports the tree and provides the water and nutrients essential to survival and growth. It is therefore very important. However, unlike climate, the soil does not dictate the choice of species to anything like the same extent. Yes, some soils require the trees which will grow on them to have certain characters, but apart from this the effect of the soil is more on tree vigour, rather than species.

The function of the soil, as far as the tree is concerned, is threefold. It is to provide the nutrients and water which are absorbed by the roots, and to support the tree.

A tree remains standing in a gale because of the volume of soil which is in contact with the fine roots. The main roots serve to keep the smaller roots in contact with the trunk. The root spread of a tree cannot be precisely estimated but as a very rough *working model* the roots can often spread with a radius of *up to* one to two times the height of the tree. Thus for a 20m tall tree, the roots may spread up to 20–40m in any direction; the actual spread will depend upon the nature of the tree species, the rooting conditions and a measure of chance. With the roots penetrating on average to a depth of 60–90cm, potentially the roots of the 20m tall tree cited above could be in contact with between 1,000 and 4,500 cubic metres of soil! This is sufficient to keep the tree standing in all winds, provided the roots remain intact. Generally, the reason that occasional trees blow down is because the roots are decayed, and therefore no longer able to keep the trunk in contact with the soil. Less often the cause is that the soil has been made plastic due to excessive rain and only in exceptional winds are healthy roots likely to break.

The provision of nutrients and water to the tree will depend upon the make-up of the soil and the availability of water and nutrients to the tree's roots. In some soils, an induced nutrient deficiency may arise because the nutrient, though present, is not in a form which the tree's roots can absorb. For example, nitrogen is one of the main plant nutrients; it is also the principal gas in the atmosphere, but gaseous nitrogen is in a form unavailable to plants.

The physical components of the soil are mineral particles of sand, silt and clay, derived from the breakdown of rocks; the soil may also include larger particles, or stones, but apart from occupying space, they make very little direct contribution to the soil. Sand is just comfortably visible with the naked eye, whilst silt and clay particles are very much smaller. Soil also contains organic matter.

Sand particles will fit together badly leaving empty spaces between the grains. This allows for good drainage and lets air circulate freely through the soil. Even when wet, though, sandy soils hold onto very little water and these soils will dry out very quickly. Sand grains have a small surface area in relation to their size and consequently they have only a limited capability to hold onto nutrients, which are thus easily washed out of the soil. This makes sandy soils essentially ones of low fertility.

Clay soils are composed of minute particles. These fit very closely together and have large surface areas onto which nutrients and surface water can be held. Because of the tight fitting of the particles, there is little space for the circulation of either water or oxygen through the soils; consequentially, drainage is very slow and poor and most plants find rooting in clay soils difficult or impossible. Also, when a clay soil dries out, it can be difficult and slow to rewet. Clay soils generally contain a good supply of nutrients and the problem can be to make these available for plant growth.

Silt particles are smaller than sand and are more similar in character to clay particles. Soils derived mainly of silt particles are usually very fertile, as they hold onto large quantities of nutrients and water, whilst permitting adequate drainage and exchange of gases. Some very silty soils can, however, have a poor structure and be poorly drained.

The ideal soils are loams composed of about fifty per cent sand, thirty per cent silt and twenty per cent clay particles, which gives a good combination of water and nutrient holding capacity, with drainage and aeration. Organic matter is also needed in the soil to keep it in good condition. Soils with increasing amounts of sand are sandy loams or sandy soils. Soils with higher proportions of clay or silt particles are clay loams or silty loams. Lists 1, 2, 3 and 4 give details of trees suitable for several difficult soil types.

Nutrients

The soil has to provide most of the nutrients needed by the tree. Half a dozen elements are needed in relatively large amounts and are called major or macro-nutrients, whilst some others are required in much smaller quantities and are termed trace elements.

The macro-nutrients are nitrogen (N), phosphorus (P), potassium (K), calcium (Ca), sulphur (S) and magnesium (Mg), as well as carbon (C), oxygen (O) and hydrogen (H). Shortage of any one of these is very damaging to growth, but an excess can also kill. The letter in parentheses after the nutrient is the international chemical abbreviation and is used to describe the contents on fertiliser packets.

Nitrogen is needed by the plant for the formation of proteins, which are essential for growth. Most nitrogen is present in the soil in the top 10cm (4in). Phosphorus and potassium are both needed for cell division and for the ripening of fruits. Potassium is very soluble, and therefore easily lost by leaching from many soils, as are nitrates. Phosphorus is much less soluble, and its very insolubility in some soils can create an artificial shortage, as far as the plants are concerned. Calcium is needed by all plants for the cell walls, and sulphur is used in root development and as a component of proteins. Magnesium is an essential constituent of chlorophyll (which traps the energy in sunlight as part of the process of photosynthesis). Carbon, hydrogen and oxygen are needed in large quantities to make all organic compounds. Carbon and oxygen come from carbon dioxide in the air and are absorbed by the leaves, and hydrogen comes from water.

Trace elements are required in very small quantities; for example, molybdenum (Mo) is only needed in the plant tissues at a concentration of one part in one hundred million, and may be fatal if more than ten times this amount is present. Molybdenum is important in the use of nitrate and nitrite forms of nitrogen. Iron (Fe) is essential for the manufacture of chlorophyll, boron (B) for the uptake from the soil of calcium, and zinc (Zn), manganese (Mn) and copper (Cu) in the formation of enzymes and proteins.

The supply of nutrients to a plant depends upon their presence in the soil in a form which the plant can absorb. Roots can only collect nutrients if they are in a water solution. Some nutrients are only available to plants between certain pH levels. Phosphorus may be plentiful in calcareous soils, but most of it is insoluble; bonemeal will not add much usable phosphorus to such soils, although it is a satisfactory way of adding phosphorus to acidic ones. Plants differ in their capability to extract nutrients from the soil at various pH levels and therefore some plants can only grow at certain pH levels. Others may naturally be found in areas where a certain nutrient is scarcely available; if planted in a soil where that nutrient is abundantly available they may be poisoned by their inability to *not* take it up – rhododendrons and calcium is one such case. Generally, a pH of 6.5 is optimum for nutrient availability and for uptake, except for certain plants for which a different pH may be better, e.g. a lower pH for members of the Ericaceae.

Rooting Depth

The depth to which a tree's roots can penetrate the soil will affect both the potential stability of the tree and also the quantities of water and nutrients upon which the tree can draw for sustenance. Trees are capable of growing on very thin shallow soils, such as over a rock formation close to the surface where the depth available for rooting may be only 15cm (6in) or so, as well as growing on much deeper soils; however, the tree with the shallow surface root system is not likely to be as stable as one with a deeper, if less widespread, system.

Primarily, the rooting depth is determined by the characteristics of the soil, although individual species of tree vary in their ability to exploit a given situation. The physical constraints on rooting include the hardness (or resistance) of the soil to root penetration and the availability of oxygen and water to the roots.

A very hard or compacted soil may be so dense that roots are physically unable to penetrate through it. The obvious example is where there is an impervious rock beneath the soil, such as granite; here the roots are only able to penetrate down through cracks in the rock structure and the tree has to root into whatever suitable material there is above the rock layer. Such solid barriers are very apparent and require either the importation of extra soil, the planting of smaller growing trees or shrubs or that the trees are more widely spaced, thereby allowing a higher volume of soil per tree.

More common, however, are situations where the impervious layer is less obvious. Compaction is a common cause of the difficulty or outright failure to establish trees on some sites. This is especially serious on new developments where the soil is consolidated by the frequent passage of machinery.

The nature of the soil and site conditions can lead to the development of an indurated layer. On podsols, there is often a layer of iron which develops from the leaching of the upper layers of the soil. Material from the upper layers is redeposited lower down as a solid iron pan, which can prevent roots penetrating to the potentially rootable zones beneath.

Tree roots cannot grow in soils where oxygen is not available or where there is a build-up of harmful gases such as ethylene. There are a few special exceptions to this, trees such as the swamp cypress (*Taxodium distichum*) have special roots or mechanisms to overcome this problem. Most trees, however, need the soil to have a free exchange of gases with the air above, both to replenish the oxygen used in respiration and to remove waste or poisonous gases.

Oxygen may not be available due to a variety of causes. The commonest one is because the space the oxygen would occupy is taken up by water; oxygen only dissolves in water in very small quantities and therefore is practically unavailable to the plant from water solution (except where the water is a well aerated fast-flowing stream). Another cause is where the soil surface is compacted or impervious, such as when capped by a solid layer of asphalt or concrete. Less common, but worth considering, is the effect of a leak of natural gases, either from the decomposition of old rubbish or a fractured gas main; this is poisonous primarily because it displaces the oxygen, thereby depriving the roots.

Modifying the Soil

Very often it is necessary to accept the constraints enforced by the soil on a site and to choose appropriate species of trees. There are, however, a number of ways in which the soil conditions can be modified to suit trees better, or to allow a broader choice of species. These include cultivation, drainage and the addition of soil amendments.

Cultivation

Cultivation techniques, such as ploughing or subsoiling, can be very effective in improving soil conditions. The act of cultivation will increase the aeration of the soil and relieve compaction, permitting the trees to root to greater depth. This will also increase the water-holding capacity of the soil.

For tree planting, ploughing will usually be carried out to depths of up to 0.6m; shallow ploughing to 0.25m, such as used for grass or cereal crops in agriculture, is of more use as a weed control measure before trees are planted as it is not sufficiently deep to benefit trees very much. Where ploughing is carried out to greater depths, it inevitably includes an element of subsoiling.

The purpose of subsoiling is to shatter the lower profiles of the soil to make it easier for tree roots to penetrate and to assist drainage. Subsoiling normally involves the drawing of a tine through the soil at a depth of 0.6 to 1m. The efficiency of the operation can be improved by using tines which have flanges or wings on their sides and thereby break-up the soil. Further refinements are to vibrate the tines, using a reciprocating mechanism. The efficiency of a subsoiling operation is greater if it is carried out when the soil is dry, as the shock waves are transmitted more effectively and shatter the soil; a wet soil behaves like jelly and less longterm benefit is achieved. Subsoiling alone using simple or winged tines will not disturb the surface vegetation or mix the soil.

Both ploughing and subsoiling should be considered when planting trees on large areas or where heavy machinery or other causes have led to a problem of compaction.

Drainage

The removal by drainage of surplus water from the soil will usually increase the volume of water available to the trees. This is because it will increase the volume of soil available to the tree.

Where the water table is high, most trees cannot root down into the anaerobic conditions below the water level; they are therefore confined to the upper part of the soil profile, with its limited water holding capacity. During the summer months, the water table may drop and the tree may make roots into the newly aerated soil, only to have these roots killed when the water table rises in the winter. The death of these roots may lead to problems with decay fungi. When the water table falls in the next spring/summer season, the tree, now one year's growth larger, may find that it has used all the available water in the upper part of the profile before it is able to make sufficient root growth to tap into the newly available layers below. This is why, on heavy sites, trees may often be observed coming into leaf in the second or third season, only to die or dieback a few weeks later.

Drainage will permanently remove the surplus water and increase the depth at which roots can survive in the soil at all seasons of the year, and therefore increase the quantity of water available to the roots.

Methods of drainage include using drainage pipes laid out in a herring bone fashion, mole drains and sand-filled slits made through the soil. Each of these methods is appropriate in some circumstances. Certain soil conditions, such as heavy clays, can be very difficult to drain effectively. The requirements of a drainage scheme for a site should be discussed with a drainage engineer.

Soil Amendments

Soil amendments are materials added to the soil to change its properties and include materials such as peat or bark.

Fertilisers are a specific amendment and can be very useful where there is a deficiency. Apart from deficiency situations, the addition of fertiliser will enhance growth without changing the nature of the soil.

The addition of organic matter, such as bark or peat, can improve the soil structure and water holding capacity of both light and heavy soils. In heavy soils, the organic matter will assist the break-up of the soil into smaller particles, getting closer to the ideal 'crumb' structure (so called as a soil in good condition will break down into crumb sized fragments when rubbed in the hand). In light soils, the addition of the organic matter increases the water holding capacity, provides places onto which nutrients can be absorbed and binds the soil particles together. In both soil types, the organic matter will increase the number of earthworms and other members of the soil fauna. Such amelioration may, however, be only temporary unless combined with other measures, such as drainage. Additionally, peat can absorb available nutrients and lead to a deficiency and if allowed to become dry, may be difficult to rewet. It should therefore be used with discretion and in limited amounts only.

Heavy soils can also be improved by the addition of some chemicals. Adding lime to a clay soil causes the clay to flocculate into lumps, although for some species of tree or shrub, the resulting rise in the pH of the soil may be deleterious.

Necessary Rooting Depth

On a reasonable loam soil, a depth of around 0.5m of soil is suitable for tree growth over much of Britain where the rainfall is around 750mm per annum. This will hold sufficient water to tide the tree over periods of drought without it suffering harmful effects, and also provide suitable support. The minimum for satisfactory tree growth on a loamy soil is likely to be around 0.3–0.4m.

On sandy sites, a greater depth will be needed, preferably 0.6–0.8m. Fortunately, on most sandy sites, the rooting depth is increased as sandy soils are usually freely drained and aerobic to a greater depth. On clay soils a depth similar to that on loam sites will be needed.

Trees growing in a moister climate will require less soil to provide the reserve of water than those growing in a drier climate; trees such as poplars (*Populus*) may require more moisture than a comparably sized specimen of a drought tolerant species such as Scots pine (*Pinus sylvestris*), although this topic requires further investigation. The presence of other vegetation will also be a relevant factor; this is especially so on shallow soils, where the surface layer of grass or herbs will use some or much of the available water or nutrients. The available volume of soil may also be limited by the presence of buildings, roads or the roots of other trees.

Where the available volume of soil is limited, the tree's growth rate and ultimate size will be accordingly curtailed, giving either a smaller final height or a tall tree with the lower branches missing, depending upon the degree of shelter, shade and climatic factors.

Topography

Topography affects how trees are able to thrive in the climate of the locality; the topography of an area strongly modifies the climate. On the windward side of a hill, the site will be exposed and growth of trees will be limited. Species with large tender leaves, like the example of *Catalpa* cited in Chapter 1, will have them torn to shreds whereas on the leeward side of the hill the conditions will be much milder, with softer winds.

One additional way in which topography can have a pronounced effect upon the trees grown is in relation to frost pockets.

As air cools, it becomes more dense, or heavier, and will flow down the side of a hill in the same way that water does. The layers of air nearest the ground cool down more quickly than the air more distant from the surface of the earth; this is because the soil radiates heat at a faster rate than air itself loses heat and the cooling of the earth cools the surrounding air. When the air reaches the lowest point, it collects in a 'pool' or frost pocket.

Frost pockets will occur wherever the air is stopped from flowing downhill. This need not be the bottom of the slope and a wall or a thick hedge can cause frost pockets to develop on the uphill side. This phenomenon can be observed when driving along a country lane at night when mist, held up by the roadside hedge or wall, may swirl across the road through a field gate when the road itself was mist-free.

Frost pockets will receive stronger frosts during the winter period and may cause damage to tender plants from sheer cold. More usually, though, the damage is caused by the frosts which occur in late spring after the buds have flushed and to a lesser extent in early autumn.

When planting in a frost pocket, it is necessary to choose either species such as birch (*Betula*), alder (*Alnus*) or Scots pine (*Pinus sylvestris*), which are fairly tolerant of frost, or selected late flushing forms of other species, so that they will come into leaf after the risk of frost damage has passed. Once the trees are 2–4m tall, they are likely to have escaped the frost pocket. Species which are susceptible to late spring frosts include English oak (*Quercus robur*), ash (*Fraxinus excelsior*), silver fir (*Abies*), larch (*Larix*) and most origins of Norway spruce (*Picea abies*).

The converse of the frost pocket is the slope on the side of the hill. Because the cold air drains away freely, the slope stays warmer and frost damage is less likely. On the sides of hills, therefore, it is often possible to grow species which are not hardy either on flat ground at the top or on ground at the bottom of the slope.

An overstorey of trees will reflect back to the earth a proportion of the heat radiated, slowing the rate of cooling. The ideal site, therefore, for tender plants is in a wood on the sheltered side of a hill.

Salt and Other Pollutants

Salt is a damaging agency to tree growth. It may come either from spray off the sea or from salt applied during de-icing operations. It is discussed further in Chapter 7, see page 125. List 22 includes genera suitable for use in coastal situations where salt spray is a problem. Other pollutants will also occur beside roads. The most damaging are some of the by-products of car engines, such as peroxyacetyl nitrates (PANs). Trees susceptible to these pollutants, e.g. silver firs (*Abies*), should not be used within a few metres of busy roads.

Buildings, Paths, Grass Areas and Services

Buildings, paths and services will have an influence on the trees planted;

and the trees potentially may affect the buildings, etc. A summary of the potential ways in which trees may affect buildings and services is given in Chapter 9, pages 137–9. This should be consulted before any new planting takes place close to existing structures, as with adequate prethought, most problems can be avoided without compromising intelligent tree planting. In this section, only the possible impact of the structures on the new trees will be considered.

The types of service or structure which may affect tree planting include paving of roads and footpaths, underground and overhead services such as electricity cables as well as buildings and their immediate environs.

Buildings

Buildings are the most obvious elements and probably have least impact. Trees planted close to the building are likely to lose the lowest branches, either from damage by rubbing against the building or from being removed to retain clearance or reduce light loss to windows. Tall buildings will also cast shade over the tree and may cause the tree to grow lanky and upwards towards the light. The trees, therefore, may not develop into the neatest of specimens. Waste heat vents and sometimes the flues from boilers, may create conditions unfavourable for tree growth, requiring the selection of more tolerant species.

Buildings also funnel the wind and can create much more windy conditions than might be expected in the area. They act as solid barriers, similar to the less effective types of shelter discussed in Chapter 1, page 17.

The climate around buildings is often warmer, due to the heat used in central heating and also that reflected off the structure, but, on the south side, the reflected sunlight in summer can cause scorch to some species. Where buildings are knocked down around established trees, the tree may suddenly be exposed to strong winds or sunlight from which it was previously sheltered.

The soil beneath any substantial building is often of little value to tree roots. Even if the roots manage to penetrate beneath the foundations, they will soon exhaust the supply of water, air and nutrients in the zone beneath the building. Only if it is possible for these to be replenished will the roots flourish.

Roads and Paths

The conditions beneath large areas of drive or road are likely to be equally barren. Apart from a finite supply of water, etc, the subsoil is likely to be heavily compacted, both during the construction of the road and by the movement of vehicles. The application of de-icing salt in winter and the general spillage of diesel and engine oil is likely to further pollute the conditions beneath the road surface.

Areas of paving and footpaths are more promising. Most paving surfaces, such as tarmac, loose gravel and paving slabs, permit water and air to pass through relatively easily. The conditions should therefore remain suitable for root growth, although there may be little recycling of nutrients. Also, these surfaces are often bedded onto a layer of sand. Water and air can usually be exchanged through the porous nature of footpath tarmac or the open joints between paving slabs. Solid barrier surfaces, such as poured slabs of concrete and heavily rolled and compressed tarmacadam surfaces as used in major roads, are unlikely to permit the exchange of gases, although if the area covered is not large exchange may take place at the sides.

Frequently, trees planted into paving surfaced areas will make much faster initial growth and establish more reliably. This is because the layer of paving acts as a mulch and because there is no competition for the available water and nutrients. However, this spurt of growth is not likely to be maintained, unless the tree can root over an extensive area. This is because there will be no recycling of nutrients. Also, there is often the risk that de-icing salt or herbicides applied to the paving surface to keep weeds down will be washed through to the roots and harm the trees.

Grass Areas Around Buildings

Grass around buildings is not an ideal medium into which to plant trees for several reasons, although very often it is the best or only place where tree planting can take place. The disadvantages stem from the frequently shallow layer of often compacted topsoil replaced on many building sites; the competition from the grass; and the prospect of damage from grass cutting machinery or the playing of games. Most of the nitrogen and other nutrients available to plants on a site are recycled in the top few centimetres of the soil and where a close mown grass sward is maintained, the grass tends to monopolise this zone. Close mown grass also dries out the soil more effectively than almost all other plant surfaces. These aspects are discussed further in the section on establishing trees on pages 82–6.

Damage from grass cutting machinery can be minimised by keeping a grass-free band around the base of each tree, which will also give some respite from the competition. A number of methods of achieving this are discussed on pages 83–6. Game playing can be allowed for in the planting design.

In the long term, however, trees in ground which is covered with a grass sward or other vegetation will generally grow better, as there will be an adequate and renewable supply of water and nutrients and less likelihood of disruption due to the relaying of paving or the application of de-icing salt or residual herbicides.

Services

Underground services will affect the trees in several ways.

Sometimes the Statutory Undertakers (Public Utilities) require that no tree planting takes place immediately above their service or for a specified distance on either side. Usually such restrictions are allegedly placed to reduce the risk of trees damaging the service, which is not a convincing argument considering the nature of tree roots and the standards of materials used in the construction of gas or other mains; more relevant is that the restriction on planting makes for easier access to maintain the service.

The service may also create a barrier to rooting. Often this will be a physical barrier, such as the mass of concrete around a large sewer, but may include chemical barriers. These may be due to toxic effects from the leakage of material from the service, such as methane from anaerobic decomposition of material in a sewer to a leak of heating oil from an underground ring supply. Where the service is known to be in a poor state of repair, sometimes chemicals are passed down it to kill tree roots penetrating through faults before they can grow large enough to cause additional damage to the main; the roots will be killed for some distance back from the service.

Overhead services are usually only electricity and telephone wires. The low voltage on which the telephones operate is not affected by trees and therefore the telephone companies do not normally worry about trees growing around the wires. With the electricity supply the situation is different as the foliage of trees, particularly when it is wet, can cause a short circuit across the wires and lead to power failures.

With high voltage transmission lines, the risk of the power arcing from the cables across to a tree (and possibly electrocuting a person nearby) is such that the electricity boards will not allow any tree planting within a specified distance from the power lines. As some main power lines are 20m across, the area sterilised can be significant but in this situation it represents a loss to be balanced against the benefits of electricity.

In low voltage systems, i.e. the final element in the power supply, the voltage is not sufficient to cause harm except if touched directly. Here the requirement is to keep the branches of trees sufficiently distant so that they cannot whip across the wires when they are wet and cause a local failure. It is prudent not to plant trees directly beneath LV (low voltage) wires, but if they are placed to one side, it is usually possible to trim the tree around the wires.

Animals, Vandals and Patience

The details of any scheme are going to be influenced by the constraints placed upon the tree planting by various wildlife factors. These may include damage by animals, vandalism and impatience.

The forms of damage by animals will depend upon the situation. In a public area, such as with street tree planting, dogs performing may cause some problems but these are unlikely to really affect tree growth or survival. Cats may sometimes claw at the base of trees when sharpening their claws but damage from this is spasmodic and probably not significant. Deer can cause much damage both by browsing the foliage and also by stripping the bark off trees. Squirrels can cause considerable damage to a number of broadleaved trees. The damage mainly results from bark stripping in the upper crown during May and June and is probably a feeding activity. Cattle, horses, donkeys and goats can cause considerable damage to young trees, and quite often to older ones. The worst damage is when the animals are kept in poor conditions without sufficient grazing, particularly in winter. Protection against damage by animals is discussed in Chapter 4, see pages 86–91.

Vandalism can be a constraint on tree planting. It is usually only a slight or intermittent problem, although there are situations where it is more likely. These include isolated new trees near footpaths or planting adjacent to pubs or other places where people congregate. Damage is less frequent in very open or exposed situations.

Vandalism can be countered in several ways. The most promising is by educating the general public and getting them involved in the tree

4 Cattle damage to the base of an oak tree

planting. This can be particularly effected around schools. Additionally, the density or size of the trees used can be increased, so that the trees are less at risk. Very often by planting a large number of small trees, cost can be saved and the incidence of damage lessened – there is, after all, nothing macho in breaking a tree the thickness of a pencil! By the time the tree has grown large enough to be 'worth' vandalising, it will probably be accepted as part of the local scene. If this approach is adopted, attention will be needed to ensure that the trees are thinned out in number as they grow.

New planting can sometimes be very effectively protected by being placed in the midst of beds of prickly shrubs. Deciduous *Berberis* species can be very effective here, as they can be planted as 45–60cm bare root plants with 2.5cm thorns in threes every few centimetres along the shoots. By comparison, gorse (*Ulex europaeus*) may be a flop, not for want of prickles but because it is not sufficiently tough *when* planted. Large trees are not necessarily any more resistant to vandalism than smaller ones. During the period when the tree is growing rapidly, the bark can too easily be stripped from trees such as Norway maple (*Acer platanoides*) and horse chestnut (*Aesculus hippocastanum*), even those with a butt diameter of 15cm (6in) or more at 1m.

Good staking, see pages 78–82, can lead to less damage from vandals.

Where damage does occur, it is sensible to tidy it up, as an air of neglect will reduce what respect there is for the planting. It is not always, however, advisable to remove and replace the damaged tree. If the tree has been in the site for a year or more, it will often make substantial regrowth and may even outgrow undamaged trees beside it by the end of the first season. Allowing this regrowth to take place should be considered, although in prestigious situations it may be better to replace the tree immediately.

The final element in considering the site is the expectations of people. People can be impatient and this may lead to demands for the planting of large trees, such as semi-mature trees 8–10m tall, to create an immediate impact, rather than wait a few years for the new planting to take hold. The demand for some instant tree planting is more reasonable where the existing tree cover is slight or non-existent. Where the planting is part of an ongoing management programme with adequate trees already on the site, this pressure should be resisted, as a better longterm effect is likely from the planting of trees in the 1–3m sizes.

People may also have ideas about the right way to do things; which species to be used, etc. These notions need to be considered, as this will assist the task of the manager when complaints are voiced. Education, public participation and gentle persuasion are the best approaches in these situations.

3

ASPECTS OF PLANTING DESIGN

THE design of any planting scheme is likely to determine the value and beauty of the work and to be evident for as long as the trees survive. It is important, therefore, that the planning of the planting is well conceived and that the plants are not thrown together piecemeal, although for a given location, one of several different design styles or arrangements may be appropriate. This chapter looks at spacing and thinning of trees and then discusses aspects of planting design affecting woodland formation, parkland, parks and gardens, avenues and formal areas, housing estates, hospitals, factories, offices, schools, street tree planting, arboreta, shelter, screening and land reclamation sites.

Spacing

In the wild, trees are usually gregarious plants. Where conditions are suitable, a number of seedlings will germinate, giving rise to competition between individuals of the same species. But there is also protection in this arrangement; if there are a number of similar individuals present, the chances of one surviving the browsing of herbivores, or damage by other causes, to reach maturity is increased. Because the trees are growing close together there is also mutual shelter from the wind. When flowering and fruiting stages are reached, the presence of a number of genetically different individuals will ensure cross-pollination. Lastly, a closed canopy will control other forms of vegetation, especially grasses, and let the trees exploit the full potential of the site. The natural system, therefore, is for a small number of trees to survive to maturity from a host of seedlings.

Tree planting should aim to simulate this natural system, with a larger number of trees being planted than are required to finally occupy the area when full grown. Such plantings will be able to tolerate the loss or removal of a number of trees, e.g. those which die or become damaged by mowers, animals or other agents, or allow the selection of the more vigorous individuals. The full application of this principle will only be possible where woodland is being planted; on more restricted sites, the extent to which this can be applied may often be limited.

In commercial forestry plantings, spacings of between 2m and 3m between plants, both in the rows and between rows, are common. This

Fig 1 Standard trees planted at 12m (40ft) spacing – like a row of lollipops! This may be acceptable where the site is not unduly exposed and if there are other larger trees to hold the eye, but it is not satisfactory on open windswept sites

allows for the planting of between 1,100 and 2,500 trees to the hectare; of these, perhaps 5–10% will fail to grow. As the final crop spacing, e.g for Sitka spruce (*Picea sitchensis*) at age 50 is 400 trees per hectare, a large number of trees will be lost or removed as thinnings. Apart from the benefit of mutual shelter, the trees will have smaller branches and less taper, giving better quality timber.

The potential benefits of planting specimen trees at their final spacings are that fewer costly trees are needed, less time and money is spent on planting and post-planting maintenance and that there is no need to thin out the number of trees. Moreover, each tree develops a full crown of healthy branches. Where mown grass surrounds the trees, there can be an appropriate easing of the cost of cutting the grass between the trees, but generally these benefits do not often accrue. Frequently, the wide spacing used results in the trees making relatively slow growth due to competition by the turf for moisture and nutrients and the lack of any mutual sheltering effect. Such trees sometimes take twenty years to make the growth achieved by closer planted trees in five or six seasons, during which time they often succumb to vandalism, damage by mowers or other perils of the establishment period. Nor do such widely spaced trees look satisfactory, or give shelter, shade or other desired effects until they have reached a fairly advanced age. There are, therefore, good aesthetic as well as financial reasons for planting trees at closer spacings initially, especially where the site is bare and windswept.

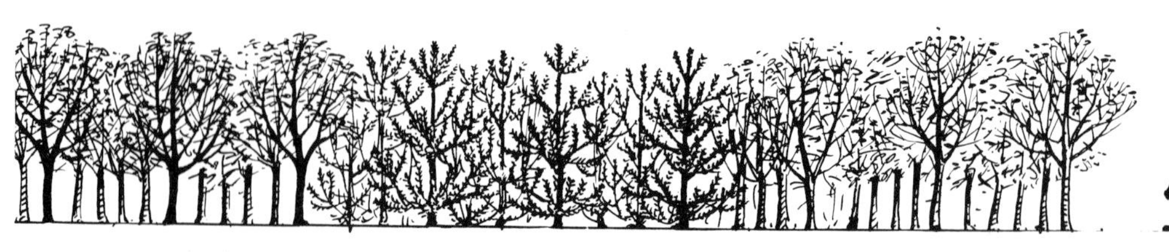

Fig 2 Belt of young trees about seven years after planting as whips or transplants, at about 3 × 3m (10ft) spacing

Thinning

When trees are planted closely together, or grow in dense stands following natural regeneration, it will be necessary to thin out the number of trees. If the trees are planted at spacings of 2–3m, i.e. with each tree potentially occupying 4–9 square metres of land, each tree will only have enough space to let it grow for a few years. The more vigorous ones will soon shade out the less thrifty. But this is a slow process, during which time the stand will contain many dead, dying or suppressed trees. Trees are sometimes grown under these conditions on forestry sites where the risk of windthrow following thinning is high, but a wood in such a condition is not usually considered acceptable in a park or garden (although it may have some interest where nature conservation is an objective, by providing deadwood for decay organisms and hole nesting birds to colonise). Also where trees are grown too close together, they become thin and weedy, frequently unable to stand against a strong storm, especially if adjoining trees are lost for any reason; they will not, therefore, be safe for as long as more spaced plantings.

With larger distances between trees, say a spacing of 5m with each tree having 25 square metres of land and light, some small growing or upright trees, such as field maple (*Acer campestre*), crab apples (*Malus*), Lawson cypress (*Chamaecyparis lawsoniana*), spruces such as Serbian spruce (*Picea omorika*) and laburnum (*Laburnum*), may be able to grow to maturity. However, at this spacing, tall spreading trees, such as English oak (*Quercus robur*), beech (*Fagus sylvatica*) or ash (*Fraxinus excelsior*), will not be naturally thinned but will only develop as very spindly specimens; with trees grown like this it is very difficult to start a progressive replacement scheme, for as soon as any trees are felled to be replanted, the neighbouring ones are likely to fall down. Large growing trees such as these need a final spacing of around 10m (i.e. 100 square metres per tree) to make good strong specimens, although as open grown mature trees they can cover 1,000 square metres (1/10 hectare).

In any amenity planting, some form of thinning is going to be necessary at some stage; the exact extent will depend upon the species, spacing and aspects of the site. What is required of the stand will also determine the level of thinning. Where a quick screen is established using trees planted closer than 2m apart with a quick growing tree such as silver birch (*Betula pendula*) or alder (*Alnus*), some thinning may be needed after only three or four seasons. Conversely in a pure planting of English oak (*Quercus robur*), no thinning may be needed for twenty years. List 9 gives details of tree genera with fast growth rates.

Removing apparently healthy trees, even when carried out to benefit the longterm development of the stand, can cause emotional criticism from members of the public. The extra work load generated to answer

such comments can lead to important thinnings being neglected until too late. It may be possible to use a mixture of species which will be naturally self thinning. Rowans (*Sorbus*) tend to develop small narrow crowns and are not as fast growing or as long lived as large trees such as plane (*Platanus* × *hispanica*) or ash (*Fraxinus excelsior*). If the extra trees to create the initial impact are mainly rowan, the group of trees will be partly self thinning and will require less management.

Woodland Formation

Where trees are planted in a woodland setting, the desired effect will normally be a high forest and for this the trees need to be able to make height growth, usually on a single straight stem. The actual purpose for planting the woodland may vary from timber production to creating a home for wildlife or a setting for a woodland garden, or a combination of these.

The layout of the planting will need to permit easy access for weeding, whilst creating a wood which does not appear contrived. The first requirement can be satisfied by planting the trees in regular rows at an even spacing between the rows. However, such a regular grid pattern can create difficulties where informality is also needed.

It can take several thinnings to remove the strict formality of the planting layout, particularly when viewed from afar. This is particularly the case if alternate rows of different trees are used. Intimate mixtures, using single trees of a species mixed together in a random manner will look better but unless the trees are carefully chosen to have similar growth rates on the soil types present on the site, they are likely to grow at different rates and only the more vigorous survive.

Satisfactory mixtures can be achieved by planting the trees in groups which cover approximately the same area as a single mature tree of that species. Thus for a large forest tree, such as beech (*Fagus sylvatica*), the group of young planted trees may cover 100 square metres, which at a 2m spacing would represent 25 young trees (or a dozen each of beech and a nurse species such as larch (*Larix decidua*), preferably planted in groups, rather than in intimate mixture). As the trees mature, the number will be reduced until only one is left. Should a disaster occur, e.g. grey squirrels destroy all the beech trees in the wood, there would be sufficient surplus trees in the adjoining plots of other species to fill most or all of the gaps.

Fig 3 Section through a belt of mature trees planted at 3 × 3m (10ft) spacing and not thinned. As a result, the outer trees are one-sided and the others spindly

Fig 4 Section through a belt of mature trees which have been progressively thinnned as they grew, resulting in better development of each remaining tree. Such a belt is easier to manage than the one shown in Fig 3, as it is easier to remove some of the trees without the remaining trees being blown down

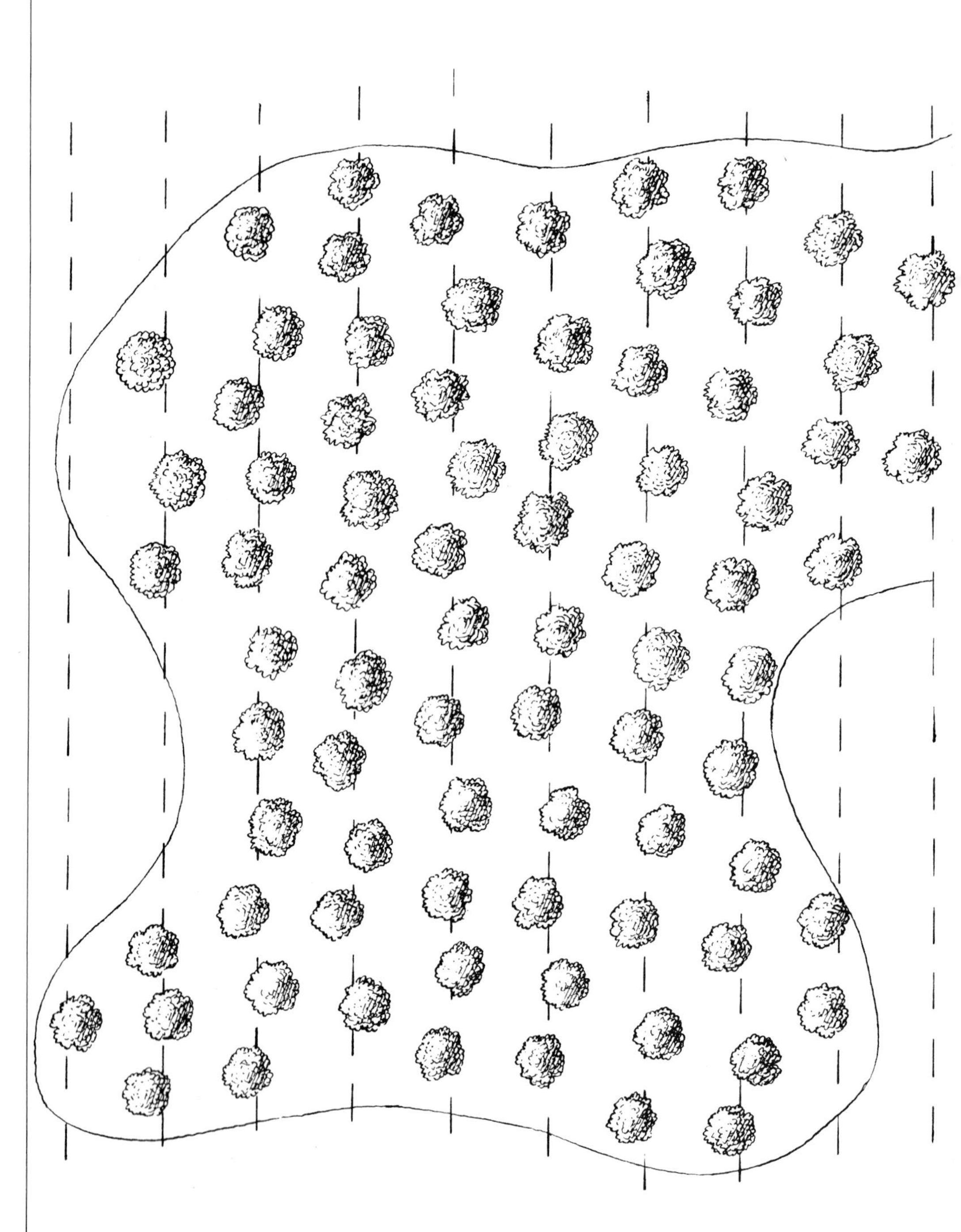

Fig 5 Trees planted asymmetrically, rather than in exactly straight lines, to reduce the regimented effect of large-scale planting

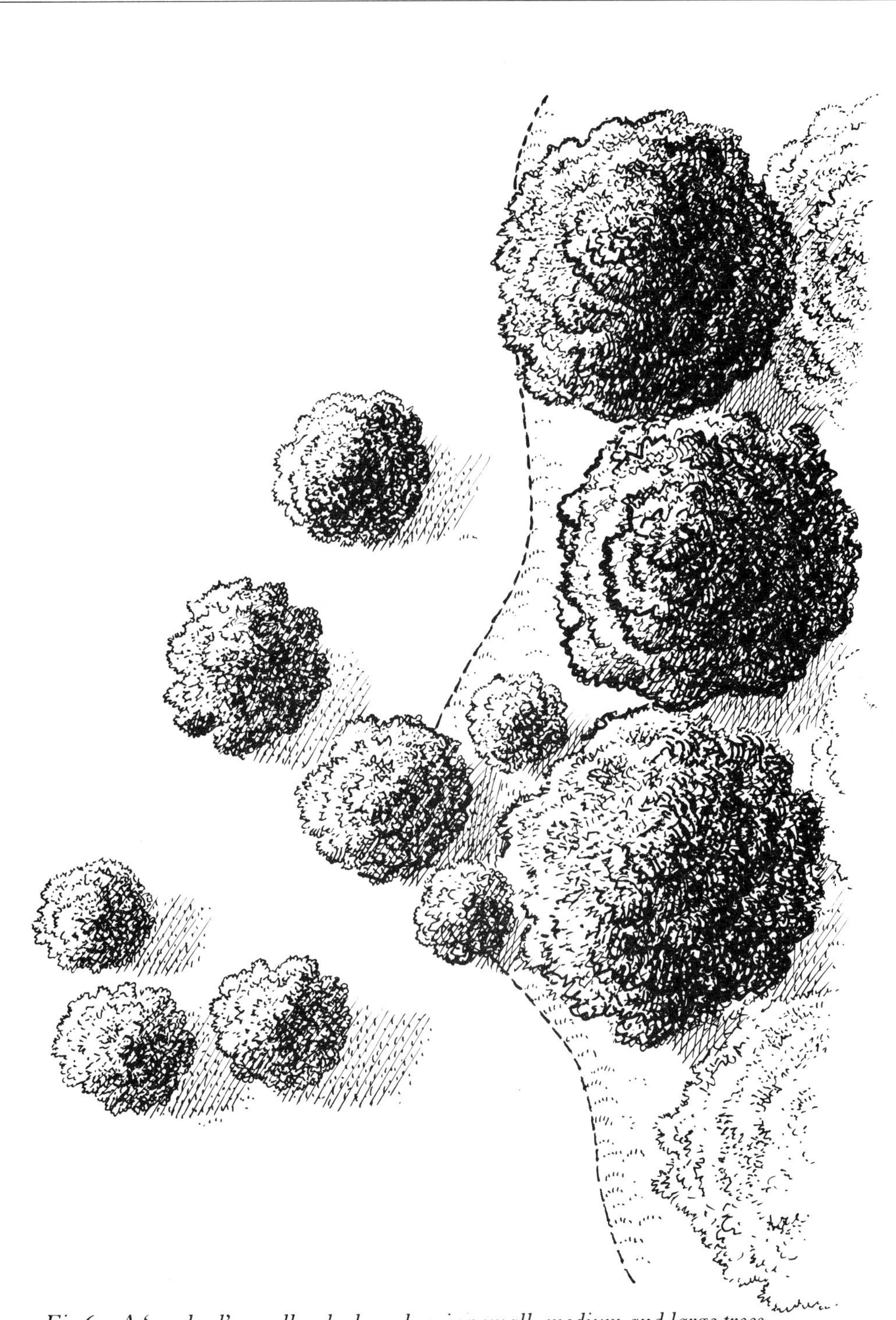

Fig 6 A 'gradual' woodland edge, showing small, medium and large trees, and the boundary edge of the frequently mown grass

Where more intimate mixtures are used, more attention must be given to the respective growth rates of the trees, and to prompt and frequent thinning of the developing stand.

In establishing any mixture, it is sensible to use one or two species as the backbone planting, with as many or more individuals of these species than of the others put together. The backbone species should give the scheme cohesion without creating dull uniformity. The species used for backbone planting should be well adapted to the site.

Care should be taken to avoid creating woodland blocks with harsh discordant lines. Many of the forestry plantings of the 1920–50 period were placed across the contours, in formal regular blocks, and left unsightly scars on the landscape for several decades.

The transition zone between tall trees and open grassed areas can be softened by using smaller trees; rowan (*Sorbus aucuparia*), cherries (*Prunus*), pussy willow (*Salix caprea*) or hazel (*Corylus avellana*) can look effective against a background of taller trees. Care must be taken, however, to avoid creating either a ragged edge to the woodland or the hard artificial edge which results from planting a complete row of small trees. A few individual trees or clumps of the 'backbone' species and a few smaller species should suffice to make the transition.

Parkland Planting

Parkland landscapes consist of prominent individual trees or groups of trees set in an open agrarian landscape. The scale of the scenery is large. Therefore, the trees need to be large or planted in bold groups, or they will appear puny. However, there must not be too many trees, or the parkland will quickly become an open woodland and lose its character. The groups of trees need to be arranged to show off the other features of the parkland. Often some groups will flank a vista, such as the view down to or around a lake, but trees can also be effectively used to conceal features, so that there is an element of surprise when something suddenly comes into view as you pass a clump of trees.

Parkland planting should generally appear informal, without the harsh use of straight lines. However, there are situations where an air of formality can be introduced by the use of straight lines or geometrical planting, much as formal 'temples' placed in the landscapes of large estates, to form a consciously constructed focal point in contrast to the surrounding informal 'natural' landscape.

In parkland, the trees will need to retain their branches and foliage to ground level or to a browse line caused by cattle eating the lower foliage. Single trees of large growing species can make effective parkland trees, but very often a group of similar trees makes a more effective 'tree', with the foliage of several growing together. Where clumps contain several

Fig 7 A clump of exotic trees deliberately planted on a small knoll to form an 'architectural' feature, contrasting with the informal surrounding scenery. This could not be repeated frequently without becoming monotonous or trite

Fig 8 Newly planted group of three trees (left). These can be reduced to a single tree after a few years or left to form a clump which is treated as a single large tree for management purposes (right)

trees, they should be spaced so that each tree has sufficient space to remain healthy and vigorous. In management terms, however, they must be regarded as being a single tree once the branches have formed a united canopy. In clumps of seven or less trees, spacings of about 3–5m are likely to be appropriate.

Where different trees are used in a single group, choose ones which will look similar or complementary. Lime (*Tilia*) and beech (*Fagus sylvatica*) will go together, having similar size and shape, whilst the excess use of spiky conifers in this situation, particularly when mixed with broadleaved trees, should be avoided. Conifers which are good in parkland are cedars (*Cedrus*), some pines (*Pinus*) and Wellingtonia (*Sequoiadendron giganteum*).

Clumps or groups in a parkland can be established by making small woodland plantings or by using a more limited number of larger trees (with the drawbacks noted above). The trees are likely to need protecting against cattle or other hazards, and more trees should be used than will remain in the mature clump. Clumps or groves will also look better either with odd numbers or in groups of over a dozen. When trees are planted in clumps of even numbers, such as 4, 6 or 8, the eye automatically pairs up the planting, and this is less restful or aesthetic than with odd number groupings.

Parks and Gardens

In parks and gardens, the scale of tree planting and the space available are generally smaller. The planting needs, therefore, to be more intimate in style and presentation. The trees used will include some tall forest trees, such as plane (*Platanus* × *hispanica*), beech (*Fagus sylvatica*) or English oak (*Quercus robur*), as these will be needed for the creation of the scale and setting. But smaller trees will also be used to a greater extent, including many 'ornamentals' such as rowans (*Sorbus*), crab apples (*Malus*) and the smaller maples (*Acer*). Attractive conifers, such as silver firs (*Abies*), cedars (*Cedrus*), spruces (*Picea*) and pines (*Pinus*), can be used very effectively in parks and gardens. Even with the larger growing trees, though, the range of species used can be increased, both by the use of a greater variety of common species and by the use of less frequent species of common genera, e.g. red oak (*Q. rubra*) as well as *Q. robur*, or silver lime (*Tilia tomentosa*) as well as large-leafed lime (*T. platyphyllos*).

There will also be a role for unusual foliage colours, or other oddities. Copper beech (*Fagus sylvatica* forma *purpurea*) can be useful in a park to make a contrast to common green foliage, whilst interest can be created by the very pendulous habit of weeping beech (*Fagus sylvatica* 'Pendula'), the contorted habit of *F. sylvatica* 'Tortuosa', or the cut leaves of *F. sylvatica* 'Heterophylla'.

Care must be used when planting unusual foliage shapes, colours or textures. Too much of one single element may soon tire, be it the blossom of *Prunus* 'Kanzan' or the dark or black foliage of *Acer platanoides* 'Goldsworth Purple'. In particular, remember that what may look attractive in flower or new foliage may well be dismal later in the year; if over-used, this can give the entire planting scheme a dull aspect.

The design of planting in a park or garden should aim to give some interest at all times of the year. Therefore more tree species should be used, as well as selected clones with larger flowers or fruits.

Except where a park or garden is being newly created, the existing trees and shrubs will provide sheltered conditions. This can influence the choice of planting material, permitting the use of trees needing shelter from wind, e.g. Indian bean tree (*Catalpa bignonioides*), or species needing protecting from spring frosts, such as katsura (*Cercidiphyllum japonicum*).

The size of planting stock used will depend upon local conditions. If vandalism is locally serious, or for political reasons it is necessary to plant trees that will make an immediate impact, larger sizes of tree may be appropriate. If there is only space for a few trees, extra cash can reasonably be expended per tree and, in theory at least, it should be relatively easy to maintain a newly planted tree in a park or garden, with staff and water available on site.

In parks and gardens, it is often possible to establish trees which are generally difficult, such as those given in list 10. They can either be given special attention by the staff or planted in the protection of a shrub bed.

In a large park, the design should cater for the taste of all likely users. This may include planting horse chestnut (*Aesculus hippocastanum*) for conkers for that part of the population which enjoys them; equally, the design should ensure that the nuisance which small boys (and their parents!) can cause when trying to get conkers down early is both controlled and confined to safe areas.

The planting of trees near site boundaries also requires careful attention if problems of overhanging branches, encroaching roots and interference with daylight are to be avoided. The latter may not be a legal problem, but loss of light to adjoining houses or gardens can be the cause of ill-feeling between neighbours.

Avenues and Formal Planting

In any formal planting, uniformity of the trees is very important. An avenue composed of a ragbag of differing species or cultivars indiscriminately arranged will generally appear ghastly. This does not mean that every tree has to be identical to the next one – variations in the site can make this impossible to achieve even where all the trees are vegetatively

Fig 9 A formal avenue in the grand style, with trees planted at 10m(33ft) spacing in two rows 30m(100ft) apart. Even this is relatively close, and some avenues are as much as 150m(500ft) wide

Fig 10 Trees planted on both sides of a road to form a closed avenue or mall. They are at 10m(33ft) spacing, in two rows 10m(33ft) apart

raised, but undue variation for its own sake, desirable in a park or garden, does not accord well with an avenue.

The purpose of the planting needs to be ascertained at the outset. If it is as a means to connect a house with the road, i.e. it flanks the drive, the length and line will be predetermined. If it is to be a feature on the landscape, there is more flexibility as to its length and orientation.

The width of the avenue is very important. Natural foreshortening of the view will mean that for a given tree size, the longer the vista, the wider it should be. The size and shape of the trees used will also affect the spacing. Tall, rather narrow trees, such as limes (*Tilia*), can be set in a narrower avenue than relatively low, broad trees, such as English oak (*Quercus robur*).

The following table gives an indication of the likely width between the crowns of the trees to make an avenue look 'right'. Closer spacing can, of course, be used if the branches are intended to close in on either side like the arches of a gothic cathedral.

Length of avenue	*Width of avenue*	*Distance between planted rows*	
		Lime (*Tilia*)	Oak (*Quercus*)
100m	10m	35m	40m
100–200m	13–15m	40m	45m
200–400m	15–18m	43m	48m
400–600m	20m	45m	50m
600–800m	25m	50m	55m

The avenue design can allow either for the trees in each row to close together, so that the effect is of two walls of foliage as you walk along the avenue, or to be spaced out, so that each tree can develop its own domed crown. With the former style, the trees should be planted around 8–10m apart, and 10–20m apart for the latter style, depending upon species.

Another consideration is whether the avenue is to be a single line on either side of the walk/drive or two or more lines. Generally, two or more lines are appropriate where the avenue is to be very long, or especially wide. The option of including two rows of trees on either side allows for a two term avenue. Quick maturing but relatively small trees can be used to make an early feature which may be enjoyed during the life of the planter; species such as whitebeam (*Sorbus aria*), some cherries (*Prunus*) and other small trees can be used for this stage. These are planted on the inner side of the avenue, to be removed after 20–30 years. Longer lasting and more majestic trees can be planted outside of the small trees. By the time they are 25 years old they will start to make a feature and take over from the small trees. Beware, however, of mixing different trees in the same rows.

Fig 11 A mall or sheltered walk, consisting of a double row of trees on either side of a path

Most successful avenues consist of only one species. Also beware of planting twice the number of trees needed for the avenue on the assumption that you can thin out the excess, unless they are trees like limes (*Tilia*) which will thrive if your successors fail to use the saw at the appropriate time.

An avenue effect does not have to be restricted to the use of long living large trees. A very effective mini-avenue can be made using smaller trees, such as a short double line of *Juniperus scopulorum* 'Skyrocket'. This can be used to create a feature in a fraction of the space needed for a full avenue, and can be very useful in some styles of gardening. Other small formal trees can be used to make a connecting feature, perhaps across only 10m of garden.

The size of plants which should be used for avenues will tend to be at the larger end of the normal range of plant sizes. This is because the trees will need to be planted at the final spacing, so natural or other losses cannot be tolerated, and a more even batch of trees will be needed, which is easier to achieve by selecting heavier standards, than from purchasing ordinary nursery stock. Also, as avenues are longterm projects, larger trees give a better initial indication of something happening.

List 24 give a short selection of genera containing species suitable for use in avenues.

Housing Estates

The role of tree planting in housing estates should be a) to create a beautiful and interesting environment, b) to give a sense of unity and individuality to the estate, and c) to provide shelter and screening between dwellings. Ideally the tree planting should enhance the architecture; too often it is needed to disguise it. The first requirement is the most important; it is, after all, where the residents live year after year. Some of these requirements are similar to those for parks and gardens, although the degree of detail is likely to be lower, with not such a large range of species used.

The scale of the buildings and open spaces on the estate should be considered. If widely spaced tower blocks predominate, very small or low spreading trees are unlikely to make much impact. Large upright and fast growing species should be used, such as maples (*Acer*) or Wellingtonia (*Sequoiadendron giganteum*). By contrast, a tall tree such as a Wellingtonia will usually look out of place beside a low row of single storey housing. Here, trees with spreading low crowns, such as may (*Crataegus*) or Indian bean tree (*Catalpa bignonioides*) are more likely to be appropriate. However, avoid making the planting appear weak and puny.

The planting should avoid restricting light to people's living room windows. Tall growing trees can often be planted beside the blank walls or windows to rooms such as toilets and bathrooms. In these locations, complaints about light loss will be minimised. Also the tree should not be planted too close to the buildings. Complaints will follow if they can rub their branches against the fabric, or if the branches can be used as a means of illegal access. There is little risk of trees causing damage to the foundations with high rise blocks of flats, but this possibility should be considered when planting around low rise structures, particularly on shrinkable clay soils (see Chapter 9, pages 138–9).

The size of plants appropriate to housing estates will very often be standard trees and larger, although it may sometimes be appropriate to use smaller trees.

Hospitals and the Like

The requirements for planting around hospitals and convalescent homes are similar to those for parks and gardens and on housing estates. The primary objective should be to create a pleasant environment which will be conducive to staff and patients alike. A pleasantly treed outlook will assist the mental state of patients and thereby hasten their recovery. It will also put visitors in a more relaxed frame of mind. A variety of trees will add interest, both by themselves and from the associated wildlife. This will include trees which give attractive features during the winter months as well as the summer, e.g trees with good bark (list 12), bold

5 *Poor choice of species, having little amenity value*

foliage (list 8) and evergreens (list 11). As with other situations, the actual species used should fit the constraints of the site, as to soil, climate, space and size of buildings. The range of trees which are appropriate is large and the design should use a variety, but in a coherent manner.

Factories and Offices

Planting around these sites should have two principal objectives, viz. to create a good environment which will be conducive to work and to screen the local populace from the complex. Screening will mitigate the noise,

6 Although the choice of species and planting design is poor, these trees succeed in breaking up the outline of this factory building

dust and visual impact of the complex on the lives of those living nearby and is discussed on pages 18 and 66. The benefits of providing a good environment for work will help to give the workforce a pride in their workplace and its surroundings, giving them a better attitude to work and therefore leading to better productivity. The pleasant environment may let them take their lunch break in more relaxed surroundings.

Creating surroundings which will give pride and joy to the staff will have similar constraints to planting in parks and gardens, housing estates and hospitals and the above sections on these topics should be consulted.

Schools

Planting around schools will have both aesthetic, screening and educational value. Aspects of the aesthetic considerations are discussed above under parks and gardens and housing estates. Screening is dealt with below. The educational aspects will include the variety of plant shapes and structures, briefly discussed under creating an arboretum (page 63), and also as aspects of wildlife (pages 21–2) and general botany (see below). In addition, on a school site consideration should be given to aspects such as poisonous plants. This may cause no concern where the school is a sixth-form college, where the students are young adults and can be

7 The dominant tall shape of the Lombardy poplars makes an unsympathetic contrast to low building on the left; the rounded smaller trees on the right mellow in with the two-storey houses there

expected to behave as such (!), but where toddlers and very young children are present, plants with poisonous berries, such as laburnum (*Laburnum*) and yew (*Taxus baccata*), may be inappropriate.

Street Tree Planting

The purpose of street tree planting is to 'humanise' the environment, to make the roads and thoroughfares pleasant in their own right, not just as places used to travel from A to B. They also help to trap dust and fumes and reduce windspeeds.

Street trees need a number of specific attributes not essential for other types of planting. In most streets, space is at a premium, and the crown needs to be upright, relatively narrow, not spreading. Only in a limited number of sites is there room for full grown forest trees. They also need to be tough. Street trees have to tolerate the winter application of salt to the road and pavement, which can cause damage to many species, including traditional street trees like London plane (*Platanus* × *hispanica*). They have to survive the occasional bashes from vehicles, lawnmowers or pedestrians; species with rather tender bark, such as the snakebark maples (*Acer*, see Gazetteer), are not really tough enough for street plantings, being too liable to damage. Street trees often have to grow in a hostile root environment. The rooting space available for the average street tree is limited and rarely contains much good topsoil. More usually the trees have to root into builder's rubble or heavy compacted clay, or in some inner city situations, find nourishment between the coal cellars! Birches (*Betula*) often do not grow well in inner city streets because of the poor compacted 'soil' and their inability to root deeply, although thriving in the grass verges of outer town locations.

Streets are windy places. The wind can swirl around corners or off high rise blocks; the slipstream created by large fast moving vehicles can add to the windiness. Trees with brittle wood, such as silver maple (*Acer saccharinum*) or robinia (*Robinia pseudacacia*), should be avoided in areas where turbulence is to be expected, although both species are capable of growing well in streets. Street trees need to develop a strong branch structure, preferably with a central stem and short spreading side branches; trees composed of a mass of erect branches, such as *Liriodendron tulipiferum* 'Fastigiata', are too likely to have branches blown or forced out of line to make satisfactory street trees, despite the narrow upright habit.

When planting street trees, there are a number of specific considerations to be taken into account. The constraints of the site will include the services running along the road or footpath, overhead telephone or electricity supplies, street lighting, and other users of the street. They must be spaced to cause a minimum of inconvenience to residents of the road; avoid planting them outside the main windows or in front of gates or sightlines. They should also be planted as far back from the kerb as is consistent with the site; this will reduce the need to prune the branches over the road and also the risk of tall vehicles colliding with the trees. Potential damage by tree roots should always be considered. Also, consider the chance of the stake being driven through the roof of the cellar, where these extend under the footpath as happens in some older towns.

The design of the planting should make the trees appear interesting. Some variation is likely to be needed, but a hotch-potch should definitely be avoided. The trees should be planted in fairly large groups or clusters of similar trees, rather than in some arbitrary repetitive manner. Blank end walls can make good locations for street trees, allowing the use of taller growing specimens which will be in scale with the buildings and the street scene.

The planting site will very often be the amount of soil exposed by the removal of one paving slab. This will limit the size of tree which can be planted. 'Select standards', with a stem girth of 10–12cm, are probably the largest size which can conveniently be planted into a single paving slab sized planting site, although where there is more space, or a grass verge, larger trees can be used, if desired.

8 Common lime and a beech forming a single clump

9 Sycamore and two Turkey oaks giving an effective clump

Creating an Arboretum

Only occasionally is it possible to plant an arboretum, but some of the joy, interest and variety to be found in an arboretum can often be incorporated in amenity plantings. The small park gives an opportunity for growing a range of different species. Rather than just beech or hornbeam, other *Fagus* (such as *F. engleriana*) or *Carpinus* (like *C. tschonoskii*) can be used. Several different rowans (*Sorbus*) can be tried in neighbouring streets, e.g. a selection of *Sorbus aucuparia* cultivars like 'Shearwater Seedling' and 'Fructu Lutes' or different species such as *Sorbus commixta* 'Embley', *S. hupehensis* or *S. rehderiana* 'Joseph Rock', can be used in adjacent roads. If only one or two species are used in each street the effect will be satisfactory; it only becomes chaotic when too many are used in a location where they can be compared directly.

Where it is possible to plant a larger collection, the objectives for doing so should be considered. These may include establishing a reference collection of small trees which may be suitable for residents of an area to grow in their gardens, or to show the folly of planting a weeping willow (*Salix* × *chrysocoma*) in a small space!; to create a pleasant landscape setting (in which case the basic layout and the framework of the background planting must be kept simple); or as a teaching exhibit, to give school children an insight into the full richness of the plant kingdom.

Shelterbelts

The benefits of shelterbelts are discussed in Chapter 1 (see page 17). The design element involves achieving the maximum reduction in wind speed possible on the site.

A belt of trees designed to give good shelter will need to retain a porosity as close as practical to the ideal of 50% for the periods when the shelter is required; in some situations this will be throughout the year, but in others, the shelter may only be critical for a limited period of time. The belt will also need to be fairly constant in the barrier it gives; if there are large gaps in it, the wind may howl through these areas as if there were no shelter on the site but large dense areas will make the belt behave more like a solid barrier and decrease its efficiency.

The belts should be aligned at right angles to the wind direction for optimum effect. As it is unusual for the wind to blow consistently from only one or two directions, this means either a series of belts effectively 'boxing in' the area, or accepting a lower standard of shelter from certain wind directions.

Different designs of belts will be needed in different situations. For example, in an apple orchard, the shelter is needed from the time the apple trees come into flower in the spring (to reduce damage to the opening flowers and create good flying conditions for the bees which pollinate the blossom) until harvest in the autumn; little shelter is required over the winter period. For an apple orchard early leafing deciduous trees, such as birch (*Betula*) or alders (*Alnus*), are well suited. In an orchard, the shelter can be a series of single lines of trees, as efficiency of operation and space are important, rather than aesthetic considerations.

Around a playing field, however, different considerations will apply. The pitches are likely to be much used during the winter months, and therefore the belt should provide adequate shelter at this season. This will entail the use of an evergreen element in the planting as deciduous trees will not give a sufficiently dense belt when out of leaf, unless the belt is very wide. However, the belts will also need to be aesthetically attractive, especially during the low levels of light which occur on winter days. The design will need to be of a higher standard than that simply dictated by the need to offer shelter. An effective shelterbelt has to keep foliage growing right down to ground level and this usually means including shrubs in the design.

Care is needed for the choice of trees for the belt. In some situations space will not be at a premium, and therefore the effectiveness of the belt can be built up over a wide band. On many sites, though, the belt will need to be relatively narrow in relation to its height. Here low spreading trees such as may (*Crataegus*) or ornamental crabs (*Malus*) are unlikely to

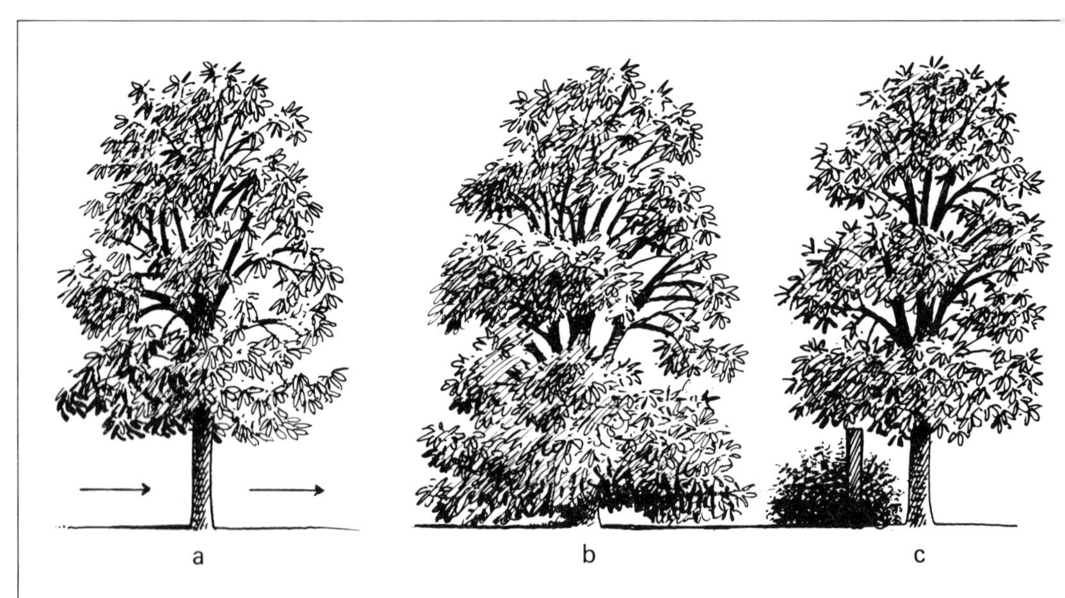

Fig 12 A gap in the canopy as in (a) creates draughts. More effective shelter is provided if the tree is branched to ground level (b), or has a solid wall or fence (or shrubs) to fill the gap (c)

10 Atlas cedar softening the outline of a block of flats; the tree is planted in front of an exterior flight of stairs

have a prominent role to play, whilst tall upright trees, such as Italian alder (*Alnus cordata*) are more useful. The trees used should be ones capable of withstanding exposure.

Evergreen trees are essential in most belts, except possibly those only needed during the summer. Some broadleaved trees are evergreen, such as holm oak (*Quercus ilex*), but these tend to present too dense a canopy of foliage and are difficult to associate well with other trees. Conifers are likely to form the majority of the evergreens used in shelter plantings. They have the advantage of being generally narrow and upright in growth and tolerating a wide range of sites and exposure. The commonly planted conifers, such as Lawson and Leyland cypresses (respectively *Chamaecyparis lawsoniana* and × *Cupressocyparis leylandii*) tend to be rather too dense for best effect when used on their own and need associating with other trees to achieve the desired density of foliage; however, they are not easy to associate with other trees and are probably best used elsewhere. More open trees, such as Scots (*Pinus sylvestris*) or other pines, make a more effective belt. Mixtures of pine with a deciduous tree, such as Italian alder, can make an effective all-year-round shelterbelt. List 22 gives details of genera suitable for use in shelterbelts, and list 11 of evergreen genera.

Shelterbelts are best started by the planting of small trees, rather than isolated larger trees.

Screens

Screens are similar to shelterbelts, except that as the shelter is visual, the screen can be as dense as is convenient. Belts of conifers like Leyland cypress (× *Cupressocyparis leylandii*) may not make a very successful screen, tending to make almost as big an eyesore as the object to be hidden. In many, though not all, situations a screen of deciduous trees can be more effective than a band of cypresses. During the winter the twigginess of the deciduous trees is often sufficient to draw the eye away from the monstrosity. Avoid using trees which will grow too large for the site, and use the trees to soften or break up the outline of the item to be screened.

Land Reclamation Sites

On difficult sites, such as quarry waste tips, landfill sites and regraded colliery spoil tips, the quality of soil and other site factors may require extra attention. The planting of nitrogen-fixing plants, such as alder (*Alnus*), or tree lupin (*Lupinus arboreus*) may be used to add nitrogen and organic matter to the soil. The degree of compaction produced by the grading machinery may require special techniques to ameliorate this condition (see page 34). Advice on this aspect of planting trees can be obtained from the Forestry Commission Research Station, Alice Holt Lodge, Farnham, Surrey, GU10 4LH, or from specialist consultants in land reclamation. List 24 gives a short selection of tree genera suitable for use on land reclamation sites, including those which can fix atmospheric nitrogen.

4

PLANTING THE TREES AND EARLY MAINTENANCE

THE actual planting of your trees is a vitally important task. As with design, the results of good planting will show for many years. It is, however, only one part of the whole spectrum of tree management, and is in many ways the simplest and most enjoyable. It should not be over-emphasised at the expense of other equally important activities, such as the careful selection of suitable and interesting tree species, the maintenance of trees already planted, cultural attention to older trees, and the design and implementation of sensible long-term programmes for the felling and replacement of trees. Nevertheless, care and attention is required at planting time, particularly with those species which do not transplant easily (see list 10).

Obtaining Nursery Stock

The first requirement is to choose and obtain good quality trees. No amount of good cultural practice will revive a dead or moribund tree, and bad handling of the planting stock can easily put good quality trees into these categories.

Size and Type of Planting Stock

The actual size or type of planting stock used will be the result of a decision involving several factors; these may include the timespan for which the planting is needed, the risk of vandalism and a judgement on how the risk of that eventuality may be reduced, the finance available for the planting, the design of the scheme and the species to be used. Some of these factors are discussed in Chapter 3 and information is given in the Gazetteer section on the ease of moving and range of sizes available for planting of a range of species and genera. This section looks at the pros and cons of different sizes of tree.

The different types of nursery stock are seedlings, transplants, whips, feathered trees, standards, extra heavy standards and semi-matures.

Seedling trees are those straight from the seedbed; they are not generally useful for planting out on a hostile site, as they are too small to

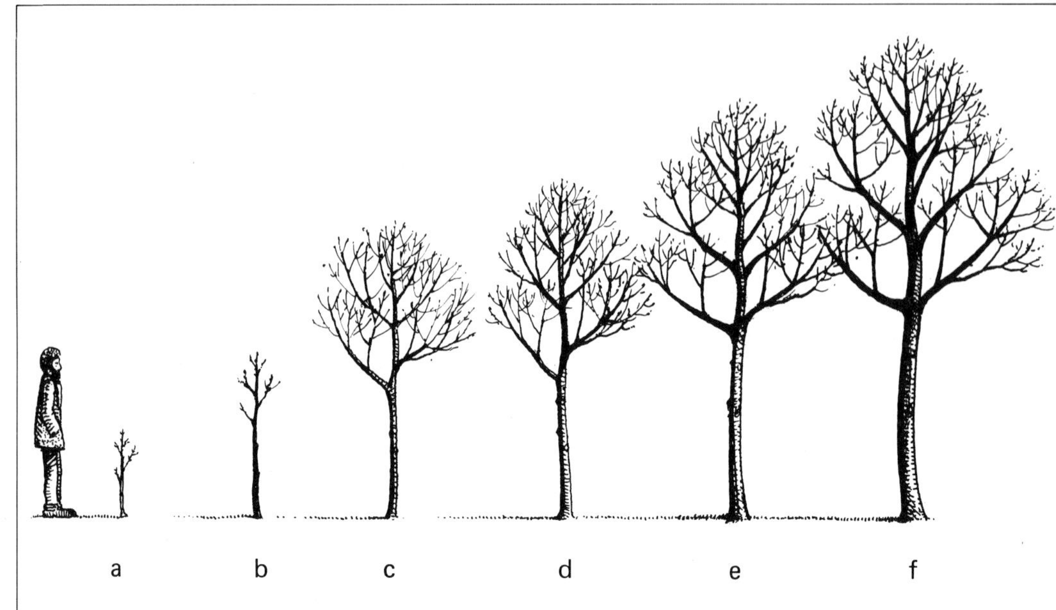

Fig 13 Comparative sizes of planting stock: (a) transplant, (b) whip, (c) half-standard, (d) standard, (e) extra-heavy standard, (f) semi-mature

handle easily, are easily lost amongst weeds and have insufficient reserves to carry them over the stress of planting.

Transplants are seedlings which have been transplanted in the nursery and are usually between two and four years old. They make bushier and sturdier plants, with fairly compact root systems. Transplanting causes the tree to slow down on height growth and to increase the bushiness of the root system, producing a thicker stem diameter at ground level. They are very useful for situations where large numbers of trees are to be planted. The age and cultural treatment received by transplants and seedlings is described in shorthand as 1 + 1 or 1 u 1 + 2, where the first number represents the time spent in the seedbed, the + sign and the period after it shows that the tree was transplanted and then spent so many years in the transplant lines, and the u shows that the plant was undercut (usually by a mechanical blade) to produce a sturdier plant without going to the expense and labour of transplanting. Transplants are usually in the size range 0.2–0.6m.

Whips are larger sizes of trees with a single whip-like shoot. They are sold by size, rather than cultural treatment. They are easy to plant and have the advantage that they are easier to see than transplants, making weeding and cultural treatment simpler. They are normally around 1m tall.

Feathered trees are from 1.5 to 2.5m. They do not have the small side branches or 'feathers' removed in the nursery, so the term feathered can be applied to various types of tree where the lower branches are retained. The advantages of retaining the feathers are that a more natural tree is obtained, and the tree is less subject to damage, either by vandals (if the top is broken there are plenty of branches lower down to grow) or by wild animals, e.g. bark stripping by deer.

Standard trees are ones in which the feathers are removed in the nursery, to give a length of clear stem. In half standards, the stem is 1.2–1.5m, but in full standards it is around 1.8m. Bush trees are similar but with a stem of only half a metre or so and a wide spreading crown on several branches. Standard trees are further divided upon the total height of the tree and the thickness of the stem at 1m. Light standards have a stem of girth 6–8cm, ordinary standards one 8–10cm, select standards 10–12cm, and extra heavy standards and advanced nursery stock have girths up to 25cm. The height generally keeps in step with the girth, although some trees, such as limes (*Tilia*) tend to have much stouter stems than normal for their height. It can be quite convenient to describe the girth in centimetres and the height in feet, as a tree of 6–8cm girth is usually 6–8 feet (1.8–2.4m) tall, one 10–12cm usually 10–12 feet (3–3.6m) and so on.

Standard trees are most useful for situations where immediate height is needed, such as beside a narrow street, or where some immediate impact is required. They are more appropriate in urban situations, being more robust (and more costly) than smaller trees.

'Semi-mature trees' are larger, up to 10–12m. They are very expensive and do not always grow satisfactorily after planting. Their advantage is that they can be used to create an immediate impact, giving scale to a situation. They are well worth considering *if* there is a definite benefit from achieving an immediate impact but they should not be used to form the ultimate basis of a planting scheme, as smaller sizes of trees will outgrow them within a few years, and outlive them. One type of site where semi-matures can be used to advantage is when creating a new urban park. Two or three 8–10m tall trees per hectare can be sufficient to give an impression of maturity in a flat and relatively formless new site and the cost can be justified in relation to the general cost of creation of the park (e.g. £200,000–500,000 per hectare).

Grafted Trees

Many ornamental species are vegetatively propagated by grafting them onto a rootstock. The benefits and drawbacks of this are discussed in Chapter 1, page 16. Grafting is often necessary for plants which will not root easily from cuttings and is a method which will make a saleable tree more quickly for some others. The rootstock may influence the development of the tree, the most prominent effect being seen with some fruit trees, where the rootstock can determine size, vigour and fruiting of the tree. Except for fruit trees, grafting should always be as near to ground level as possible, especially where the bark of the rootstock is markedly different from that of the scion. Topworked trees (i.e. grafted higher up the stem) are only acceptable in special situations, e.g. for pendulous trees. With any 'worked' tree, be on the lookout for sucker growth from the rootstock, as if left this will often grow faster than the scion and crowd it out.

Unusual Shapes

In some situations, multi-stemmed trees are required. These can sometimes be purchased. It is possible to achieve the desired effect by planting two or three small trees close together, or in the one hole. With trees which will coppice (i.e. grow from the base, which includes most broadleaved trees except those grafted onto a rootstock) a better result can be gained by cutting the tree down to ground-level after it has been planted for about two years and letting several stems grow. Curved or crooked stems can be created by planting the trees at an angle; subsequent growth will be vertical, creating a curved stem at the base.

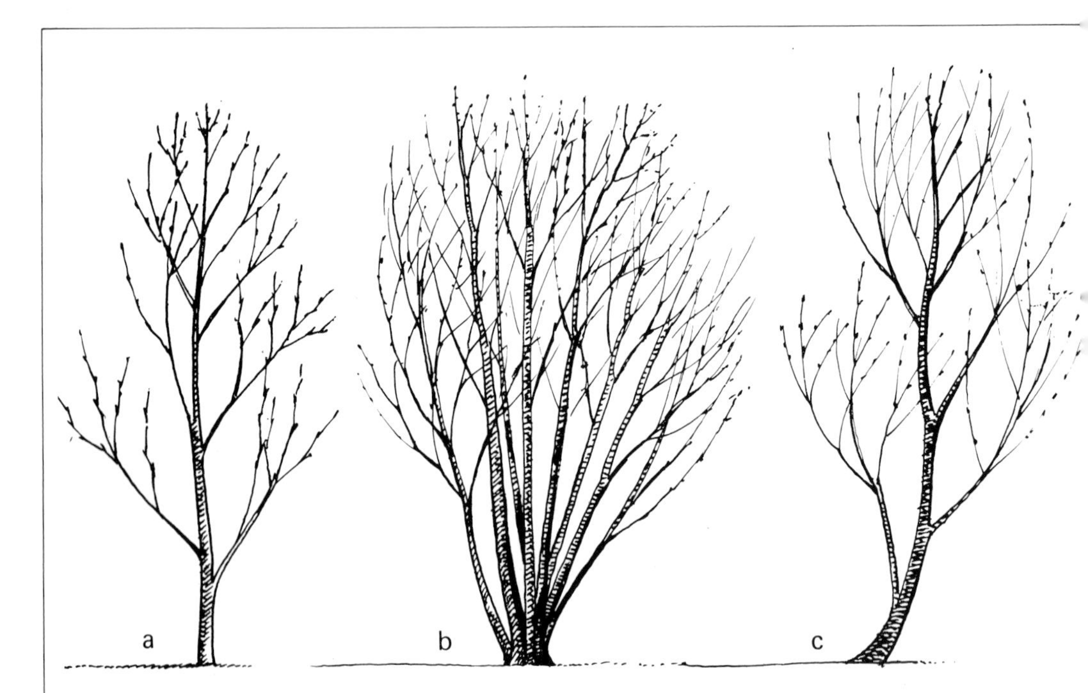

Fig 14 (a) Single-stemmed tree, (b) multi-stemmed tree, (c) curved-stemmed tree

Bare Root, Container Grown or Rootballed?

Bare rooted plants are generally cheaper, both to purchase, transport and to plant than other types. Where the trees are in good condition, they can establish very effectively after planting and this is the best method for most tree species and sites. There are a number of tree species, however, which can be very difficult to transplant bare rooted (see List 10). With deciduous trees, bare root stock can, also, only be safely used during the dormant season; although it is possible to move broadleaved trees in leaf, this can only be carried out over short distances and when watering is possible. For evergreens, such as conifers and trees like holm oak (*Quercus ilex*), only very small plants, effectively less than 0.75m, can be moved bareroot with a reasonable chance of success. Bare root stock is restricted to the traditional autumn/winter/spring planting season when the trees are dormant and leafless and is not amenable to out-of-season planting. This is discussed on page 75.

Container grown stock is more expensive and bulkier. The size of the container needs to be adequate (as does the root system of a bare rooted tree). The main justifications for using container grown stock are a) that the trees can be transplanted with the entire root system, thereby making establishment quicker and more reliable, b) for temperamental species (such as tulip tree – *Liriodendron tulipiferum* which resent root disturbance) losses are substantially reduced, and c) out of season planting is possible (see page 75).

This last point can be of major significance in some circumstances, such as on development sites when the planting has to follow the completion of the building works; delaying the planting till the next planting season can involve considerable cost in maintaining the areas to be planted, as well as losing a valuable opportunity to get the site established from the outset.

Rootballing is used for trees which are not easy to move bare rooted. The plant is dug up with the soil still attached to the root system, and the entire system wrapped in hessian. The soil keeps the roots moist and should lead to a greater proportion of the roots being moved with the plant. The system is particularly useful for the larger sizes of trees. It adds considerably to the weight of the tree and thereby the cost of planting. Rootballing is not a good option for small sizes of trees, as to be useful the rootball has to remain intact and most small trees do not produce suitable rootballs; there is no benefit if the rootball falls to pieces somewhere along the line. Because of the extra weight, there is a temptation for the root system to be cut smaller than it would be for a comparable bare root system. Generally, rootballing is a valuable option for broadleaved trees of 4–5m and over and for conifers and evergreens above 1.5–2m.

Good Quality Stock

Planting stock should be vigorous and disease free. The top should be in good condition but even more important is the state of the root system. The trees should have been transplanted or undercut in the nursery at intervals of no more than two years, in order to produce a compact root system. Such a root system will have many small roots, between 2 and 5mm in diameter, whereas the root system from a tree grown for a longer period in one place will consist of fewer but larger roots. The more small roots the tree has, the less roots it will lose when it is lifted; trees with a few long roots will inevitably lose much of the system when the tree is dug up and thereby be less suited to being planted out. It used to be thought that the small feeding or fibrous roots, those usually less than 1mm in diameter, were the most important ones but research has shown that the very finest roots often die and that new root growth is made from the somewhat larger roots, 2–5mm in diameter. Keeping the finest roots, though, is beneficial, as the care which needs to be taken ensures that the root system as a whole does not suffer from desiccation.

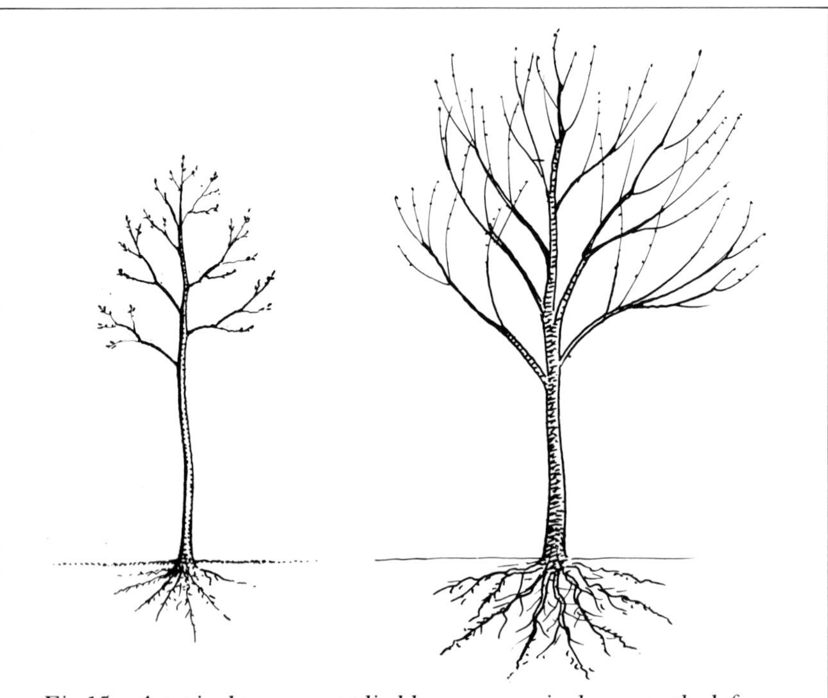

Fig 15 A typical tree as supplied by a nursery is shown on the left – a cheap plant with spindly stem and roots. By contrast, the ideal type of plant (right) has a sturdy stem and a well-developed, but compact, root system

11 Root system of a potbound tree, eventual failure guaranteed !

Some species naturally produce a better nursery root system than other trees. Ash (*Fraxinus excelsior*) usually makes a fibrous system, whereas cherries (*Prunus*) have coarse roots with relatively few small roots. It pays to know the characteristics of the species when making comments upon the root system.

Spindly close grown trees with vestigial root systems should be avoided or returned to the supplier.

When purchasing trees which have been grown in containers, it is even more important that they have not been in the same container for more than two growing seasons, and preferably just one. Trees kept in pots have a pronounced tendency to make roots which spiral around the container; if they are kept in the same one for more than two years, these spiralling roots will become woody and the plant potbound. When planted out, the roots often continue to grow from the ends of the spirals but do not spread out evenly into the surrounding soil. For a few years growth may be rapid, but after a while one of two consequences often develops. Either the lush tree is blown over during strong winds – this can be a particular problem with some of the pines (*Pinus*) which are rather tender when young (the temptation is to keep them for several years in pots until planting them out when mature foliage is produced), or the roots can strangle each other, depriving the top of water, nutrients or stability. Also, trees kept for more than 18 months in the one container are difficult to keep in the best vigour. With all container grown trees, if the roots show any tendency to spiral, they should be straightened out at the time of planting, or if this is not possible, cut so that new roots can grow out radially from the stem.

Conversely, avoid buying trees which have been too recently potted up. It takes about three months in the growing season for a containerised tree to form a reasonable fibrous root system which will remain intact when the tree is planted out.

Containers used for pot grown trees should be sufficiently large to give the tree a sizeable root system. Avoid tall trees in small containers. As a general rule, the container should have a diameter equal to between a quarter and a sixth of the plant's height.

Caring for the Tree Prior to Planting

Always ensure that the tree's roots are moist and never allowed to dry out. This is important with bare root stock and with container grown plants, the latter can easily dry out during cold frosty spells over winter. With bare root plants, avoid exposure of the roots or the shoots to drying winds or to strong sunshine, even a few minutes can kill or damage the roots of some species, such as rauli (*Nothofagus procera*). List 10 gives details of tree genera which require extra care when handling or planting.

The interval between lifting and planting should be as short as possible. Also keep the plants cool, although avoid freezing (frozen roots are unable to absorb moisture and can die from desiccation). The roots of bare rooted plants should be wrapped in damp straw or enclosed in polythene bags. Enclosing the roots in polythene is a very satisfactory way to keep small trees (those less than 0.75m tall) in good condition but the parcels must not be exposed to the sun, as this can very easily lead to overheating, which will kill the trees. Evergreens in particular benefit from total enclosure in polythene, provided the foliage is not wet, (moulds may develop on the leaves in the humid conditions).

If plants have to be held for more than a few days, they should be taken out of their wrappings and the roots placed either in damp organic matter such as peat, bark or chopped straw, or in garden soil. An alternative is to keep them in a special low temperature cold room. Whichever method is used, check regularly that the material around the roots is moist. Bundles of trees with their roots in soil or organic matter can quickly dry out under certain conditions, and remain dry even after periods of rain.

Experiments involving the dropping of bundles of trees suggest that rough handling of bare root trees can affect the ability of the trees to make new root growth; so avoid flinging the bundles of plants about!

A 'Code of Practice for Plant Handling' has been prepared by the Joint Liaison Committee on Plant Supplies, and is available from the Horticultural Trades Association (HTA), 19 High Street, Theale, Reading, Berks, England, RG7 5AH. Tel: (0734) 303132

Soil Condition

The condition of the soil will have been considered before the choice of species was made, but on most soils and with nearly all tree species, some form of cultivation or amelioration is beneficial. The benefits may be shown both by better survival of the plants and faster initial growth. The period prior to planting is the only time during the life of a tree when the soil may be cultivated without damaging the tree. The types of amelioration of the soil which may be considered or are sometimes recommended are cultivation, and adding nutrients and organic matter. The components of soils and ways in which the soil can be modified or improved are discussed under 'Assessing the site' in Chapter 2.

Season for Planting

The normal planting season is in the autumn/winter/spring period but different plants are best planted at varying times within the season. With bare root plants (see page 71 above), it is unwise to move the tree very far before they have naturally shed the leaves in late October or early November, although with care they can be satisfactorily moved over short distances when in leaf. They are best planted as soon as possible after this period, although they can be planted at any time before they come into leaf in the spring. Evergreen trees are better planted either earlier in the autumn or in late March or early April; midwinter is better avoided. This is because evergreen trees are always going to lose moisture from their foliage, even in midwinter, and it is better to plant them when the roots are immediately capable of making new growth but when the tops are not growing. Evergreens can therefore with advantage be planted out later in the spring, as they flush later; they can also be moved very satisfactorily in September (if water is available in case it turns out to be a dry month) when top growth has stopped but the roots are still active. Some trees with thick fleshy roots, like dove tree (*Davidia involucrata*) and magnolias (*Magnolia*), though deciduous, should be treated as honorary evergreens and should be planted when the roots are able to make new growth immediately.

Container grown trees can be planted out during most of the year. If they are planted in the middle of the growing season, they will need to be watered for several weeks. When planted at other times, a check should be made to see that the compost has not become dry, as the effect of the foliage can be to act as an umbrella and deflect water away from the roots; always remember that in the nursery the plants were regularly watered.

Periods to avoid are when the soil is very dry, when the ground is covered with snow and when it is deeply frozen. The problem with both snow and frozen ground is that it is very difficult to firm properly the plant into the soil, and that airpockets or patches of snow or ice are left around the roots; as soon as the weather improves this melts and the roots dry out. The actual temperature is less likely to affect plants, unless they have been kept inside. If the crust of frost is only shallow, e.g. less than 2cm, it should not affect planting.

Planting

The stages in planting are: to excavate a suitable pit or hole, place the tree at the appropriate level in it, and backfill.

Sometimes it is suggested that the pit should be excavated in advance; this can be beneficial on heavy soils if there is no risk of the pit filling with water – the action of frost and drying out of the soil will improve the structure, but generally is not worth doing, and if the pit fills with water a new one will be needed anyway.

The pit needs to be large enough to accommodate the roots of the tree. It is better if the soil is dug out to make a larger pit and the sides broken down to permit the roots to spread outwards. When digging the pit, the top layer of soil with turf should be chopped up in the bottom of the pit; on no account should it be replaced at surface level around the tree after planting, as the competition from the grasses will seriously affect the growth and survival of the tree (see pages 82–6). It is important that the tree is planted more or less at the original soil level, and not buried at the bottom of the hole.

The tree is placed in the pit and the roots spread out. Only roots which have been badly damaged should be pruned, all other roots will be needed by the tree. The nursery soil mark on the stem should be at or just above ground level at this stage.

Soil is then gently placed on top of the root system, the tree shaken to work the soil between the roots and when the roots are covered by a layer of soil, this is firmed to make good contact with the roots. The object of firming the soil is to make contact between the tree and the soil, not to compact the soil into rock! Further soil is placed on top of the root system until the tree is planted at the same level it was in the nursery. At this stage, the soil will probably be found to be on a slight mound of 3–5cm; this will settle. If the soil is in large clods, it is worth importing some friable soil from elsewhere, although it should be similar to that on site; importing different soil may lead the tree to grow in a 'plug' of the better soil and fail to root into the surrounding ground. When planting

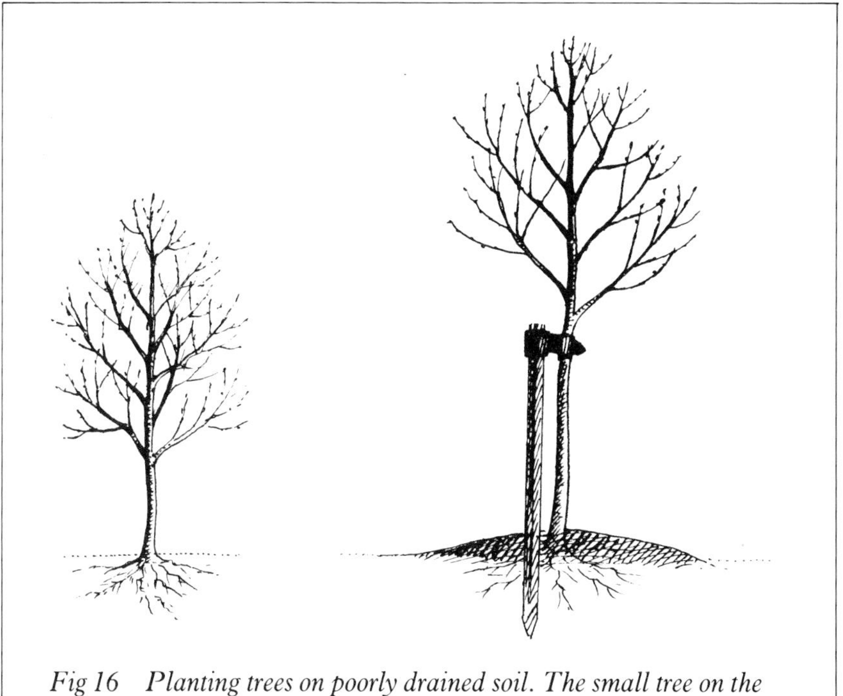

Fig 16 Planting trees on poorly drained soil. The small tree on the left is planted fairly shallowly, while the larger tree is also planted shallowly but in a slight mound of soil

container grown trees, it is wise to mix some peat or other organic matter in with the backfill soil.

When planting into very light sandy soils, it is possible to plant in a small depression, so that it will be easier to water the tree. On other soils a slight mound is preferable, especially as the soil will settle. On very heavy soils, or wet shallow clays, planting on a definite mound is advisable. This leaves the tree a greater depth of soil into which to root, before encountering the waterlogged layers. When planting on a mound, it is imperative to control weed growth and on very heavy sites, it is better to use smaller stock.

The above describes 'pit planting', which is appropriate for all sizes of tree. When planting larger numbers of transplants, as in forestry schemes, there is an alternative method which can be satisfactory. This is notch planting. It is not quite as good as pit planting, but is significantly faster, and a few failures can often be tolerated when planting thousands of trees.

In notch planting, the blade of the spade is pushed into the ground and rocked back and forth to make a notch in the soil. The roots of the transplant are pushed into the notch and gently pulled up and down, so that the roots are spread out in the space and the soil is at the correct level on the stem. The notch is then closed by the spade being driven into the soil a few centimetres from the previous place and wriggled; finally, the soil is firmed around the plant using the heel of the boot (using the toe of the boot does not firm the soil adequately). On rough or stony ground, a mattock is often used instead of a spade, for both pit and notch planting of small transplants.

Staking and Tying

The diagram which has appeared in one form or another in thousands of posters or leaflets over the past couple of decades shows the planting of a standard tree (i.e. a tree with a stem 1.8m tall) tied securely in several places to a stout stake which is almost as tall as the tree. This prescription has been dutifully followed in the planting of thousands of trees; and the sight of trees rubbing against the top of the stake, being slowly strangled by unloosened tree-ties, or manfully supporting stakes which have rotted away at ground level, has become an accepted commonplace in areas which have been 'landscaped'. In fact, such planting has become the 'norm', so that areas which have been treated more professionally have sometimes given rise to complaints that proper care is not being taken of the trees.

12 A well-planted stake, pity about the tree. Weed control might have saved it!

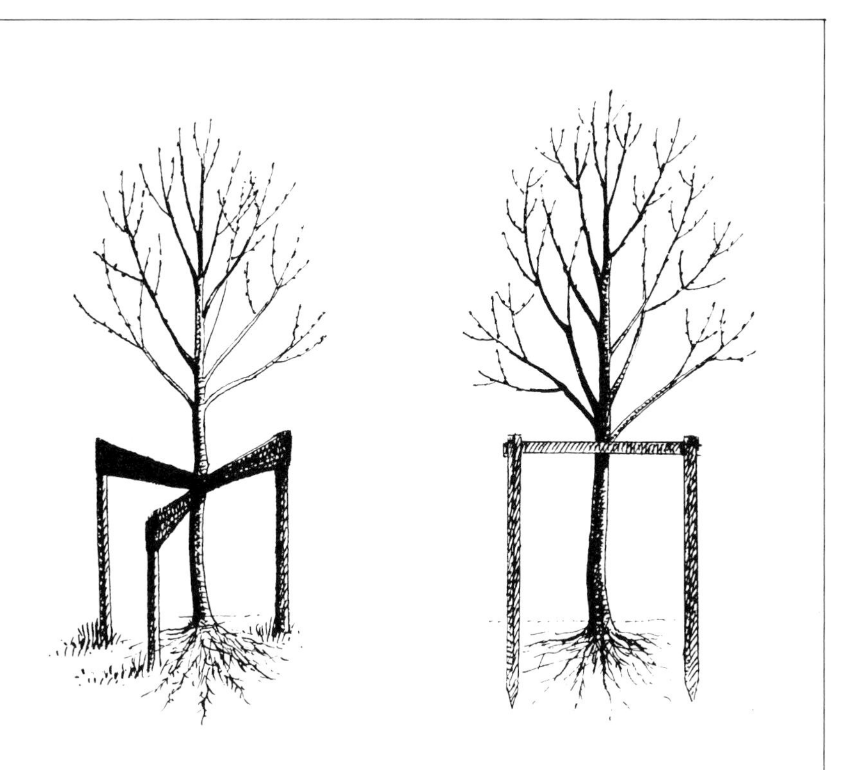

Fig 17 Double staking is necessary on a windy site for trees which have been 'root-balled' or are very branchy – single stakes would be inadequate or impractical. The tree can be fastened to a cross-piece (right) or by three tree-ties pulling in opposite directions

It is pertinent to remember that trees naturally grow without stakes! However, where a tree is closely grown in the nursery (particularly thin stemmed trees such as some *Malus*, see Gazetteer) and when a tree has then been planted out in a windswept site, some form of support is going to be needed until it is established.

The function of staking should be to hold the roots firm so that new root growth can be made. This does not require holding the stem in place.

Trees only thicken the stem in response to the natural bending that the stem receives as it is moved in the wind; hold it rigid against a telegraph pole and it will not get the necessary stimulus to thicken. In fact, such 'over-staked' trees are often narrower at 1m than they are above the top tie. Eucalypts (*Eucalyptus*) will show this very clearly if over-staked. If the stake breaks or is abruptly removed from trees like this, even after several years, the tree invariably falls over.

The best way to stake normal sizes of nursery stock, i.e. standards, is to use a very short stake with no more than 30–50cm above ground. This is

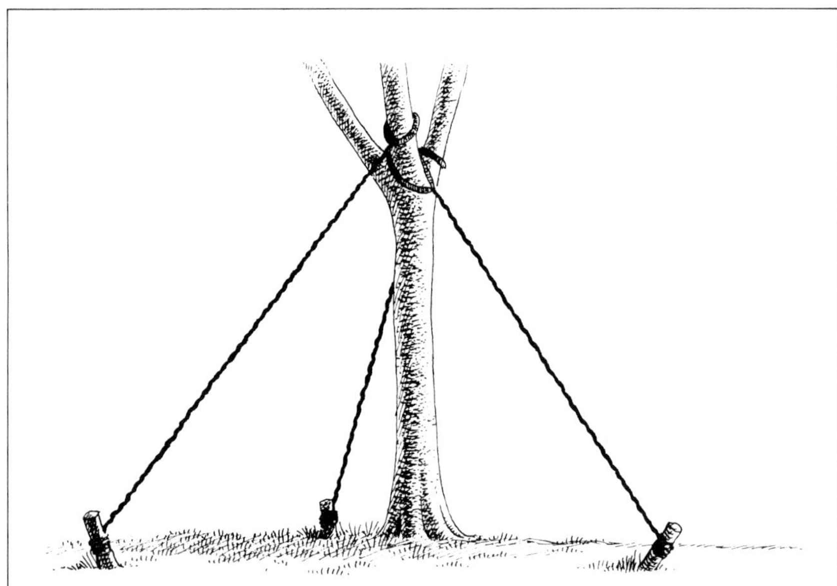

Fig 18 Securing a heavy tree with guy wires until firmly rooted. The tree must be protected against chafing by the wire, and the wires must be kept reasonably taut to hold the tree firmly

placed in the planting pit close to where the stem will be; the tree is attached to the top of this stake by an expandable tie. The tie should have a spacer to keep the tree away from the stake so that it can't rub against it. String and webbing are disastrous materials for ties. Far better are plastic materials; although these appear very rigid and tough in winter temperatures (when they are put on) they become softer and more flexible during the summer and will expand to some extent as the tree grows, although even these should be checked and loosened as appropriate. The stake should not be treated with preservative, or it will neither rot down nor be easily removed without causing damage.

Stakes applied as prescribed above should not be needed for more than two seasons, or at very most three, provided the trees are properly looked after, including adequate weed control. If it is necessary to support the stem whilst it thickens (as with the *Malus* example above), a bamboo cane will allow it to move, and therefore to thicken naturally. This should be considered as a separate exercise from staking the roots.

Larger trees can be staked by using either three short stakes or three guy ropes. With the larger sizes, the stem should be sufficiently strong, so it is only a case of holding the roots firm until they have established. Care must be taken to ensure that where the ties are in contact with the tree they do not damage the stem.

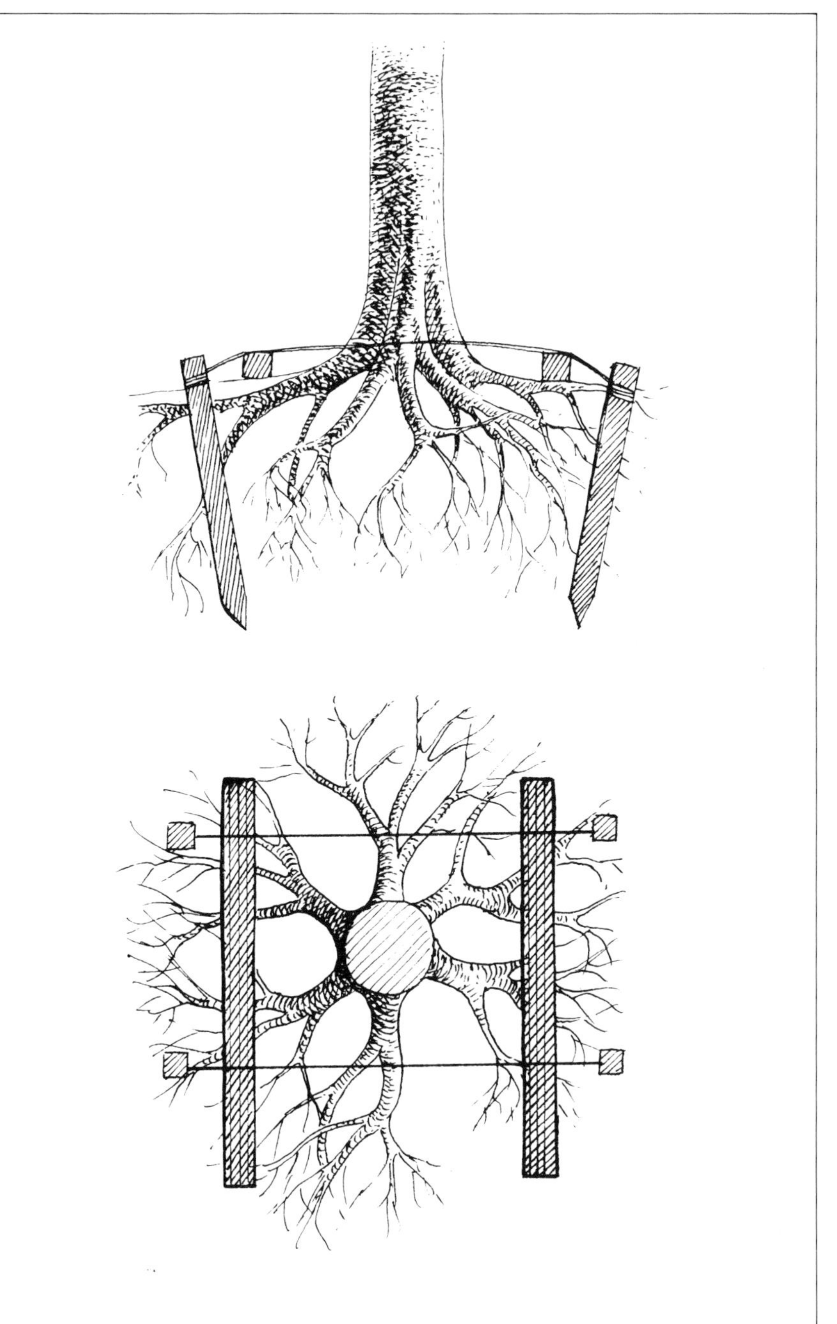

Fig 19a Heavy tree secured by wooden bars placed over the roots. The bars are held down by wires attached to metal stakes. Cross section and plan view shown

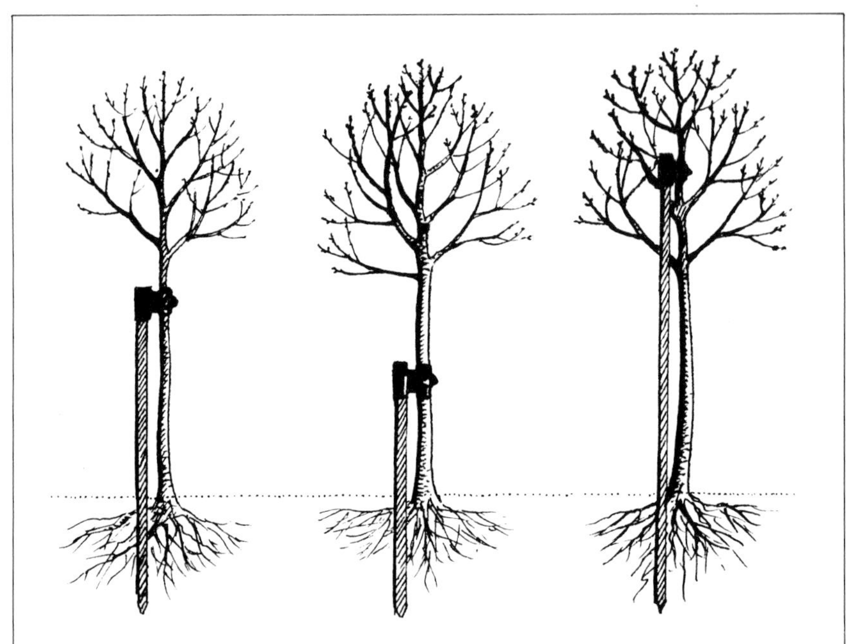

Fig 19b Conventional staking, with a single tree stake: (left) for a tree with a weak stem (perhaps grown too close together in the nursery); (centre) for a tree with stronger growing stem; (right) with a very tall stake to prevent vandals snapping off top of tree

Sometimes, because of the risk of vandalism, it may be thought necessary to use a longer stake, although a short stake may in fact result in less vandalism. The topmost tie should be within 3cm of the top of the stake in all cases.

Establishment/Weed Control

The establishment phase involves getting the tree to recommence normal growth. To achieve this rapidly it is necessary to control weed growth, either by hand, by chemicals or by mulching, but watering may also be necessary or helpful in the first couple of seasons, if dry.

Grasses, clover and, to a lesser extent, other plants growing near to a tree compete for available water and nutrients (and if the tree is very small, for daylight also). Some trees can survive such competition better than others, although all will grow more slowly because of it; may or hawthorn (*Crataegus monogyna*) and English oak (*Quercus robur*) can successfully colonise neglected pastures, competing effectively with the rank herbage, whereas species such as pine (*Pinus*) or birch (*Betula*), are less effective competitors and typically only colonise bare earth or very poor soils where competition is less. Even may and oak grow faster on bare soil.

As a rule, grasses compete most strongly for soil moisture and nitrogen. Tall herbs, such as rose-bay willowherb or hemp agrimony, are less troublesome, although they can outgrow and smother trees less than 1.5m tall. Shrubs such as bramble (*Rubus*) and gorse (*Ulex europaeus*) also tend to use less moisture but can overgrow even quite tall trees unless cut back periodically. They can also be a fire hazard. The best conditions for tree growth are created by eliminating all competing vegetation within the rooting area.

Control of weeds by cutting is largely ineffective – close mown turf will actually depress the growth of trees more than uncut grass by exerting greater competition for the available water and nutrients. Cutting is only useful where rank vegetation is taller than the young trees and is shading them out. Hoeing is better, but must be shallow, or the roots of the tree will be damaged; it is better to pull the weeds out by hand, shake off the soil, and leave the weeds as a contribution to the mulch around the trees.

Herbicides

Herbicides can be very effective in removing competing vegetation, provided they are properly used and safely applied. They divide into two groups, soil-acting and contact herbicides.

Contact herbicides are applied to the plant foliage, being absorbed through the cuticle. Only living tissue can be treated, which means that most of these chemicals can only be used during the period when the weeds are in leaf and growing. They are not persistent. Contact herbicides are very useful for preplanting applications, which are best carried out in the autumn. The most commonly used contact herbicides are paraquat and glyphosate.

Paraquat interrupts the plant's photosynthesis; it only affects the portions onto which it is applied and is not translocated. This means that it is ineffective against perennial weeds with underground rootstocks, but fairly safe if accidentally applied to tree foliage (the tree will be partly defoliated but probably not killed). Paraquat is very poisonous to people and is covered under the Poisons Act. Paraquat is marketed as Weedol, Gramoxone and under other trade names.

Glyphosate is different and acts by interfering with respiration. It is easily translocated through the plant, thereby being useful against deep rooted weeds, but is slow acting. Because it is readily translocated, it can cause damage if accidentally applied to tree foliage. By contrast with paraquat, glyphosate has a very low mammalian toxicity and is very safe for the operators. Glyphosate is marketed as Tumbleweed and Roundup. Both paraquat and glyphosate are rendered inoperative on contact with soil. Several other contact herbicides are available.

Soil-acting herbicides are applied to the soil surface. They are bound in the top few centimetres of the soil and taken up by the roots of seedling plants. Trees are less affected because they are deeper rooting. Soil-acting herbicides are persistent, giving effective weed control for up to 8 months. Useful ones include simazine, propyzamide, napropamide, oxydiazon and dichlobenil.

Simazine is cheap but at too strong a dose will kill trees along with weeds. It can be applied at any time of year, provided the soil is moist, or can be moistened. Simazine is usually applied as a water-based spray, but is also available as an oil-based formulation or in granular form. In some parts of Britain, groundsel (*Senecio vulgaris*) has developed a resistance to simazine. Simazine is marketed under a number of product names.

Propyzamide is much safer, in weed control experiments only showing foliage damage to trees when applied at four times the recommended rate. It is very effective against grasses, but much less so against broadleaved weeds. It has to be applied in the October-December period (to January in northern England and Scotland) as it is only bound into the soil at low soil temperatures; this is because the active ingredient is volatile. Propyzamide is very useful, as it can be used as either a pre-planting (if notch planting is used) or post-planting herbicide. It can be applied either in granular form or as a water-based spray. Propyzamide is marketed as Kerb.

Napropamide is a new herbicide which shows considerable promise; it can be mixed with simazine and be used on newly planted stock. It is particularly suitable where groundsel has developed resistance to simazine. It may also be a useful management tool, to use a rotation of herbicides, such as napropamide and simazine, rather than continually use a single one, which runs the risk of resistance to it being developed by weed species. Napropamide is marketed as Banweed and Banweed-S with 10% simazine.

Oxydiazon is similar in application to the other soil applied herbicides, but is actually a contact herbicide. It is bound into the soil surface layer and kills by contact, not root uptake, any young plant tissue which grows through the surface layer. It is not translocated. It can be useful where bindweed is a problem, acting as a chemical hoe, although not killing the root system. Oxydiazon is marketed as Ronstar.

Dichlobenil is useful around established trees but is not recommended for newly planted ones. It will control established weeds, depending upon the rate of application. It can cause damage to the base of trees if granules are allowed to lodge against the bark but otherwise is reasonably safe. It should be applied in late winter or early spring, to moist soil. Dichlobenil is marketed as Casoron.

When using any herbicides, the manufacturer's recommendations, as given on the label, should be followed.

Application methods include knapsack sprayers, controlled droplet applicators, wick applicators and granular applicators. Knapsack sprayers are useful for water-based sprays, but require a fairly large quantity of water, which is heavy, tiring and time consuming, particularly when out in the woods. Also, because the spray is produced from a nozzle at pressure, there is little control over the droplet size and drift is a problem. Knapsack sprayers should only be used in still air conditions.

In the controlled droplet systems, a spinning disk throws out a fairly precisely defined spray of droplets of herbicide. As the size of the droplets is even, there is much less risk of drift than with a knapsack sprayer, which increases the number of days in which spraying can be carried out. Controlled droplet systems use special oil-based formulations of herbicide, applied as a concentrated emulsion at very low volume. The system is useful for herbicides such as simazine and glyphosate but cannot be used with paraquat, as this is too poisonous a chemical to apply in concentrated form.

Wick based applicators ('Weed Wipers') can be used to apply glyphosate to vegetation. The herbicide is fed from a reservoir to a fabric wick and rubbed onto the weed. The method allows for accurate application, with no risk of any drift. Currently, it only has clearance for use with glyphosate and must not be used with paraquat.

Granular herbicides can be applied either by special applicators, or from a pepperpot. A pepperpot applicator works on the principle of having a reservoir of granules and a perforated lid; the granules are shaken onto the area to be treated.

With all application methods, it is very important to be familiar with the method and rate of dosing. Experience can be obtained by measuring the area treated in a certain time, or by applying granules to a sheet of polythene and measuring the dosage given to work out how the correct dose looks on the ground.

Mulches

Mulches are a marvellous way of controlling weeds without resorting to chemicals and some types can give enhanced growth. There are esentially two types of mulch; organic materials such as peat or bark, and inorganic ones like polythene sheeting or gravel. The purposes of a mulch are to keep the soil moist, by inhibiting water loss from the surface, and to prevent the growth of weeds.

The area covered by the mulch needs to be sufficient to benefit the tree. For a small transplant or whip no more than a metre high, the minimum area should be a quarter square metre, but an area nearer one square metre would show considerably more benefit. For all trees, the area covered should be of radius at least 30cm larger than the spread of the root system at planting. For heavy standards, this means a minimum radius of nearly a metre, i.e. about 3 square metres in area.

Organic mulches include bark, peat, straw or wood chips. They are slowly broken down by soil bacteria and incorporated into the soil. Organic mulches may need to be topped up on a regular (annual) basis. Ideally, an organic mulch should retain an open structure; one such material is coarse conifer bark, and this is the most effective organic mulch, lasting for 3–5 years. Other materials, like sawdust and fine grades of peat, may become too dense, restricting the free exchange of air and water with the soil; and some mulches may provide good germinating conditions for weed seeds, although they are usually easily pulled. Wood chips can provide a growing medium for harmful decay fungi, but usually there is no problem. Organic mulches need to be in a layer at least 5cm (up to 10cm) thick to prevent light reaching the soil surface. Materials like fresh lawn mowings can be included but are not recommended for use on their own as they will make a rather impenetrable layer, and a fairly deep layer may also give off heat on decomposition, damaging the trees.

Inorganic mulches include polythene sheeting, bituminous roofing felt and gravel. Gravel is used in the same manner as organic materials. It is slowly incorporated by worm activity. It can be quite effective, although of most use on scree beds for alpines or to show off dwarf conifers.

Polythene sheeting is a very cheap and effective mulch, although less sightly than some other materials. One advantage of polythene sheeting (and roofing felt) is that in addition to controlling weeds and moisture loss, the higher surface soil temperatures generated under the polythene leads to an increased mineralisation of nutrients, giving a further boost to growth. Also, a larger area can economically be covered by polythene than for other mulches. 500 gauge black polythene should be used, as this will cut out light and should last approximately three years (which is sufficient to get a tree established); redundant fertiliser sacks can be used. The mulch is placed over the root system at the time of planting and can be held down by placing clods of earth or stones over the sheet. A more effective method is to make a slit with a spade about 10cm in from the outline of the sheet and to use the spade to push the polythene into this slit. If this is done on all four sides, this will hold a sheet one metre square in place. Polythene mulching is a very effective method for establishing trees in places such as farms, where labour is available for planting during the winter, but is not available for maintenance during the busier early summer period.

Watering

If properly planted and with good control of weeds, newly planted trees in the average British summer should not need watering, except possibly on some very shallow or freely drained soils, such as light sands. However, all summers are not equally wet and if the planting was late or other site factors are against the trees, some watering may be needed.

The amount of water to be given can be related to the amount of water likely to be consumed by the tree, and the amount which will be evaporated from the area of soil in which the roots occur (see Chapter 2, page 26). In practice, about 50–75 litres (10–15 gallons) per square metre of root area will suffice, provided weed control measures are instigated (i.e. all weeds are pulled when applying the water). It is better to apply the water on a weekly or fortnightly basis; more frequent waterings may induce waterlogging and lead to a shallow surface rooting system, whilst the soil may become too dry and difficult to rewet if longer intervals are used.

Water applied quickly to the surface of fairly dry soil will almost invariably lead to runoff. If using a hose, the nozzle can be forced into the soil to apply the water below the surface (provided the pressure is not such as to wash soil away). It can be useful to place a perforated plastic pipe in the soil at the time of planting. With large trees, this can be laid around the hole and be capable of holding several gallons. On sloping sites on light soils, the trees can be planted in a slight dip, which will hold the water until it soaks in.

Protection

Newly planted trees often need protecting against wild or domestic animals, vehicles, machinery and man (see Chapter 2, pages 37–42). Some tender species also benefit from frost and wind protection, whilst growth of many species may be enhanced by using individual tree shelters (see below).

Where the tree planting is in grazed land, some form of protection is essential. The options are either to fence the entire planting area or to protect each tree individually. The cost of fencing an area is such that it is often more economic to give individual protection. Also, where a fence is breached all the trees within are at risk, whereas when an individual protection is lost, only one tree can be destroyed. The relative costs can be determined on the basis of a critical area index, where

$$\text{Critical Area Index} = \frac{\text{Cm} \times \text{P}}{\text{N} \times \text{Ci}}$$

where Cm is the cost of fencing per linear metre, Ci the cost of providing an individual tree shelter, P is the length of fencing needed to enclose the

Fig 20 Protection against livestock: (left) a short fence at a wide distance from the tree; and (right) a tall fence close to the tree

area and N the number of trees to be protected. If the index is less than one, it will be cheaper to fence, if more than one, cheaper to give individual protection. Further details on this, and other aspects of individual tree protection, is given in Arboricultural Leaflet 10, produced by the Forestry Commission Forest Research Station, Alice Holt Lodge, Farnham, Surrey, GU10 4LH.

Protection may be needed against browsing of foliage and against rubbing or damage to the bark. Of these the latter damage is more catastrophic, as trees can tolerate a certain amount of browsing. To protect the stem against damage, a certain amount of protection can be provided by a wire or plastic mesh guard around the stem. For protection of foliage, the guard must either keep the animals away, or keep the leading shoot out of reach, so that the tree grows away. Animals can be kept away from the foliage by constructing a post, rail and netting guard. For horses and cattle, the protection must be at least 90cm high and placed 1.5m radius away from the tree. The corresponding figures for sheep are 90cm and 60cm. Where the tree is planted on the far side of a fence, this can be made taller for a metre or so either side of the tree.

Animals can be effectively kept away from the leading shoot by tall narrow guards. These are made of plastic mesh and are either 7.5 or 15cm in diameter. For rabbits, they should be 60cm tall, for hares 75cm tall, for sheep 1.3m, for roe deer 1.2m and for red or fallow deer 1.8m. Metal guards can also be used, but are less sightly, more likely to cause damage, more expensive and will not bio-degrade after 5–10 years (which may, however, be an advantage where on-going protection is needed). Where

13 Protecting trees from cattle using posts and rails

14–15 Mound planting used to protect trees in a parkland setting

protection is needed against voles, smaller mesh is needed for the lower portion of the stem, up to 5cm above the top of the summer vegetation (cutting the grass short for a year or two will give good control). Spiral rabbit guards are frequently advertised but have several limitations, particularly tending to get blown over on windy sites, and the plastic mesh ones are generally more efficient. Details on these guards are given in Arboricultural Leaflet 10.

Grey squirrels can be a particular problem. In late spring and early summer, the friendly little beasts strip the bark from the stems of young trees, or the branches of older ones. Maples, especially sycamore (*Acer pseudoplatanus*), and beech (*Fagus sylvatica*) are most likely to be affected, but a wide range of other species, including English oak (*Quercus robur*), poplar (*Populus*) and willow (*Salix*), can also be affected. Shooting is ineffective, as one never shoots all the squirrels. In woodland, poisoning using Warfarin in special hoppers is useful, but unlikely to be appreciated by the general public in a park; (also Warfarin may not be used in those parts of the country where the native red squirrel is still to be found, and it will kill any mice or voles which manage to gain access). The simplest method may be to replace badly damaged trees with less susceptible species. Outbreaks of bark-stripping are variable and unpredictable, and even in years when there are a lot of squirrels around you may find that a combination of reducing the number of dreys (nests) and providing alternative food during the susceptible period, from May to July, reduces damage to an acceptable level.

In urban areas, trees may need protecting against damage by vandals. The traditional welded metal guards used in many inner city sites give some protection, but probably kill as many trees as the vandals; when the tie breaks the tree gets damaged and ringbarked by the top of the guard, or the guard is filled with litter, which is then set alight. Traditional heavy iron guards can be used, but are very expensive and damaging if the tree grows over them. Some trials have been made with plastic mesh guards and they appear, from limited experience, to be at least as effective as other materials, at lower cost.

Trees may also need protection around car parks. This can be given by the use of kerbs or bollards. If using bollards, make them tall enough to be visible to a driver reversing and place them, and kerbs, some distance from the tree.

In areas where grass is regularly mown, one of the main causes of damage to trees is from the mowers striking the base. Better trained staff is one answer, but more likely to yield results is to remove the need for the mower to come close to the tree. If a radius of 0.5m (preferably 1m) is kept free from grass, damage will be much less frequent. Either herbicide or mulch can be used to maintain the grass free zone.

Tree Shelters

These are translucent plastic tubes which create around a seedling tree conditions similar to those found in a greenhouse and enhance its height growth. The results are particularly promising with traditionally slow trees, such as English and sessile oaks (*Quercus robur* and *Q. petraea*). The tubes are approximately 1.2m long and about 10cm in diameter; they are supported by a small stake and can also serve as protection against rabbits or deer. They also make it easier to locate the trees in rather overgrown woodland or grassland and protect the trees if herbicides are applied. Height growth is enhanced, particularly in fairly weedy sites, but total biomass is not increased when compared with trees on sites with full weed control. The short-term benefits are often clear and as a means of establishing a wide range of slow growing trees, they are good. The long-term effect on tree growth is not known.

Pruning

Some pruning may be useful when a tree is planted, in order to redress any imbalance between roots and branches, or to produce a better shaped tree. It is much easier to remove weak or crossing branches from a 5m tree when it can be laid on its side, than when it is planted. Some expert opinion believes that as some roots are inevitably lost during lifting a similar reduction in the branch system will help remedy the situation. There is probably some truth in this line of thought, but any pruning should not be too drastic for the following reasons: a tree can accommodate the loss of some roots; the newly planted tree will need all the leaves it can support to make new top and root growth; food reserves are stored in all the woody tissues, so removing branches is depriving the tree of stored reserves. Generally, good planting stock and practice, with proper weed control, should obviate the need for such pruning, other than that needed to remove crossing branches or double leaders. Pruning is discussed further in Chapter 5.

5
CARE OF ESTABLISHED AND AGEING TREES

EXISTING trees represent the capital accumulated over the years. They need to be effectively managed both for present safety and enjoyment and so that trees of comparable or better quality can be passed onto future generations. The successful guardian will need to combine patience (trees take a while to make giant specimens) with foresight (trees need to be replaced for the benefit of future trees and treescapes) and management (to know when to thin, remove dead wood, brace, etc, or when to do nothing) to have the best of the present beauty and to leave a worthwhile inheritance for future tree lovers. This section looks at the various aspects of tree surgery and tree removal.

Tree Surgery

This is an all embracing term to describe procedures carried out to trees either for the benefit of the trees, or of those living around them. The main aspects of tree surgery are pruning of young actively growing trees, activities to lengthen the safe life of old trees, and removal of surplus or dangerous trees and their stumps. The following discussion is not intended as a treatise on tree surgery but as a relevant résumé. For a fuller treatment, the reader is recommended to consult *Tree Surgery – a complete guide* by Peter Bridgeman (David & Charles); this gives information on many aspects of tree surgery, including equipment and safety, although some of the recommendations for tree work may not be supported in the light of current research.

Pruning Established Trees

This can be carried out either to improve the longterm prospects for the trees or to enable people to live with trees. Pruning newly planted trees is discussed on page 92.

A little early attention to trees can often prevent problems in later years and enable the trees to live longer without becoming unsafe. If unwanted branches are removed when they are only 3–5cm in diameter, the cut surfaces will callus over within a short space of time, with little prospect

16 Branch removal scar on an oak with well developed callus

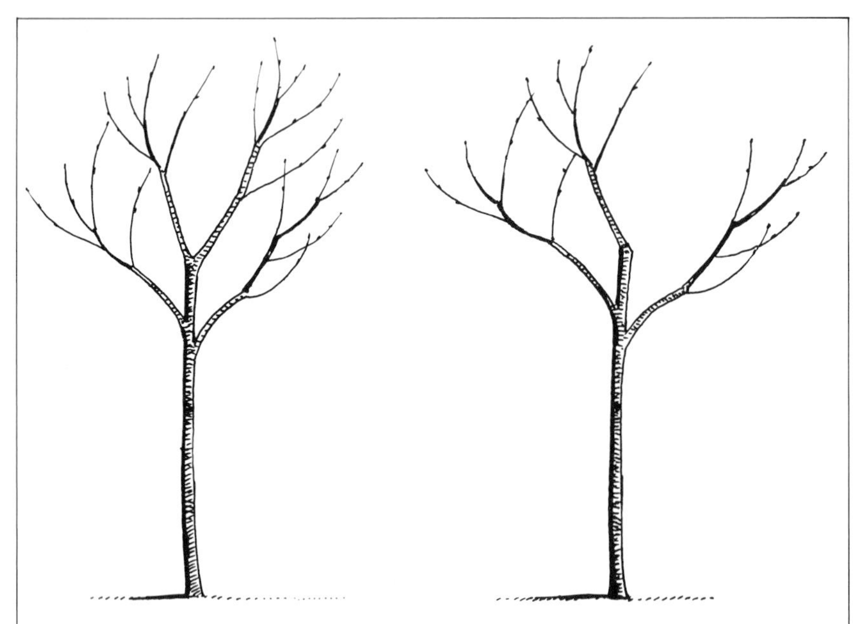

Fig 21 If one side of a young tree's forked stem is to be removed before it gets too large, the stem will straighten as it grows, producing a sounder structure

of decay organisms gaining entry; but if the pruning is left until the branch is 15–30cm across, the wound will take years to close over (or may never!), and there is a much greater risk of decay fungi gaining entry, not to mention the effect on the amenity value of the removal of a substantial branch.

The main cultural requirement is to form a sound branch system which will be capable of withstanding the gales, falls of wet snow and other natural calamities to which the tree will be subjected during its life. It is particularly important to remove at an early stage any double leaders which make a narrow crotch. As the two stems grow together, their increase in girth results in an outward pressure on each other. Also narrow crotches are weaker and easier to force apart than ones nearer a right angle. If left, there is the prospect that one side will be blown out during a storm, taking half the tree with it and leaving the remainder unsafe.

Crossing branches should be removed; the bark will be removed where they rub together and decay fungi may gain entry; the point of contact may also act as a fulcrum in strong winds, leading to branch break (also, they will often let out weird shrieking noises in windy weather, which will disturb those living nearby and raise fears that the tree is about to fall over). Broken or diseased branches (and weak ones which are going to die within the timespan of the cycle of dead wood removal) should also be removed. Sometimes it will be appropriate to remove branches to improve the visual balance of the tree.

When living branches are removed, they should be removed reasonably close to the main stem. Long snags should not be left as they will prevent the callus from growing over the wound, but the older recommendation to cut as flush as possible is now found to cause some unnecessary damage. In many species, there is a collar of growth which is angled across a branch, being closer to the stem on the top side and further away on the lower side; to cause least harm and for speedy callusing, the cut should be positioned just outside this line. In species where the collar does not show up clearly the best current advice is to cut along the line of an imaginary collar. If the cut is made here, the wound will be smaller than with a flush cut and will heal much more quickly than if a snag is left. 'Callusing' occurs when the tree makes new growth from the sides of a wound, ultimately occluding, but not actually 'healing', the wound which is usually left in an inactive state inside the growing tree, rather than acting as a continuing point of potential infection.

When a large branch has to be removed, it should be removed in two stages. The first cut is made from beneath and 30cm or so from the stem; this cut only extends between a quarter and a third through the branch. The next cut is made a few centimetres beyond the first cut (i.e. towards

Fig 22 The lower branches can be retained (left), or removed to give a clear stem (right)

Fig 23 A tree's size can be reduced by cutting branches back to the nearest suitable fork

the tip). By using this cutting technique, there is no risk of the branch tearing a strip of wood and bark off the main stem, and the cutting can be kept under control. Finally the remaining stub is cut off at the point discussed above. In many situations, it will be necessary to use ropes to lower branches. For the sake of safety, it is advisable to leave all above ground and major work in trees to professional tree surgeons.

Where a branchless bole is required, the unwanted branches should be removed when small. This should not be carried out too precipitously, or the tree will decline in condition due to loss of foliage! It is not advisable to prune up to more than about one-third the height of the tree; nor to remove more than one-third of the total foliage in any one year. Of course, where the branches are dead, as often happens with old pines (*Pinus*) or monkey puzzle (*Araucaria araucana*), no harm is done by removing these otherwise unsightly branches. Removing the lower live branches from a tree is termed 'lifting', as the centre of the crown is raised by the loss of the bottom end.

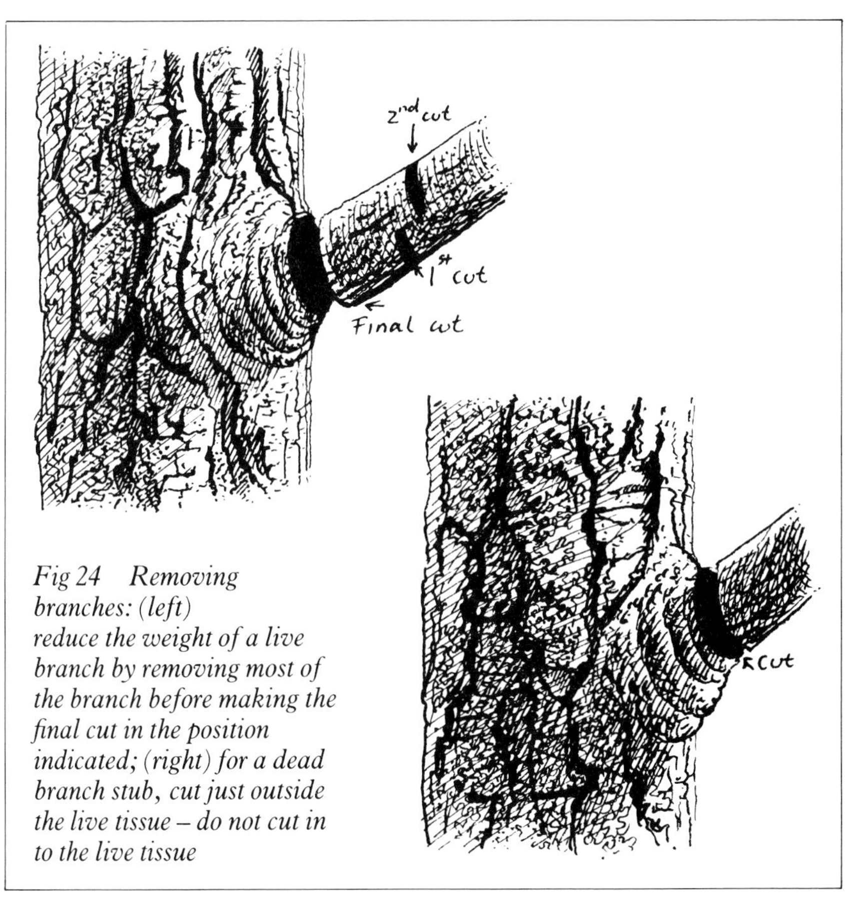

Fig 24 Removing branches: (left) reduce the weight of a live branch by removing most of the branch before making the final cut in the position indicated; (right) for a dead branch stub, cut just outside the live tissue – do not cut in to the live tissue

Crown Thinning

In many situations there is a need or desire to thin out the crown of trees so that less shade is cast. This can be carried out by removing a percentage of the foliage bearing smaller branches in the crown, and will significantly improve the amount of light which filters through the canopy. Crown thinning needs to be carried out by skilled operators, as if a tree is over-thinned, it will produce a mass of new vegetative foliage and very quickly become as dense as before. Even when expertly carried out, the tree will slowly redress the loss of foliage and the operation will need repeating after perhaps five years. Crown thinning can also be used to remove the weaker branches which will die naturally within a few years. It can, therefore, form part of a programme of good husbandry, where deadwood and incipient deadwood are removed on a regular (three or five year) cycle.

When to Prune

Most trees can be pruned at any time of the year, it making really very little difference. However, there are a few occasions where certain times should be chosen. A few species, such as maples (*Acer*) and birch (*Betula*) will bleed if cut earlier in the year than late May and so are better left unpruned until then as the loss of sap may weaken these trees, although is unlikely to kill them; maple syrup is extracted from some North American species at this season. Walnut (*Juglans regia*) and magnolias (*Magnolia*) should only be pruned when in full leaf, as this prevents bleeding and improves healing; mid to late summer, around the end of July is the most suitable time. Members of the large genus *Prunus*, the cherries and plums, are best pruned when they first come into leaf, as this avoids excessive bleeding and also reduces the risk of infection by silver-leaf disease (caused by *Condostereum (Stereum) purpureum* – see page 121).

Pollarding and Coppicing

Pollarding and coppicing are extreme forms of pruning which have been and are practised for a variety of reasons. All the branches are cut back to the main stem at an interval ranging from one year to 20 or more years. The system gives a regular, sustained yield of poles and other products. In recent years, there has not been much demand for these products in Britain, so these systems have declined; there is, though, a revival of interest in coppicing for firewood and as a means of nature conservation.

In coppicing, the trees are cut back to the stump to ground-level. They then make fast initial growth, soon yielding the next crop. The system requires no replanting and little management. Also, when the canopy is removed, the forest floor receives full sunlight, giving an immediate boost

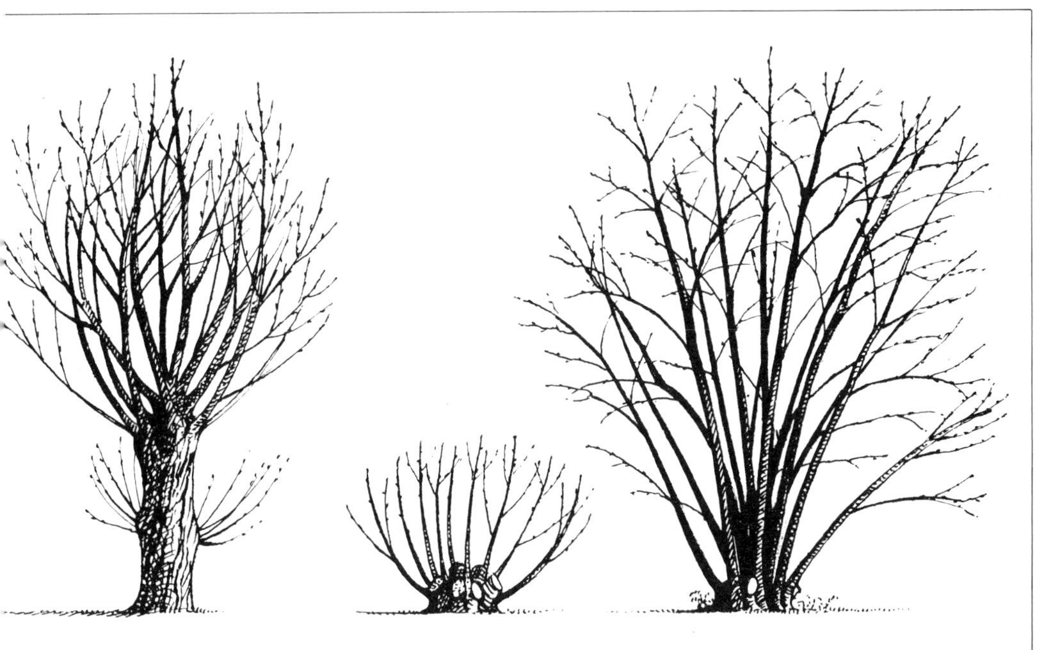

Fig 25 (left) Pollarded tree with new shoots, (centre) coppice stool with new shoots, (right) coppice stool with poles ready for cutting

to the ground flora. Over the years this leads to the build-up of a richer flora and fauna, particularly wild flowers and butterflies. The system is, therefore, beloved by nature conservationists and useful for small areas where there is a demand for either the produce or the enriched wildlife.

Pollarding is similar to coppicing, except that the cutting back occurs at a height above the reach of marauding cattle. Originally, it was used for poles and foliage for winter feed or fodder for the cattle during dry spells. If carried out regularly, every ten to fifteen years or so, the trees can have a very long life, as the branches never become large and therefore the stem can support them, even when part rotten. In many species, such as willows (*Salix*), the bole will rot away in the centre, leaving a trunk of circular or horseshoe shaped cross-section, or in several segments. In some places, particularly with willows along river banks, this system is traditional and completely acceptable in the landscape, although possibly costly to perpetuate in the absence of any modern demand for the foliage and timber. It is also the way to keep an old oak tree alive for 600–800 years!

The practice of 'lopping and topping', alias urban pollarding, is similar to pollarding and was a feature of many urban streets. Fortunately, there has been a reaction against it in most places, as the trees look ugly for much of the year and the cost of annual cutting is quite high. Once a tree has been severely lopped considerable care and patience is needed to restore it to a natural aesthetic appearance; if it has been lopped on several occasions, there may be extensive rots associated with the old cuts and it may not be possible to develop a safe crown of branches. The choice then has to be between continued periodic lopping or felling and replacing with a new tree. Pleaching is similar to pollarding but gives a rather rudimentary two-dimensional shape, being useful in hot sunny climates, (e.g. the south of France), to give dense summer shade, at the expense of a rather weird winter silhouette.

Pruning Wound Treatments

Over the past three or four centuries a number of materials, ranging from cow dung with soot to bitumastics, have been recommended for putting on cuts and wounds in trees to assist healing or prevent decay. The debate has warmed up recently following research which has shown that virtually all these recommendations were of no positive benefit, and possibly harmful. The situation appears to be as follows: there are vast numbers of fungal spores in the air at any one time; when a branch is cut, the tension between the roots and the foliage (i.e. the transpiration stream) is broken, causing a sharp inrush of air which sucks some of these spores into the wood (only 0.1cm or so, but sufficient); and that by covering these spores, they are kept moist and able to germinate freely. If the wound is left uncovered, natural drying of the tissue will prevent most of them growing. Adding a fungicide to the sealant does not appear to help. The reason is partly that such fungicides are toxic to tree tissues and partly that there are so many different fungi which can enter wounds, that some will be resistant to whichever fungicide is applied. Only where there is a specific problem, such as *Nectria* canker (see page 123) in fruit orchards, is the addition of a specific fungicide beneficial. Research is continuing into the possibility of using biological control, i.e. applying spores of a benign fungus, such as *Trichoderma viride*, to the wound, so that the decay fungi are kept out.

The only definitive benefit of using a tree paint is to prevent the cambium layer (that is the layer of tissue between the wood and the bark where growth in girth occurs) from drying out and therefore dying back. The best recommendation is to paint the bark and the outer rings of wood but to leave the central portion alone. Lac-balsam and Seal'n'heal have both shown good properties for inducing callus growth when applied to the cambium zone, without being phytotoxic (i.e. damaging the tree). There may be a demand for the painting of tree wounds on the grounds that otherwise the trees are not being properly cared for, but if possible, it should be resisted.

Root Pruning

Root pruning is a technique sometimes used to curb the vigour of fruit trees, and thus lead them to fruit more heavily. It is not recommended for controlling the vigour of other trees. Firstly, although trees can withstand the loss of a fair percentage of the root system without appearing to suffer (many trees on development sites lose at least a third or a quarter), it is not possible to know what is going on underground and the removal of a percentage of the roots may lead to instability, and can cause the partial die-back of branches. Also, the wounds will permit the entry of decay fungi into the roots. If a tree is too large and vigorous for its situation then it should be removed and a more suitable one planted instead.

Care of Ageing Trees

As trees grow older they tend to be more highly valued. Old trees have a particular attraction, due in part to their large size and gnarled appearance, to the feeling of permanence which they give to their surroundings, and from the fact that they take many years to grow. Yet trees are living beings, and like all of them, there comes a time when they die. Often, before trees die, there is the question of safety, or unsightliness. The manager needs to maintain his trees in the best possible condition so that they have the longest safe life consistent with an acceptable appearance. This requires attention to any necessary early pruning, and the careful thinning out of tree numbers where overcrowding occurs. There are also aspects of tree surgery appropriate to ageing trees.

When a tree has become mature, pruning should be restricted to the very minimum. Usually all that is needed is the removal of broken branches and those which have been shaded out and died, i.e. deadwood. Some trees, such as pines (*Pinus*) and oaks (*Quercus*), need plenty of sunlight and in these the shaded branches die quickly.

Both natural prudence and the responsibilities of management demand that mature trees should be inspected regularly for any obvious signs of fungal decay, dead or broken branches and anything else which might affect their safety. As some aspects are better inspected when the tree is in leaf and others when leafless, the general recommendation is to give the trees a thorough inspection from the ground approximately twice a year, i.e. every six months. Periodically, a more detailed inspection should be considered.

The signs to look out for include: smaller and thinner foliage than normal, late flushing in spring or early leaf fall in autumn, retention of leaves or fruit beyond the normal period, abnormal fruiting (extra heavy crops on just one tree or a group of trees), exudation of slime or water from the bark, branches which are rubbing against each other, fungal fruit bodies, holes on the main stem or branches, and lifting of the soil around the roots. Particularly difficult to see are some root decay fungi which have the fruit bodies at or around ground level. Just because a tree shows some of the above signs does not make the tree unsafe, merely suspect. In all cases of doubt, the advice of a qualified arboriculturist should be sought.

Trees you wish to keep beyond what might be regarded as their normal age require particularly close inspection, and may require some additional remedial treatment, such as detailed below.

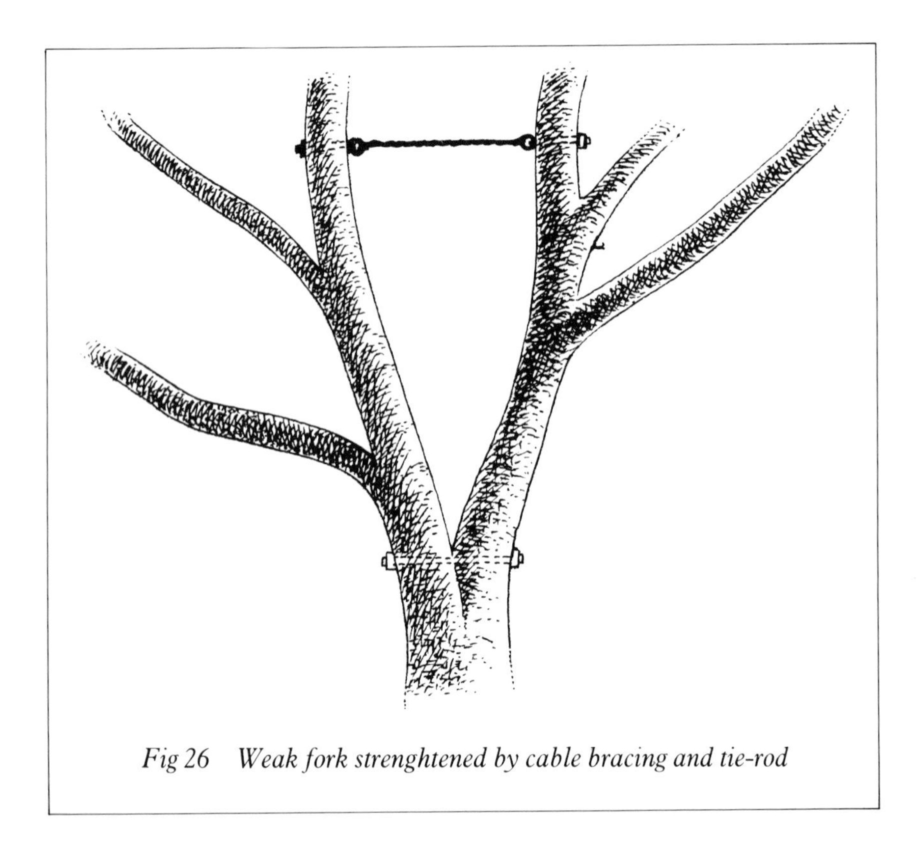

Fig 26 Weak fork strenghtened by cable bracing and tie-rod

Bracing

Bracing is the term used when two or more parts of a tree are joined together to give mutual support. It can be used where there are weak forks or heavy or weakened limbs, or with trees like cedar of Lebanon (*Cedrus libani*) which have large areas of flat foliage carried on long branches and are very vulnerable to damage by the weight of wet snow. The usual method is to attach a galvanised cable to bolts fastened into or through the main stem and branches; in some situations, such as with certain weak forks or slits, the two parts can be held together in a rigid fashion using solid metal rods. Bracing should not be considered as a panacea, but can be a useful way of extending the safe life of a tree or reducing the risk of storm damage. Bracing should only be attempted by a skilled arboriculturist and subsequently checked as part of the regular inspection programme.

Propping

Where there is no suitable point for the anchorage of a cable brace, as in low spreading trees like the Indian bean tree (*Catalpa bignonioides*) or Japanese pagoda tree (*Sophora japonica*), the lower limbs or whole tree may be supported on wooden or metal props. The top of the prop is a U shape, with a piece of old car tyre or some similar padding to cushion the tree. The prop needs to be firmly placed on the ground, so that it cannot move. This method of supporting an old tree is much more conspicuous than bracing and should only be used as a last resort.

17 Spreading branch of a cedar supported by a prop

Crown Reduction

Trees which have a small amount of decay, or are becoming old and brittle and have large spreading branches which are too numerous or awkward to brace satisfactorily, or have lost many roots in building development, can sometimes be retained for a few more years if the larger branches are cut back. This is most successful where there are major forks in the branches to which you can cut back without giving an ugly appearance nor leaving stubs which will die back and decay. It is a measure of last resort, which will lead to more decay in the long term, even with such decay resistant trees as English oak (*Quercus robur*), but can be used to extend the useful life of a tree, possibly for several decades; during this time, new planting can be established to take over. With oak trees, all the really old ones, i.e. trees believed to be over 600 years old, are old pollards which have been cut back regularly (probably in the past for bark for tanning).

This short-term treatment should not be confused with haphazard lopping, in which branches are crudely cut back with no regard to preventing tearing down the stem or the aesthetic appearance or future growth of the tree.

18 Weak crotch on a beech; the tree will almost certainly fail at this point at some time in the future

19 The same beech shown in Plate 18, from the other angle

Fertilising

Trees which grow slowly have a greater chance of living to a ripe old age than those which grow fast, since the longevity of an individual tree of a given species is partly a function of its size. Fast growing trees, such as willows (*Salix*) and poplars (*Populus*), will soon make large trees on fertile sites but do not last for very long, yet cuttings can be made from the wood so that they effectively live for centuries; the growing or meristem tissue of a tree does not age and trees are always growing whilst they are alive. The oldest living biological entities are some of the ancient pines (*Pinus longaeva*) growing in the White Mountains of California. These have been dated (by counting the rings) as up to 5,000 years old, yet the trees are gnarled, half dead (and have been for years!) and less than 10m tall. In the White Mountains, the climate is very severe and exceptionally dry, and no other plants can survive except for the pines; lower down on richer soils the trees can grow to 30m but live for only 400–600 years. To live to a good old age, a tree should have adequate amounts of nutrients but not a super-abundance.

However, if a tree has suffered damage to its root system, due to excavations or disease, or if it has suffered from extensive damage to the foliage, it may benefit from some form of fertilising. This will help it to recover, and reduce the risk of it succumbing to attacks by harmful fungi or insects. Perhaps the soil is naturally deficient in some nutrient, or maybe the tree has exhausted the supply of nutrients in the limited soil in which it is growing. Wood contains only a limited amount of nutrients and trees are very efficient at recycling nutrients, but if the rooting zone is finite, the tree may have used up all the available supply, particularly if the leaf litter is not returned to the soil; in these situations, it may be useful to increase the supply of nutrients in order to increase the vigour of the tree. Fertilising tends to become more important as the tree grows older.

Where trees are growing in open ground, the application of manure, compost or granular fertilisers is straightforward; simply spread an appropriate quantity over the rooting area of the tree every two or three years; in the short term the grasses and surrounding shrubs may pick up most of the added nutrients, but eventually they will enrich the soil and reach the tree's roots, unless they are taken up by a lawn where the mowings are removed from site. An alternative would be to kill the grass, which would give a more immediate boost to the tree, even without applying extra fertiliser.

Where the tree is grown in close mown grass or in a paved area, or where an immediate effect is needed, the fertiliser can be placed in holes drilled within the root spread of the tree. The holes are usually about 5cm in diameter and drilled to 30cm, on a 60cm spacing. The fertiliser is mixed with soil, and about 100–150gm applied per square metre. Slow release fertilisers, such as Osmacote or Ficote, are best, and can be used at slightly higher concentrations. Enmag releases its nutrients more quickly, but also suitable. If the fertiliser does not contain them, extra trace elements may also be given.

Treatment of Cavities

Old trees often develop rots and decaying areas in the bole and main branches. Several methods of treating these have been suggested or tried in the past. Recent research has found that trees isolate decay by creating a number of barriers around the decay, and that the recommendations to drain all cavities or pockets of water are only likely to cause fresh damage to the tree by breaking these natural barriers. Research is continuing on the potential treatment of cavities but until more is learnt about the biological sequence in decaying cavities, precise recommendations on how to deal with cavities cannot be given.

Tree Removal

Felling large trees is a skilled and potentially dangerous job which should not be attempted by those unfamiliar with all aspects involved. The manner in which a tree is felled will depend upon the location. In an open parkland, there may be plenty of room to fell it, whilst in a build-up area, the tree may need to be taken down piece by piece, at much greater cost.

Stump Removal

When a tree is felled, there is a choice as to whether the stump is left to rot away naturally, or whether it should be removed. If there is no particular reason for removing a stump and it is not in the way, it can probably stay where it is. It will be worth applying a herbicide, such as ammonium sulphamate, to kill the root system (although this should not be used where root grafts between trees are likely, or all may be killed), as potentially this will let all the available wood decay fungi colonise the roots, and therefore give some biological control over honey fungus (see pages 118–19).

Short of total stump removal and complete cultivation, as used in forestry on some sites severely affected by the fungus *Heterobasidion (Fomes) annosum*, any method will leave much of the root system in the ground; only the base of the stem and the main roots nearest the stump will come out. The different methods are detailed below.

Stump Chipping

Stump chipping machines use a revolving disk on which are set a number of cutting teeth. The machine grinds down the stump, turning it into a

20 Stump chipper removing a stump

mixture of wood chippings and soil. The machines are either independently powered, with some small models designed to enter confined spaces, or work from a tractor PTO. They give a neat finish, taking the stump to below ground level, but not removing much of the root system. They are inappropriate for stony ground, due to the large number of expensive teeth which will be lost on the stones. They are fairly economical and are not very likely to cause damage to subterranean services.

Explosives

Explosives can be used to clear stumps in areas where the explosion will not cause damage, but are unlikely to be useful in urban areas. They work particularly well on clay soils and wet sites, where the use of alternative machinery is difficult or messy.

Grubbing

Grubbing involves digging around the stump and severing the roots. The stump is them pulled or pushed, usually by some form of excavator, winch or tractor. The stump can be removed with a proportion of the root system, leaving a large hole. If this method is going to be used, it is better to leave the stump a couple of metres high, so that leverage can be gained, either by the blade of a dozer pushing against the stump, or the winch pulling. Winching can be dangerous, especially if the cable or stump slip.

Burning

Burning is sometimes recommended, with a number of dubious materials being sold as aids. It is generally unsuccessful.

6

CREATIVE MANAGEMENT OF TREES

THE fact that trees are biological entities, which live and die, cannot be over-emphasised. They do not have infinite lives, although the actual growing tissues can theoretically continue for ever. However, trees give the appearance of being immortal and many live very much longer than people; occasional trees can be traced through historical records over several generations.

Most tree species will not live beyond one or two centuries, with some common trees like cherries (*Prunus*), rowans (*Sorbus*) and birches (*Betula*) living for substantially less than a century; although some large trees, such as oak (*Quercus robur*), Scots pine (*Pinus sylvestris*) and limes (*Tilia*), may regularly live for up to two or three centuries. A few other species may generally live for longer periods, such as Wellingtonia (*Sequoiadendron giganteum*), ancient pine (*Pinus longaeva*) and ginkgo (*Ginkgo biloba*), at least under certain conditions. Within any species there is always the individual which survives for much longer, and just as man's three score and ten years results in some people living to be 110 or more, so some trees live for much longer. Yew (*Taxus baccata*) and pollarded English and sessile oaks (*Quercus robur* and *Q. petraea*) are particular examples, where trees over 500 years are known, probably up to a maximum of around 800–1,000; these, however, are the exceptions, even within their own species.

Good management has to perceive and put across this fact; that trees have finite, if often long, lives and therefore need to be creatively managed, not just maintained or preserved. There are several stages in creative management of trees, including ascertaining what you have to manage, what is wanted from the trees (or the purpose of the management), and how to perpetuate and enhance the assets represented by the trees.

Assessing the Current Situation

The gardens and grounds of many large houses, institutions, hospitals and parks in Britain were planted more than 100 years ago and, therefore, contain a large proportion of trees which are likely to die, fall down, or become unsafe over the next fifty or so years. In situations like these, there is a real possibility of there being virtually no tree cover in five decades unless action is taken now, yet to a casual observer the grounds may appear to be full of healthy trees (which they may be at this stage). The manager in this situation could take the view that all is fine for the duration of his working life, but that is scarcely good or responsible management.

The assessment of the site should look at the existing stock of trees, including their species, age, lifespan, location and general condition, and how that stock is likely to be altered over the coming years. Ideally, the foreview should stretch up to 200 years hence, although positive planning can only be made for a period of two or three decades. The assessment will indicate a likely lifespan for the current trees, and from this a prediction of how many trees presently on the site will be there at a given period in the future.

In the grounds of a house or hospital where there are forty trees whose average lifespan is expected to be around 120 years, in a normal or steady state situation, three or four trees would be felled and replaced every decade; this will be preferable to replacing the entire stock every century or so, or half every 50–60 years. Also, by carrying out the work bit by bit, there is less likely to be public uproar than if substantial numbers need to be felled at one time, even if by this time the trees are unsafe!

21 Beech partly blown over. The retention of a tree in this condition is probably negligent

22 Pollarded street trees – replacement with new smaller growing trees is economically and aesthetically desirable

What is Wanted from the Site?

This is going to vary enormously from place to place, perhaps in different parts of the same site. Where the site is historical, the retention of a venerable old tree and the planting of young trees propagated from it may be an important aspect of the purpose in the site. In many parks, beauty, safety and serenity are the main requirements. On a golf course, it may be the need to frame a fairway and green, or the provision of shelter and screening between adjacent fairways. In other places, timber may be a consideration, or the development of the wildlife associated with the trees. In parkland, it may be the pleasing agrarian view created by isolated large trees.

All of these requirements are going to make different demands upon the trees, and how they are maintained. In an extensive private parkland, there is only a slight risk of somebody being under a tree if it drops a branch and therefore a lower standard of tree husbandry may be acceptable, but in a public park, golf course or housing estate, people are likely to be about in larger numbers, at odd times and in all weathers, so high standards of maintenance are essential. Where trees are situated beside a road, where cars and buses pass whatever the weather, and at speed, no risks can be taken with safety.

The sort of treescape which is wanted will also differ. Along the fairways on the golf course, the tree may not be wanted to grow to maturity, or the fairway may be in shade all day, whereas in a park, both large groups and colourful trees are going to be needed. This aspect is discussed in Chapter 3.

How to Perpetuate and Enhance the Value of the Trees on Site

After assessing the existing situation and what is wanted, the next action will be to try to marry these together, for both the benefit of present users and for the longer term. All management will need to contain an element of compromise, as the best course for the long term benefit may be unacceptable in the short term. The manager needs to know what are the short, medium and long term consequences of any course of action, e.g. by not thinning out a group of trees, the short term effect may be very little, in fact a saving of cost, but in the medium term the trees may become lanky and attentuated with some starting to die from excess shading, and in the long term, the group may become unsafe due to the development of small high crowns on long thin stems, and may be subject to windthrow in a gale.

One of the difficulties and bedevilments of dealing with trees is that few decisions or actions have to be taken at a specific time; most can be carried out at any time over a short number of years. There is a natural temptation to take the 'mañana' option, and leave the problem for someone else. Also the general public, often only taking a short term view, may not fully understand or accept the need for certain actions, and thereby create 'difficulties' to good and effective management. At the same time, however, because any individual action (except where safety has become suspect) can be carried out in one of several years, it does allow the good manager time to get everything properly organised; for instance, if a group of trees needs thinning out in number either this year or within three years, the manager can plan the work for the current year but if outside pressures require that more ground work is put into explaining the need for the work, there are two years for this to take place before any damage is caused. Alternatively, the manager may consider that the essential work he has to carry out at another site or part of the same site, means that he would appear in the public's eyes to be doing too much felling (or his budget may be overstretched!) and therefore this item can wait a year or so.

Management Phases in a Tree's Life

The growth characteristics of most trees can be divided into four phases for management purposes:

1. Establishment and early growth, or 'young tree' phase. This is likely to occupy about ten to fifteen per cent of the tree's lifespan. Apart

Fig 27 Small-leaved lime tree at different ages: (left) 10 years old, mid-way through the young phase; (centre) 60 years old, mid-way through the simi-mature phase; (right) 150 years old, mid-way through the mature phase

from the initial establishment, during the early growth phase the tree will be growing quickly in height and reach approximately a third of its likely height. By the end of this period, the tree will have started to form a significant part of the landscape. Formative pruning in this phase can often significantly increase the potential lifespan (see Chapters 4 and 5).

2. Later growth or 'semi-mature tree phase'. This is the period when the tree makes most of its height and crown growth, and covers the period from phase 1 to around midway through its lifespan.

3. Maturity. This phase will occupy the last half of the tree's life, during which it will significantly increase the diameter of the bole but the height and crown will only alter slowly – in fact imperceptibly in the eyes of the average passerby. During this phase the tree remains relatively unaltered as a prominent feature in the landscape, until such time as it starts to become overmature, shedding limbs, dying back and becoming rotten. It is this phase which gives the impression that trees are static objects, like buildings, which do not grow or become senile.

4. Overmaturity. When trees have reached this stage, they are starting to become unsafe and safety should always be considered. In the average situation, trees in this category should not be kept.

Bearing in mind that these phases take up different lengths of time, the park or garden with an 'ideal' tree population would have about 10% of the tree covered area occupied by young trees, 40% by semi-matures and 50% by mature trees, with perhaps the occasional venerable specimen where it is safe to do so. However, as young trees are generally planted at relatively close spacing, there should be roughly equal numbers of young trees, semi-mature trees and mature ones. The mature and semi-mature categories should cover several age classes, thereby avoiding the need to fell too many trees at one time.

In the table below is an example of a park with 90 trees. The trees might be of the age, class and number shown.

Out of this population of 90 trees, about three mature ones would be felled in each five year period, along with about seven younger trees as thinnings. Ten replacement trees would be planted.

In most gardens, the distribution of age-classes of the trees does not resemble the 'ideal'; usually there are either far too many young trees, where the park is of recent construction, or too many old ones. In such circumstances, it is better to fell a number before they reach maturity, to avoid you or your successors having to fell a substantial proportion of the trees at the same time in the future. However, this course of action requires determination and strength of character! It is likely to be opposed by those who see trees as everlasting features of the landscape, as all having useful lives of 600 years or more, or who are only concerned for themselves and what they see and enjoy now.

As an example, consider a park with 100 trees all planted approximately 150 years ago; they are all fully mature, bordering on the overmature and will not last more than 30–50 years. In the absence of any planned management, there will effectively be no trees on the site in that timespan, although they may look beautiful now. The selfish approach is to say 'I won't be here in fifty years' time,' and to enjoy the present beauty. Creative management must, however, look to extend the present beauty through to future generations and will suggest something along the following lines. Approximately half the trees should be felled and replanted in the next 5–10 years; this will give a significant element of 40–50 year old trees in fifty years' time, whilst requiring only the annual loss of 5–10 trees in the short term. A further batch of 20–30 trees can be

	Age of trees (up to x years)															
	0	10	20	30	40	50	60	70	80	90	100	110	120	130	140	150-200
No. of short-lived trees e.g. birch, cherry, rowan		10	6	4	3	3	3	1								
No. of medium-lived trees e.g. ash, field maple		6	4	3	3	2	2	2	1	2	1	2	2	1		
No. of long-lived trees e.g. oak, lime, sycamore		4	3	2	2	2	1	1	1	1	1	1	1	1	1	6

replaced over the 15–35 year period, leaving the soundest and safest trees to be retained for as long as possible.

In planting a new park from scratch, the pitfalls of having the entire park composed of relatively long lived trees of a single age-class can be avoided. Areas should be planted with short and medium term trees, so that they have lived out their natural spans before the longterm trees are near full maturity.

Thinning to reduce the numbers of trees is an essential aspect of management. In Chapter 3, pages 43–4, reasons for planting trees closer together than their final mature spacing were discussed. Thinning operations should be carried out before they become really essential, rather than later. If thinning is delayed, the remaining trees will be tall and spindly, with few branches on one or more sides; they look less attractive and are more likely to be blown over or to lose branches in windy weather. Where thinning has been neglected, it will need to be executed very cautiously, removing only a few trees at a time but repeating the operation as soon as the remaining trees have grown into the extra space provided by the thinning.

The need for thinning, felling and replacement planting should be considered at least every five years. There may be no need for any action, especially in some smaller parks, but that does not excuse ostrich-like behaviour. In larger parks, containing 50–100 or more trees, some action will almost certainly be needed at least once in every five year period.

Avenues and Lines

Avenues and lines make very formal features in the landscape (see Chapter 3, pages 53–6) and their management will be fraught with difficulty. It is always very difficult to come to a satisfactory scheme to replace and renew an avenue. This can be used as an argument against creating avenues, as even the loss of two or three trees through accident or disease can disrupt the formal appearance. Gradual replacement of an avenue is unlikely to create a bold feature which future generations will venerate; the end effect will be one of a mixture of trees of different characters and ages, scarcely the formal dignity of the original.

When the time comes to replace an avenue, there are three practical ways to proceed:

1. Fell all the trees and replant. This will strike most people as very drastic and cause a vast amount of debate. It also has the disadvantage that there is effectively nothing for a number of years whilst the new trees grow. It is, however, the only way in which the original effect can be recreated, all other methods giving at best a parody. This option can be made more acceptable by delaying the replacement of the avenue for as

long as possible, provided the temptation to replant trees which fail is resisted.

2. Fell all the trees on one side or in clumps along the length. This will often prove more acceptable but will not recreate the avenue, although what is achieved may be very attractive. However, where the original avenue was composed of a double or treble line of trees, it may be appropriate to fell the inner (or outer) rows and replant, then later fell the next rows. Such double or treble avenues can sometimes be acceptably regenerated by piecemeal replacement of individual trees if the primary viewpoints are from the ends of the avenue.

3. Create a new avenue effect elsewhere in the vicinity. Where there is space, this may be the best option, whilst awaiting the death from natural causes of the trees in the first avenue. However, it is unlikely to be satisfactory to plant a new avenue to the outside of the existing one, as it will tend to be too wide to be effective.

7

PESTS, DISEASES AND DISORDERS

TREES are usually most attractive when in the best health but they can be affected by a range of damaging or debilitating conditions. Apart from general lack of vigour when they are growing in conditions which do not suit them, trees may suffer from various pests, diseases or non-living agents, which are briefly described in this chapter. Some of these cause only minor damage, although others can be more serious, sometimes resulting in death. Prevention of damage by large animal pests is discussed in Chapter 4 (see pages 87–91). The best reference work on fungal and non-living agents is *Diseases of Forest and Ornamental Trees* by Phillips and Burdekin (Macmillan), which should be consulted for more detailed information. Information about all pests and diseases affecting trees in Britain can be sought from the Forestry Commission Forest Research Station, Alice Holt Lodge, Farnham, Surrey, GU10 4LH, telephone 0420 22255. In addition, the Forestry Commission publish the Arboricultural Leaflets and Research Notes referred to below.

Insect Pests

Many different species of insects are found on trees. English oak (*Quercus robur*) is recorded as supporting over 300 different species of insect, although they have not all been found on the same tree; on many other tree species from 40 to 80 different insect species have been recorded. Consequently, trees can be of high value for nature conservation, where invertebrates are of interest, either for their own sake, e.g. butterflies, or as food for spiders, bats and birds. Generally insects are not particularly serious pests on trees and damage is usually minor. Where an insect is involved with a fungus, the disease can be quite severe, but it is usually the fungus which is the devastating agent, with the insect as vector, such as in Dutch elm disease.

Trees are often defoliated by caterpillars. English oak (*Quercus robur*) can be completely defoliated by one of several species, but the effects are only short term, causing some loss of growth. Occasionally with some insects damage can be severe, such as in the recent outbreak in northern

Scotland where lodgepole pine (*Pinus contorta*) was defoliated and killed by the pine beauty moth. However, where trees are in rude health, the main complaint is likely to come from caterpillars with irritant hairs, such as the browntail moth.

A number of trees are hosts to various aphids, i.e. greenfly or blackfly. These insects suck the sap from the leaves or shoots, but because the sap contains an excess of sugars in relation to proteins, the surplus sugars are voided as 'honeydew'. Honeydew will coat all surfaces beneath a tree, and, apart from being sticky, is soon colonised by sooty moulds and collects dust. Honeydew may be found under a wide range of trees, including English oak (*Quercus robur*), maples (*Acer*), birches (*Betula*) and cherries (*Prunus*, particularly plums), but common lime (*Tilia* × *europaea*) is most renowned for it. Occasionally, in wet weather, paths covered by honeydew can become slippery.

Another group of insects causing relatively minor nuisance is the scale insects. These are sap-sucking insects which secrete a protective shield around themselves once they have found a suitable feeding site. They also secrete a significant quantity of white, woolly wax. Scale insects often affect trees which are under stress, such as from drought, overcrowding or poor soil conditions. They are mainly unsightly, but felted beech coccus can, in association with a species of *Nectria* fungus, cause significant loss of beech trees (*Fagus sylvatica*). Another increasingly common one is the horse chestnut scale. This is found on horse chestnut (*Aesculus hippocastanum*), limes (*Tilia*), maples (*Acer*) and some other species. It can appear unsightly, and presumably weakens the tree, but will not kill it. It is more likely to be serious where the leaves are removed and not left to rot down around the tree, as the scale insect overwinters on the bark but its main predator overwinters on fallen leaves. Some control of both these scale insects can be achieved by the application of a tar oil spray.

Weevils and other beetles can sometimes be a problem, particularly to young trees.

Fungal Diseases

Many fungal diseases occur but most cause only minor or insignificant damage. Some, however, are much more serious, killing, disfiguring or rendering trees unsafe or in other ways unsuitable for the purpose for which they are grown.

Honey Fungus

Honey fungus can be identified by the sheets of white fungal mycelium which grow beneath the bark of roots and the trunk near ground level of affected trees. It probably kills more ornamental trees each year than any other non epidemic fungal disease and is caused by several species of *Armillaria*. The disease does not, usually, kill many trees at once, but kills them here and there in ones and twos. It is a fungus which feeds on and decays woody tissues. It spreads by means of rhizomorphs, which are black strands of fungal mycelium which grow through the soil. The honey coloured mushrooms may be produced in autumn.

Honey fungus is most troublesome where susceptible species are planted into old broadleaved woodland or hedgerow sites. The disease has a generally slow spread through the root system. Death will occur either when most roots have been killed or when the stem is girdled. The speed of a tree's death will depend upon its inherent susceptibility to the disease, its size, the number of infections present, the growing conditions and which species of *Armillaria* is involved. Where roots are lost, the trees can become unstable.

The best control is to remove as much as possible of the infected woody material and wait for a few years for the fungus to exhaust what remains before replanting. Where this is not practical, it is necessary to live with the problem and concentrate the planting on resistant plants. Some species of tree are very resistant, including silver fir (*Abies*), oaks (*Quercus*), ash (*Fraxinus excelsior*), may or thorn (*Crataegus*), beech (*Fagus sylvatica*), lime (*Tilia*) and robinia (*Robinia pseudacacia*), and only occasionally killed, except as young plants which can be more susceptible. Others, such as monkey puzzle (*Araucaria araucana*), Wellingtonia (*Sequoiadendron giganteum*), pines (*Pinus*), cedars (*Cedrus*), cypresses (*Cupressus*), maples (*Acer*), common walnut (*Juglans regia*), willows (*Salix*) and cherries (*Prunus*), are much more susceptible and are frequently killed. Yew (*Taxus baccata*), Californian walnut (*Juglans hindsii*) and box elder (*Acer negundo*) appear to be virtually immune; interestingly, with the latter two, most other species in their genera are susceptible! There is no proven effective chemical aid for use in the control of the disease in British conditions.

Arboricultural Leaflet 2 – *Honey Fungus*, gives a full account of the disease.

Phytophthora Diseases

Several species of *Phytophthora* are damaging. The species are microscopic and can only be seen and identified positively in the laboratory.

***Phytophthora* root disease** can kill the roots of a number of broadleaved and coniferous trees. Damage shows as dead or weak plants. Susceptible genera include maples (*Acer*), horse chestnut (*Aesculus hippocastanum*), sweet chestnut (*Castanea sativa*), Lawson cypress (*Chamaecyparis lawsoniana*), eucalypts (*Eucalyptus*), beech (*Fagus sylvatica*), apple (*Malus*), yew (*Taxus baccata*), and lime (*Tilia*). It is most troublesome in nurseries, but also occurs on older trees. The disease is spread by contaminated water, soil or plants and usually found on wet or poorly drained sites. Control is best achieved by improving the drainage, planting a less susceptible species and ensuring that planting stock is free of the disease. The disease is only annual on the roots, needing a new infection if it is to continue for a second (and subsequent) year.

***Phytophthora* bleeding canker** causes the death of areas of bark, but the disease may be perennial. It gets its name from the gum exuded by the tree. It affects mainly horse chestnut (*Aesculus hippocastanum*) but can occur on some other broadleaves. The affected tissue with both bleeding canker and *Phytophthora* root disease can quickly be invaded by wood decay fungi, e.g. honey fungus following *Phytophthora* root disease. Arboricultural Leaflet 8 – *Phytophthora Diseases of Trees and Shrubs* gives more information.

Fireblight

Fireblight is caused by a bacterium (*Erwinia amylovora*) which affects trees and shrubs in the apple subfamily in the rose family (Family *Rosaceae*, subfamily *Maloideae*). It can be serious in orchards and is a notifiable disease (details of a suspected outbreak should be communicated to the nearest Ministry of Agriculture office). The disease gains entry to the plants mainly through the flowers, from where it may spread to kill the adjoining area of stem or the entire plant. It is spread through a bacterial ooze, containing spores, which is given off from the affected plant tissues. Diseased trees or branches should be burnt, and the tools used sterilised using a 10% solution of domestic bleach. The Agricultural Development and Advisory Service (ADAS) of the Ministry of Agriculture has published a leaflet giving more information on fireblight.

Verticillium Wilt

This causes either the foliage to suddenly wilt and turn brown or to prevent the tree flushing in the spring. It is a soil borne disease, caused by the fungus, *Verticillium dahliae* (and occasionally by a closely related species), which can only be confirmed in the laboratory. The disease is spread from infected soil, through wounds to the fine roots. It penetrates the wood tissues and can lead to death of entire trees, or parts of trees. It is most serious on small trees but can occasionally cause damage on larger plants. Maples (*Acer*) and Indian bean tree (*Catalpa bignonioides*) are particularly affected but it can cause damage to limes (*Tilia*) and a few other broadleaves. It does not affect conifers. It is mainly a problem in nurseries. The disease is annual, so a tree which only suffers dieback may recover in the subsequent years, unless re-infected. More information is contained in Arboricultural Leaflet 9 – *Verticillium Wilt*.

Anthracnose Diseases
Anthracnose diseases can completely defoliate a tree, particularly if killing all the buds as they flush. They are caused by fungi which kill the new foliage, leaves and small twigs and can lead to cankers on shoots. Generally, anthracnose diseases flourish in cold wet springs and summers. They only rarely kill trees. Anthracnose of willows, caused by the fungus *Drepanopeziza (Marssonina) sphaeralis*, is most severe on the common weeping willow (*Salix* × *chrysocoma*). Plane anthracnose (*Gnomonia platani*) is most severe on (and will cause the death of) the American plane (*Platanus occidentalis*), which is rarely planted for that reason, whilst Oriental plane (*P. orientalis*) is more or less resistant; London plane (*P.* × *hispanica*) is intermediate between its parents in susceptibility, with some clones being more resistant than others. Willow anthracnose can be controlled by spraying but there is no effective control for plane anthracnose, but to await the normal recovery later in the season or next year. Arboricultural Research Note 46/83/PATH gives an appraisal of anthracnose of planes.

Silverleaf Disease
The fungus causing this disease, *Condostereum (Stereum) purpureum*, is very common in the wood of many trees. The disease is mainly a problem with cherries (*Prunus*) where it shows as a silvery colour to the foliage and debilitates the tree.

Coral Spot Fungus
Nectria cinnabarina produces coral coloured fruit bodies on the bark. It mainly affects dead branches, but can cause the death of live tissue, especially with maples (*Acer*).

Coryneum Canker of Cupressus
This disease causes spreading perenniating cankers on the stem, which girdle and kill the distal portion. The disease causes considerable death of twigs, leading to the death of the tree, although it may first become so unsightly that it is felled. Disease is caused by the fungus *Seiridium (Coryneum) cardinale* and mainly affects Monterey cypress (*Cupressus macrocarpa*), although other cypress species have been affected in Europe. In Britain, several cases of the disease have now been discovered on Leyland cypress (× *Cupressocyparis leylandii*). Arboricultural Research Note 39/84/PATH gives more information on coryneum canker.

Dutch Elm Disease
This disease probably needs little introduction. It causes the wilting of foliage, usually leading to the death of the tree and is caused by the

fungus *Ceratocystis ulmi*. The disease is spread partly by root grafts between adjacent affected and healthy trees but mainly by the feeding and breeding activities of elm bark beetles. They breed in the inner bark of moribund elms and, on emerging in early summer, fly off to have a 'maturation' feed on the bark of small twigs on healthy elms; if carrying the disease, the beetle can pass it to the elm at this stage.

Apart from most species in the genus *Ulmus*, species of *Zelkova* can also be infected, although the beetles rarely breed in them. Elms do vary in their tolerance of or susceptibility to the fungus, with some eastern Asiatic species being very tolerant. Various attempts have been made to breed resistant elms but time is needed to assess the longterm potential of the resulting trees.

Watermark Disease of Willows

This disease affects various willows (*Salix*) but is only serious on a few clones, notably the cricket bat willow (*S. alba* 'Caerulea'). The foliage wilts in April and May, following infection to the wood by the bacterium (*Erwinia salicis*). Trees are rarely killed but become stag headed and the timber is stained and rendered brittle, making those grown for cricket bat blanks valueless; for this reason certain local authorities in southeast England have the power to order the felling of diseased trees as a means of control.

Stem Cankers

Cankers are caused by a number of agents and found on several trees. A number of cankers are perennial, resulting from the ebb and flow of recovery by the tree and death caused by the disease; over a period of time, one or t'other gains the upperhand and either the branch is girdled, killing the distal portion, or the disease dies out. Some common cankers are ash canker, which is caused by a bacterium; cherry trees (*Prunus*) are sometimes affected by a canker which occasionally can kill the entire tree by girdling the stem; apples often have a canker caused by *Nectria galligena*, which forms small cankers on the twigs, often girdling the shoot and reducing yield. Poplar canker is caused by a bacterium (*Xanthomonas populi*) and is widely spread throughout Europe. It produces cankers on the bark of twigs, branches and stems. Some poplars are quite resistant, such as white poplar (*Populus alba*) and many selected clones, but others are much more susceptible; unfortunately, in the latter category is the very striking *Populus × candicans* 'Aurora'. Horse

23 Holm oak with fruit bodies of a Ganoderma *species, indicating extensive decay of the bole. Immediate felling is indicated*

chestnuts (*Aesculus*), particularly red horse chestnut (*Ae.* × *carnea*), are frequently affected by what appears to be a powdery canker, but this is due to a proliferation of buds, possibly caused by a mycoplasma-like organism.

Decay Fungi

All trees can be affected by decay fungi of one sort or another. They will rot the stem or branches, or kill and decay the roots, in either case making the tree unsafe. A number of these fungi are described in Forestry Commission Arboricultural Leaflets 1, 2 and 5.

Non-living Agents

Some of the adverse effects of compacted soils, unfavourable climate and building operations are mentioned in Chapter 2. These and other physical or chemical causes of decline or death of trees may be confused with the effects of various diseases. The chance that it is a non-living agent causing a particular set of symptoms should always be considered.

Gas Leaks

Natural (methane) gas can indirectly cause the death of trees where it escapes into the soil from underground mains. Natural gas is not actually toxic, but bacteria which thrive on it remove oxygen from the soil, replacing it with carbon dioxide (CO_2), thus asphyxiating the roots. The effects of a natural gas leak on the trees are similar to those caused by poor soil aeration due to compaction or waterlogging, or to some root diseases, and includes sparse foliage, with leaves dying prematurely; eventually branches or the whole tree may die, or roots be killed. Confirmation of a gas leak may require chemical analysis of the soil, although the presence of work on the gas main along the street can be useful circumstantial evidence.

Town gas contains carbon monoxide and other toxic substances and is more damaging, but is only produced to a limited extent these days.

Oil Spillage

Spillage of fuel or heating oil is not uncommon. The effects are primarily due to either the replacement of the oxygen in the soil by the oil or the production of toxins by the bacteria which break down the oil in anaerobic conditions. The effects of an oil spill will last for some time, until the oil is broken down or flushed from the soil, although usually there are no longterm toxic residues. Trees which will tolerate a degree of oil spillage, and therefore may be appropriate for screening storage tanks, are those thriving on anaerobic soils, such as western red cedar (*Thuja plicata*).

Road Salt

Salt can affect trees in several ways. The most immediate is likely to be the scorching of buds and foliage splashed by salty water or a mixture of salt and snow, from the spray behind cars and lorries (or from the sea). Once washed into the soil, the effects of salt are less immediately obvious. A high concentration is toxic to plants and can also alter the structure of clay soils, leading to poorer aeration and drainage. Branches on the side of a tree nearest to a road (as the salt source) are likely to show symptoms before branches on the other side, whether caused by salt spray or salt in the soil. Typical symptoms are the death of leaves on some branches shortly after the leaves flush in the spring, or a paler colour or scorched appearance later in the season. Many conifers and evergreens will quickly show dead brown areas of foliage from the effects of salt spray. Severe damage is usually limited to trees close to roads following cold winters (when large amounts of salt is used in de-icing operations) or in trees adjacent to uncovered heaps of salt. Many species of tree can be affected. Oak (*Quercus*), robinia (*Robinia pseudacacia*) and Japanese black pine (*Pinus thunbergii*) are more resistant than most to salt damage. If the soil has become affected by salt, the application of gypsum (calcium sulphate) will help to remove it and improve soil structure. A number of salt tolerant seaside herbs are colonising the edges of inland roads due to the increased use of de-icing salt.

Herbicides

Trees can be damaged or killed by the indiscriminate use of herbicides, either by wrong application rate or by permitting drift or wash from a treated area. Usually, if trees are large the damage shows more as deformation or death of foliage and leaves or retardation of growth, than in their death, as because of their large size they need more herbicide to kill them than is required to kill the weeds. 2, 4-D (2, 4- dichlorophenoxyacetic acid) is commonly used on lawns and is quite toxic to trees, and can be absorbed through the bark. Simazine and dichlobenil can both cause damage at strong concentrations, whilst sodium chlorate can be washed onto root areas. Where damage follows herbicide application, some form of mis-use should always be considered as one possible explanation.

Lightning

Lightning can damage all sizes of trees, there are even some records of hedges being killed. It more frequently affects the tallest trees in a neighbourhood. The commonest types of obvious damage are when a strip of bark down one side of the tree is killed, or the top is killed. Much less frequent, but rather spectacular, is when the entire tree is shattered in small pieces! Where no such damage occurs, death from lightning is not easy to diagnose. Lightning conductors can be fitted to trees, but the cost is high and not often justified, unless the tree is very exposed and will inevitably be used for shelter during storms.

Frost and Drought Cracks

Frosts in late spring or early autumn can affect leaves and twigs, sometimes even killing the cambium under the bark. The damage is usually not severe, except to young trees. Very cold periods can sometimes cause cracks in the bark and timber of some trees, such as oak (*Quercus*), poplar (*Populus*) and walnut (*Juglans*). Frost cracks usually heal over within a year or two, although the timber may be affected and decay fungi may enter the bole.

A rather similar effect, most frequently seen in some conifers, can be caused by summer drought. Some silver firs (*Abies*) and spruces (*Picea*) are most frequently affected; it degrades the timber but is of little further concern.

Sun Scorch

The bark of thin barked trees can be killed if it is suddenly exposed to strong sunlight after previously being shaded by branches, other trees or buildings. Beech (*Fagus sylvatica*) is particularly prone to such damage, but maples (*Acer*), hornbeams (*Carpinus*), spruces (*Picea*), poplars (*Populus*), cherries (*Prunus*) and some other trees can also be affected. Wrapping the trunk with hessian or coating the stem with white paint may prevent damage but these remedies are unsightly. If possible, avoid sudden exposure of thin barked trees.

Snow Damage

Heavy falls of snow, especially wet snow, can cause extensive damage, as the snow clings and adds appreciably to the weight of the branch. Cedar of Lebanon (*Cedrus libani*) is particularly susceptible to wet snow and may be braced (see page 102) to reduce the risk. Very late snowfalls can affect deciduous trees in leaf. Damage can also occur where freezing fog or freezing rain leads to a build-up of ice on the branches and occasionally causes devastating damage.

Atmospheric Pollution

Atmospheric pollution is mainly caused by local emissions from chemical and other processes or from the burning of fossil fuels. Sulphur dioxide is released by burning coal or oil, whilst peroxyacetyl nitrate (PAN) is formed under certain conditions from exhaust gases emitted by petrol engined cars. All of these substances can kill leaves, twigs and even whole trees. Damage is often more severe to evergreen trees, partly because more fossil fuels are burnt during the winter, and possibly because the tree's economy relies on the individual leaves for longer.

Fire Damage

Obviously if a fire is lit close to the base or under the branches of a tree, the heat emitted is likely to kill both foliage and bark. Yet it is common to see trees which have been damaged in this way. Leaves and weeds should be used as a mulch, or composted, rather than burnt, and any bonfires should be kept well away from the trees.

Summer Branch Drop

In summer branch drop, branches may be lost in the apparent absence of either decay, strong winds or any other known predisposing factor. Summer branch drop can occur in several species of broadleaved trees, including elm (*Ulmus*), oak (*Quercus*), beech (*Fagus sylvatica*), horse chestnut (*Aesculus hippocastanum*), ash (*Fraxinus excelsior*) and less often on several other genera or species. The fracture may show some decay, or abnormal growth of tissues, but often no cause is obvious. Several possible explanations have been suggested, but the most plausible includes reference to internal stress occurring in the branch due to the different response characteristics of the vessels and tracheids in the wood when subject to tension as part of the transpiration stream; however, in the absence of proof, this explanation remains a theory, not fact. When summer branch drop has occurred from a tree, the tree should be closely inspected to check that there is no suggestion of other branches being about to fall and therefore likely to cause damage. Trees with exceptionally long branches and trees which have passed the stage of rapid growth (e.g. horse chestnut, *Aesculus hippocastanum*, over 100 years old) are most likely to suffer, typically during or at the end of a period of warm dry weather, and on days with little wind.

8 Costs

AN indication of costs is useful to the newcomer but extremely difficult to give with any validity. Costs are always going to vary, from the complexity of an individual site or tree to local factors of supply and demand, let alone allowing for inflation and how it may affect prices over the next decade. Costs will also vary with the numbers involved, e.g. the planting of 100 small transplants on a site will involve much the same travel to site as the planting of 10 or 1,000, with fewer or more trees over which to spread the cost. In this chapter, the intention is to give an indication of approximate costs and discuss what may influence those costs.

Where labour is not paid, i.e. in most private gardens, the cost of an operation is likely to be the sum expended on buying the materials used, such as trees, herbicides or fencing materials. In other situations, the cost of labour is likely to feature as a significant element in the cost of establishing, maintaining and felling a tree.

When preparing an estimate of the likely costs in a tree scheme, the first element should be to obtain current prices for the type of operations involved. These can be obtained relatively easily by phoning suppliers and contractors and discussing the project with them. Most will be very willing to give a brief outline of the range of prices for basic supplies, e.g. trees, or for materials, such as bark mulch, and will look upon answering your telephone call as part of normal public relations. Only if you require a site visit to give a detailed estimate may there be a charge for the time and expense involved.

Plants and Planting

Trees, particularly in the smaller sizes, are really very cheap and the cost is unlikely to prove a major obstacle if you only require a few. Often, a whip or transplant will be less expensive than a shrub or a few bedding plants, and, bearing this in mind, there is no reason why trees should not be used as temporary features, in addition to those planted for 'posterity'.

Costs of plants will vary according to the size, species, number purchased and whether bare root or container grown.

The size will appreciably alter the cost. With a 1m whip as a bench mark, costing one unit, you will get 2–6 small transplants (less than 0.5m tall) for the same money, but expect to pay 3–4 times as much for a tree 2m tall, 6–8 times for one 3m tall, 15–40 times for one 4m tall, and from several hundred to over 1,000 or more times for trees around 10m tall.

The species is likely to affect the cost in two ways. Where a species is rare, the numbers produced in the trade are small, and therefore the cost of production is invariably higher per plant than for common species. Some species and selected forms are difficult to propagate, needing special techniques, which may significantly increase the cost, perhaps by up to 10 times. Some plants are also subject to Plant Breeder's Rights, which means that a royalty has to be paid to the breeder or person who discovered the select form. Where a number of trees of one species or size is purchased, there is likely to be a quantity discount.

Container grown stock will be more expensive because extra labour is involved in potting, growing, watering, weeding and transporting the plants, as compared to a similar sized bare root plant. Also, there is the cost of the pot and compost. At the smallest sizes, container grown stock may be 3–4 times as expensive, decreasing to only 1.5–2.5 times as much for larger sizes, and possibly no more than bare rooted plants for some very large or difficult to move items.

The cost and labour involved in planting will increase in line with the cost of the plant. A skilled forestry worker can plant from 500–1,000 transplants per day in the forest using notch planting, or 200–300 per day using pit planting. With larger trees, particularly those over 4–5m, special machinery is likely to be needed to lift them and move them around the site, and to excavate the planting pits, leading to a greater cost, though not disproportionate to the cost of the tree.

The cost of transporting the trees from the nursery to your site will vary with the size of tree. Transplants and whips are usually bundled in fifties, and many bundles can be moved in a van or covered lorry, whereas a tree 10m tall may be the only one you can fit on the lorry, and as few nurseries produce this size of tree, delivery may require the lorry for one day to the site and a second for the journey home. Normally, delivery will work out at around 10–25% of the cost of the plants but may vary widely depending upon location or individual situation.

Fencing, Fertilising and Weed Control

The cost of the materials can be obtained from local suppliers. The cost effectiveness of fencing as compared to individual protection can be worked out using the formula given in Chapter 4 (see page 87). The cost of labour involved in applying herbicide or fertiliser, or erecting fencing, is likely to work out at from 50 to 250% the cost of the materials, normally somewhat exceeding the material costs. Obviously, where the number of trees is small, the 'dead' time goes up as a proportion of the total, increasing the cost.

Early Pruning and Maintenance

Pruning during the early years of a tree's life may only involve a few minutes every year; it usually consists of inspecting the tree and removing crossing branches, double leaders, unwanted lower branches, stakes and ties and repairing any storm or vandal damage.

Maintaining a Tree in a Park

A study by R. Helliwell for Cobham Resource Consultants Ltd. estimated that the basic cost of maintaining a young tree in a public place was around 0.1 man-hours per year, i.e. one man would put in one hour over the course of a year to maintain 10 trees, although this figure needed to be increased according to one or more specific factors. The specific factors are: site type, number of trees per unit area of site, vandalism, standard of tidiness required and proximity to roads, buildings and services.

Site type. On very difficult sites, the costs might increase by a factor of up to 1.5 times.

Number of trees per site. With very few trees, or if the trees are widely scattered over a large site, costs per tree can be increased by up to 3 times.

Vandalism. Where vandalism is fairly severe, costs may be increased by 2 times or more, if replacement trees have to be planted.

Standard of tidiness. In areas where a very high standard of tidiness is required, costs can easily be doubled.

Proximity to roads, services and buildings. Where trees are close to roads and/or buildings, costs may be increased by as much as 3 times.

In the worst possible situation, where all five special factors are operative, a single tree could require the equivalent of $0.1 \times 1.5 \times 3 \times 2 \times 2 \times 3 = 5.4$ man-hours per year. Even this, however, is likely to be only around a tenth of the cost of maintaining 100 square metres of bedding plants, which would occupy the same area as the mature tree, and it is considerably less than the expense of an intensively maintained lawn.

Removal of Trees and Tree Surgery

The main factor in cost is the size of the tree. A small tree, with a stem diameter of 30cm or less, will rarely prove difficult to fell. A tree 40m tall with a butt diameter of nearly two metres will contain perhaps 100 times as much timber and branchwood and will take much longer, even if it can be felled as it is. Also, the larger tree is invariably the older one, and more prone to have decay or weak branch forks which require additional care.

The next factor is location. A tree in the middle of a large field can be felled without the need to take it down piece by piece; the extra size only results in more work to clear away the residue. By comparison, if the tree is at the corner of four properties, each with a glasshouse or shed beneath its branches, in a smoke control zone where all rubbish has to be wheel-barrowed or even carried through the small side gate, it is not difficult to realise why that tree may be so costly to remove; or where the tree overhangs a busy road, and two or more men are needed to control the traffic. In these situations, each branch will need to be roped and lowered carefully, so that no damage is caused by its fall; and the crown of a large tree may weigh 10–40 tonnes or more.

The final factor which will influence the cost of felling is whether there is an economic use for the timber and branchwood. The cost of a two man team of trained tree surgeons, complying with sensible health and safety regulations, is likely (in 1987) to be from £150 to £250 per day, allowing for wages, machinery and overheads; for a number of jobs, a three man team is needed, increasing the cost proportionately. The cost of felling a given tree can be expressed in the number of such gang days to carry out the task.

The cost of tree surgery can also be expressed in gang days, with from half to one, sometimes two, to deadwood a large tree, or fit bracing cables to a big Cedar of Lebanon (*Cedrus libani*). Crown thinning may take from a quarter to one day, depending upon the size and location of the trees. Other tree surgery operations will be similar in range of cost.

The cost of tree surgery or tree felling involving dead or dangerous trees can be higher, as the operatives will need to take more care, and pay extra attention to their own safety, to that of passers-by and to ensure that damage is not caused. There may also be a need for the hire of a heavy crane to lower large pieces of timber safely.

9

TREES AND THE LAW AND DAMAGE BY TREES

THIS chapter discusses the law affecting trees in England and Wales and possible ways in which trees may cause physical damage, either by their roots or their tops.

Trees and the Law

In England and Wales, two systems of law are found. These are Common law and Statute law. Both affect trees in some ways and where appropriate a solicitor should be consulted.

Common Law

Common law is based on case law, i.e. the decisions made by judges over the years, as opposed to Statute law which is based on Acts of Parliament. Common law is the basis of much of civil (as opposed to criminal) law. Aspects of Common law which are of relevance to trees include ownership, overhanging branches (and roots), and damage caused by trees.

Ownership of Trees

A tree normally belongs to the land on which it is growing, regardless of how it got there, and is the property of the owner of the land, although where a tenancy or lease is in operation, the ownership of the tree may be assigned under the terms of the tenancy or lease. An exception may be where a tree is growing on land which is dedicated as a public highway, the land is owned by the adjoining property owner but the planting and maintenance of the trees is usually taken over by the highway authority. The land on which a tree is growing is considered to be the position where the tree first grew or was planted, so it is the position of the trunk which determines ownership. Thus a tree which is growing out of the soil one metre from the boundary but which has most of the crown over the fence, is the property of the owner of the land on which the tree makes contact with the ground. The tree includes the roots, branches and fruit, as well as the timber. Where the tree is growing on a boundary and it is not possible to say on which side it arose, the ownership of the tree may be shared between the two parties.

The owner of the tree is entitled to the rewards offered by the tree, ranging from timber to fruit, but is also liable should the tree cause any damage.

The owner or lawful occupier of land is entitled to the enjoyment of the air above and the soil beneath his land. Where trees overhang land, the neighbour may cut the overhanging branches back to the boundary where they are causing a nuisance. He is not entitled to enter the neighbouring land to do this, nor to cut the branches back beyond the boundary. The cut branches remain the property of the owner of the tree, and cannot be disposed of except with his permission. This includes any fruit or firewood from the overhanging branches.

Where roots extend across the boundary, the neighbour may cut them back to the boundary.

The occupation of land gives rights to air and soil vertically above or below the land. It does not confer on the occupier any right to light coming from the side of the property, i.e. a person cannot claim in law that a neighbour's trees are blocking out the light if they do not overhang the property, because in law the occupier of property is only entitled to light which falls vertically. A tree on neighbouring property is most unlikely to interfere with 'rights of light' established under Common law, as a tree is never constant, always growing or moving in the wind, so that a static interference with the right of light is not created. There is, also, no complaint in law against leaves blown onto a property from trees not overhanging it; after leaves have fallen, they are considered wild uncontrollable items (like cats) which may be blown where the wind takes them.

Damage and Dangerous Trees

The basis of actions concerning damage by trees is a case in 1868 when the following principle was established. Where an occupier of land brings something dangerous onto his land, he is liable for any damage should that object escape. Where a tree 'escapes' from one piece of land and causes damage on another, the owner of the tree may be liable for any damage caused if it can be shown that he was negligent in allowing the tree to escape.

The courts have suggested that the owner or occupier of land with trees growing on it should have a greater degree of knowledge about trees than an ordinary layman, and that he should regularly inspect his trees to check that they are safe. Regularly is imprecisely defined but will probably mean at least once a year. It fact, it is much more sensible to inspect trees at least twice a year, as certain features are better seen in

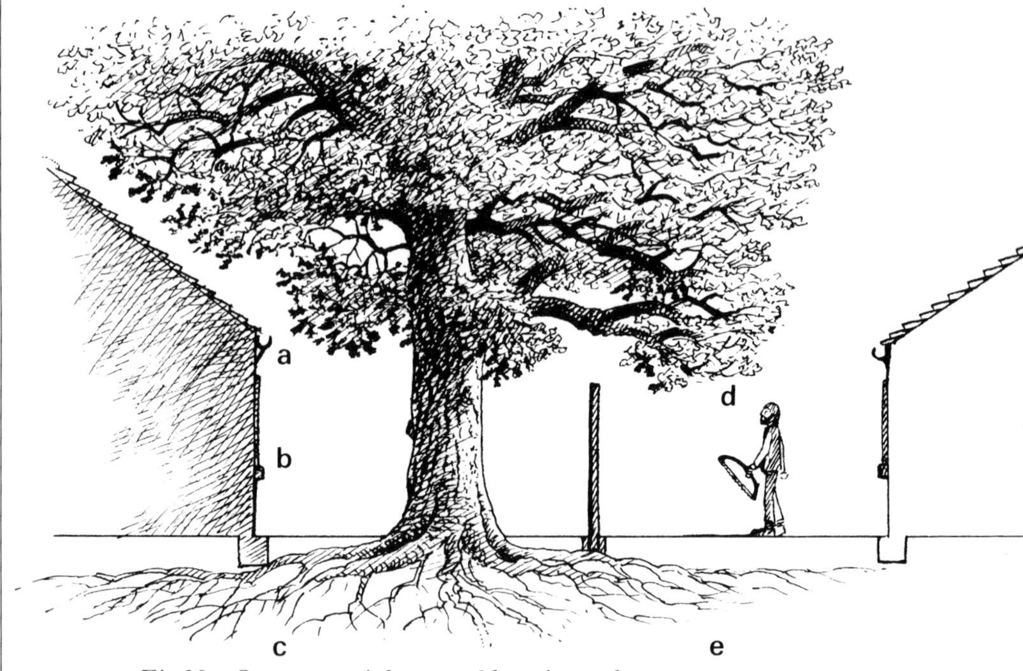

Fig 28 Some potential tree problems in gardens:
(a) guttering blocked by fallen leaves; (b) windows and garden heavily shaded; (c) foundations of buildings and walls affected;(d) branches overhanging adjoining property; (e) roots which cross boundaries, and may cause damage to drains or foundations

leaf, e.g. size of leaves and general vigour, whilst other things are clearer when the tree is leafless in winter, such as the presence of weak crotches, broken branches or fungal fruit bodies. These aspects are discussed in Chapters 5 and 7. When the trees are inspected, a record of the inspection should be kept.

If the owner or occupier fails to regularly inspect his trees, or fails to act upon the results of an inspection, he may be adjudged negligent, and therefore liable for any damage caused.

He is not liable for any defect which could not reasonably have been apparent from an inspection, nor for damage which results from exceptional weather conditions, or similar unpredictable factors. Liability may extend to roots which cross a boundary and cause damage, either to drains or by causing subsidence, as discussed below.

Normally, cover against damage by trees or their roots is included in the Public Liability element of household insurance, although if you knowingly refuse to rectify or prevent a possibly dangerous or damaging situation, your insurance company may contend that you were in breach of the conditions of your policy.

Where a tree is poisonous, the operative principle is whether it has escaped from the land. If a yew (*Taxus baccata*) overhangs a boundary and the foliage is eaten by a neighbour's horse or cow, the owner of the tree will be liable, but not if the horse had to enter his land (or lean over the fence) to eat the foliage.

Statute Law

This covers all laws established under Act of Parliament. Statute law normally has precedence over Common law.

Tree Preservation Orders

Local authorities in Britain have the power under several Acts of Parliament concerned with planning matters to make Tree Preservation Orders. The purpose of a Tree Preservation Order (or TPO for short) is to safeguard, from indiscriminate felling or lopping, trees which make a significant contribution to the amenities of an area.

A TPO is served on a property and represents a charge upon that property. It must be properly served on the owner (and any other interested party, e.g. a leaseholder) to be valid. Although the TPO is served on the property, it only covers the trees specified in the schedule. These can be single numbered trees, trees specified by area, groups of trees or units of woodland. A unit of woodland covered by a TPO cannot overlap another category of protected tree.

The presence of a TPO requires the owner to apply to the local authority for permission to fell or cut back any trees affected by the TPO. The local authority may either give or withhold permission for the tree work, or may give consent subject to certain constraints, or for only part of the proposal. Where the local authority refuses to give absolute consent, the owner may appeal to the Secretary of State against this refusal, or the granting of partial consent. The procedure for objecting to a TPO or appealing against an unfavourable decision is outlined in the formal notice of the TPO. If you are affected by a TPO the local authority will discuss these aspects, and provide a copy of the notice, if needed. Where a person suffers a financial loss due to the action of a TPO, a claim for compensation can be raised, but no compensation is payable where you reach an agreed compromise, or where the refusal is judged to be in accordance with the practice of good forestry.

The presence of a TPO does not remove from the owner or occupier of land any responsibility for the safety and general management of the trees and the owner still has a responsibility not to be negligent. Specifically, the legislation leaves with the owner the duty to fell any trees which are dead, dying or dangerous; also felling is permitted where a covenant with the Forestry Commision exists, where a tree stands on land directly affected by a development which has planning consent, or where statutory undertakers require the felling or tree surgery under their enabling legislation. However, except where immediate danger exists, the local authority should be given five days' notice of any felling in this category. Tree work may also be carried out to abate a nuisance, but remember that under the law, your own trees cannot cause *you* a nuisance. Fruit trees are outside the TPO legislation.

Normally, replacement trees of a suitable size and species must be planted where trees are felled, although the local authority can agree to dispense with this requirement.

Contravention of a TPO can leave the owner of the trees liable to a fine not exceeding £1,000 or twice the value of the trees on summary conviction or an unlimited fine on indictment, with a smaller daily penalty for continuing offences.

TPOs should not be looked upon as 'preserving' trees; the trees must still be managed creatively (see Chapter 6). A TPO is a useful tool for retention of trees on development sites or on industrial estates and to ensure that new planting takes place where trees have to be felled. They have less moral integrity in established situations, such as old residential areas. The choice of the word 'preservation' is unfortunate, as it is only possible to preserve trees in the negative sense of not allowing them to be cut down; trees are living things and cannot be indefinitely 'preserved'.

Conservation Areas

In a Conservation Area, six weeks' notice of any proposed tree work must be given to the local authority; the exemptions and fines for breaches of this rule are similar to those outlined above under TPOs. The purpose of the six week period is to allow the local authority to assess the amenity value of the trees and, if appropriate, place a TPO on them. If no response is received from the local authority after the six weeks have elapsed (and you have proof of sending the notice!) you have two years during which to carry out the proposed work.

Felling Licences

Felling of timber is controlled, mainly as a measure of ensuring that woodland is not converted into farmland without permission. A felling licence must be obtained from the Forestry Commission, unless one of the following exemptions applies. No licence is needed if:

a) the felling is in accordance with an agreed plan of operations under one of the Forestry Commission's grant aid schemes;
b) the trees are in a garden, orchard, churchyard or public open space;
c) the trees are all below 8cm diameter measured at 1.3m above ground

level, or 10cm if they are part of a thinning operation, or 15cm in coppice or underwood;

d) the trees are interfering with permitted development or statutory works by public bodies;

e) the trees are dead, dangerous, causing a nuisance or are badly affected by Dutch elm disease;

f) the felling is in compliance with an Act of Parliament.

Also, a small amount of other felling is permitted. Currently this is 5 cubic metres (of timber) in any calender quarter, of which no more than 2 cubic metres may be sold. This concession was reduced from a more generous figure in 1985 to cut down the conversion of woodland to other land uses.

Any questions on felling licences should be addressed to the local office of the Forestry Commission, or to the headquarters at 231 Corstorphine Road, Edinburgh.

Trees and Highways

Highways legislation gives the local highway authority the right to cut back or fell any tree which interferes with the safe or efficient use of the highway, including the pavement and street lighting. This specifically includes trees which are unsafe and within falling distance of the highway. By the Highways Act of 1835 it is illegal to plant a tree within 15 feet of the centre of a highway, a rather archaic restriction in these days when most highways and pavements are considerably wider. Local authorities have exemption from this constraint.

Local Government (Miscellaneous Provisions) Act 1976

This permits, but does not force, local authorities to enter private land for the purpose of removing dangerous trees which overhang or risk falling onto neighbouring land. The cost of this work will become a charge on the land.

Damage Caused by Trees?

Trees, despite their innumerable attractions, can sometimes cause problems or damage. For example, the shade which can be a welcome relief on a hot summer's day may be less welcome where windows are unduly darkened or greenhouses or vegetable patches shaded. Areas of grass beneath trees will grow with less vigour, and if subjected to heavy wear, will the sooner become bare; in damp shady conditions where the sun cannot reach, some forms of paving may become covered with algae and require treatment to prevent them becoming slippery. These examples illustrate common problems of relatively minor significance (although very important to the people involved) which should be avoided with forethought and planning, as discussed in Chapter 3. However, there are a number of ways in which trees can or may cause actual damage and these are discussed in greater detail below under the headings 'Damage by aerial parts' and 'Damage by roots'.

Damage by Aerial Parts

The most obvious problem emanating from the aerial parts of a tree arises when branches are lost or the whole tree is blown down. The owner, or his manager, should check the condition of his trees regularly to ascertain, as far as is practical, that the trees are in reasonable condition, as discussed in Chapters 5, 6, 7 and above, and take appropriate action.

Parts of trees may be poisonous or give off harmful substances. Poisonous trees include nearly all parts of yew (*Taxus baccata*) or the seeds of laburnum (*Laburnum*), whilst others may give off irritant hairs, such as plane (*Platanus* × *hispanica*), or have poisonous sap, as with some species of *Rhus*; although with *Rhus* in particular, not all people are sensitive to the sap. These are mentioned under the appropriate species in the Gazetteer.

Damage by Roots

Roots can cause or be implicated in damage in three different ways.

Where a root is growing under a rigid structure, such as a garden wall, the root may cause damage as growth leads to an increase in diameter. Damage may occur if the root is growing between a solid lower layer and the structure above, or where the tree is very close to the structure and the roots, or lower portion of the bole, are increasing in diameter. Where the structure is brittle and not of flexible construction, damage may follow the lifting of the foundations. This form of damage is common to garden walls or where tree roots grow beneath rigid drains, but is much less common where buildings are concerned; normally the loading on the foundations of the average building and the depth at which they are placed act to preclude damage.

Trees can grow in and thereby block drains. Only some trees are capable of exploiting the damp and usually anaerobic conditions inside a drain, such as willows (*Salix*) or poplars (*Populus*). What trees cannot do, except as discussed in the above paragraph, is grow into an integral drain. The drain must first be faulty in some respect, either fractured (by vibrations from traffic or lifting by tree roots) or with failed joints; tree roots cannot grow through fired clay, plastic or concrete drains!

The third way in which trees can be involved in damage or cause a problem is in the extraction of moisture from the soil. Trees, with their extensive root systems and large crowns, will use an appreciable quantity of water in transpiration during the summer season and dry out the soil.

On shrinkable clay subsoils and some organic soils, the extraction of moisture from the soil may lead to subsidence. This does not occur where the soil or subsoil is not a shrinkable one. Where the soil shrinks, the effect may be to cause differential settlement of the foundations and, in rigid structures such as brick houses, lead to cracks in the fabric. Modern building regulations and standard of foundations should be adequate to prevent damage to new houses on these soils (unless the trees are very close), but older properties, especially those with foundations to a depth of less than 1m may be at risk. During the winter season, the soil moisture deficit will be partly or completely removed by the winter rainfall and the soil expands ('heaves') towards its original volume. Problems with heave can occur when houses are built on land which has had trees for a number of years and these have been felled prior to building commencing; if there was an accumulated soil moisture deficit, it may take up to ten years for this to be made good, during which time the resultant heave may cause damage.

Where the soil or subsoil is, or might be, a shrinkable clay the possible effects of tree roots on properties nearby should be considered. However, there are many instances of trees growing close to buildings on shrinkable soils and the possibility of roots causing damage should not be used as an excuse for no tree planting; the problem can, after all, be resolved by taking suitable precautions to build houses capable of withstanding the site conditions. For further guidance, see the National House Building Council (NHBC) Practice Note 3 (1985), *Building near Trees*, obtainable from NHBC, Chiltern Avenue, Amersham, Bucks, HP6 5AP.

GAZETTEER OF TREES

THIS section is intended to assist in the selection and management of amenity trees. The information presented is weighted in favour of the commoner species in each genus, with less common but interesting plants being given proportionally less space. More experience has been gained over the years from the commoner and more established tree species; however, even for common or native species, new cultivars are being developed regularly and it is only in the light of experience that the longterm potential of any individual species or cultivar can be ascertained.

The details and comment in this section should be used to expand upon the information provided by the lists of trees for various sites given on pages 214–19. Comment is made about the amenity value of the species and the principal cultivars so that a realistic choice of potential trees for any site or feature can be made. Some of this information takes the form of highlighting useful characters but the intention is not to identify trees *per se*; for this and more details about the foliage, flowers, fruits or bark of individual trees, the reader is referred to the books listed in the bibliography on page 220.

A likely height of a mature tree is given for each species. Usually this takes the form of a range of heights, e.g. 15–25m. The higher figure is the maximum height recorded for the species, or likely to be recorded; this is a rather artificial measure as generally it is only on exceptional sites that this figure is reached. More relevant in the choice of species for planting is the bottom end of the range, as this is the figure which the tree will most probably reach on an average soil, given sufficient time to grow to maturity.

Most of the trees included in this section are available at a range of sizes from a number of commercial nurseries. However, a number will be available only as small plants, especially evergreens and less common species. These are not trees to be specified for large scale plantings but make interesting choices for special or commemorative trees for parks, for intimate areas around private houses and such occasional uses where an element of the uncommon or special is pertinent. A small number make shrubby trees and are usually considered and planted as shrubs; with time they will make small trees and can be useful to succeed a fast tall growing tree removed as too large.

The genus name, botanical family to which the genus belongs, appropriate common names and the approximate country or region of origin is given for each species. Details such as colour, size and shape of foliage, flowers, fruits and bark are given in the discussion, as is information about either soils or sites for which the species or cultivar is expressly suited or which it does not tolerate. Most trees will grow very adequately on the full range of soils encountered in Britain and repeated reference to this ability is not made. Similarly, information on potential pests or diseases is only given here where the tree is particularly susceptible or resistant to the disease or pest, and therefore where there is individual information to impart. For instance, a common disease such as honey fungus is only mentioned under a species which is particularly marked in its tolerance (e.g. the resistance of incense cedar (*Calocedrus decurrens*) to honey fungus), or susceptibility, e.g. monkey puzzle (*Araucaria araucana*). For more general information, see Chapter 7.

ABIES

Silver firs Pinaceae

This is a genus of evergreen conifers, containing around fifty species. The genus includes some of the tallest and fastest growing trees, although a number of species make only small trees. Nearly all are very tolerant of shade. The trees have a single straight stem with the branches in whorls; the habit may be slightly open although as trees age they become denser. Silver firs are rarely blown over or uprooted and are generally windfirm, unless attenuated from being grown too close together in a plantation. They are also generally resistant to honey fungus (see page 118). Most are not tolerant of pollution and they thrive better in moist soils; some species will grow well on chalk or limestone sites. They are better planted as small seed raised trees, preferably around 30–60cm but can be conveniently planted up to 2–3m with care. The common name comes from the silvery bands of stomata on the undersides of the leaves in many species. They are useful for foliage colour, neat habit and attractive cones.

A. concolor
White fir Western North America

A fast growing tree with a distinctive bluish foliage and corky bark, it is hardy throughout the country. It makes a taller tree in the cooler and moister north but is better suited to drier conditions than some other species. It deserves wider planting, particularly in the best blue foliage forms, 'Violacea' with glaucous blue foliage, and 'Candicans' with vivid grey or silvery-white leaves. It is not affected by the green spruce aphid (see page 188) which can mar the appearance of Colorado blue spruce and can be used as a colourful alternative to this tree. The maximum height is 50m but 20–25m is more likely, particularly in the drier parts of the country.

A. grandis
Grand fir Western North America

This is a very fast growing tree and one of three conifers to have reached 60m in Britain. The origins from coastal Washington state are much more vigorous than those from the drier parts of its range in the Rocky Mountains. At its best, it will make 1.5m for several years. It is frequently the tallest tree after fifty years on most sites but old trees when exposed to the wind are likely to become ragged. On all except the best sheltered sites, therefore, it should be managed for what it is, a fast growing attractive tree for 50–100 years, and then be felled and replaced. It will grow on a wide range of sites, including on limestone, although it may become somewhat yellower in leaf. It is shade tolerant. The bark is thin and may be damaged by roe deer. It is not suited to polluted sites.

A. koreana **Korean fir** Korea

Korean fir makes a small tree to a maximum of 10–15m, although usually less than 8m. It is slow growing and frequently produces the blue or blue and brown cones when less than a metre tall.

A. nordmanniana Caucasus &
Caucasian fir Northeast Turkey

This species is a more luxuriant relative of European silver fir and is more suitable for general planting, although it too can be affected by the aphid, *Adelges nordmannianae*, which has restricted the planting of European silver fir. It will thrive on a wide range of sites and develops a columnar habit, well furnished to the ground. It is shade tolerant. Trees of 40m are recorded but 20–30m is more usual.

A. pinsapo **Spanish fir** Southern Spain

This species is usually planted as the cultivar 'Glauca' with bluish foliage. It is unusual in the leaves being radially arranged around the shoot, like the erect spines of a hedgehog. It tolerates dry sites and both acid and alkaline conditions. It is inclined to become rather rough when old but is a neat tree for the first fifty or so years. It can grow to over 30m tall but 15–20m should be considered as a likely attractive maximum height.

A. procera
Noble fir Western North America

Noble fir is a very attractive species, both for the generally blue foliage and for the silver-grey trunk. The branching habit is very open and whorled in young trees. The cones are very large, to 25cm, and may be carried on trees less than 6m tall. It is better suited to moist acidic soils and will not tolerate dry chalky sites. It has a maximum height of 50m but will only reach this in the moist cooler parts of the country; where the soil or climate is at all dry, a height of 15–25m is more likely. On sites which dry out during the summer, or in dry years, it will produce 'drought cracks' in the stem (see page 126). Noble fir is more tolerant of exposure than are other species.

A. veitchii **Veitch fir** Japan

Veitch fir is a robust species similar to but more vigorous than Korean fir; the foliage is as silvery below but longer and the cones are a better violet blue. Extremely tough, it thrives beside the A9 at the Spital of Glenshee in the Highlands. A maximum height of 25m and a likely one of 15–20m.

ACACIA

Wattles Leguminosae

This enormous genus is mainly found in tropical or subtropical parts of the world, especially Australia and Africa. It belongs to the Legume family. Only the following species is commonly cultivated. The name 'Acacia' is sometimes used for Robinia, *quid vide*.

A. dealbata
Silver Wattle Eastern Australia

This is a fast growing evergreen tree with fernlike or feathery twice pinnate or bipinnate foliage. It bears masses of attractive yellow flowers in spring and is the 'Mimosa' of florists. It is rather tender and likely to be cut back or killed by hard frosts. It is only worth growing along the south and west coast and with shelter against a wall elsewhere, but even here it is not reliably hardy.

ACER

Maples Aceraceae

Maples are a large and rather diverse group of more than 100 species with many cultivars. They range from large trees, such as Sycamore, to small shrubby species. They are particularly useful for their attractive foliage. In most species, such as Sycamore, the leaves are palmately lobed, but they may be undivided in some, such as the Snakebark maples, and pinnate in Box Elder. The appearance ranges from the dense leafy aspect of trees like Sycamore or Norway maple, to the more open appearance of those with pinnate leaves, such as Box Elder. Various foliage colours are present in the genus. Most species are outstanding for autumn colour. Only in a few species are the flowers showy, although they are quite attractive in detail and valued as a honey source by beekeepers. The bark is very attractive in some species, especially the Snakebark maples which are discussed as a group at the end of the section.

Maples will grow on all soils, although preferring a respectable depth of topsoil over chalk. They are very susceptible to bark stripping damage by grey squirrels. They may be affected by verticillium wilt and coral spot fungus (see pages 120–1). They will move as large trees.

The following list includes the commoner species, which are all deciduous. There are also a number of evergreen species which are hardy but these are mainly shrubs.

A. campestre
Field maple Britain & Europe to Iran

Field maple is the only maple native to England and Wales, where it is found on lime-rich soils. It often is a rather shrubby tree to 10–15m, although capable of growing to 25m. It may need to be trained to force it to develop a single stem. It is used as a hedge plant and withstands trimming. The leaves turn a good yellow in the autumn and often the new growths, particularly from hedges, are a neat reddish colour. Field maple is easily moved at all sizes and will tolerate a wide range of site conditions.

'Postelense' has the leaves a striking golden colour in early spring, later changing to green.

'Pulverulentum' has motley leaves blotched with white.

'Schwerinii' is a form with the leaves a rich reddish purple when they flush in the spring, later becoming green.

A. cappadocicum
Cappadocian maple E Turkey to China

This makes a tree 15–20m, occasionally to 25m. It has an attractive rounded habit with neat foliage which turns to one of the best and most reliable golds in autumn. It grows well in damper situations, although flourishing elsewhere and has a moderate growth rate. The tree normally suckers from the root system (not the bole); this may be a disadvantage near to shrub beds or in formal grass areas, although possibly an advantage in vandal strewn areas!

'Aureum' is one of the best yellow foliaged trees, making a small tree of 10–15m. The leaves flush red, turning golden-yellow for the summer and then a brilliant gold in autumn. It is slow growing but can make an excellent tree.

'Rubrum' is the common form of the species available from nurseries. The new foliage, either in spring or on extension growths, is a blood-red colour, changing to green.

A. circinatum
Vine maple Western North America

The Vine maple is similar in foliage to the more commonly planted Fullmoon maple; it makes a small rather shrubby tree to 6–10m. Often it is broader than tall and the lower branches will root where they touch the ground. The flowers, produced in spring, have plum red sepals and white petals and the almost circular leaves will turn shades of orange and red in autumn. The main horticultural attribute of the tree is its tolerance of dry shade.

A. griseum
Paperbark maple Central China

One of the best of all small trees, this has an outstanding bark which exfoliates in small papery rich red-brown flakes. The leaves are composed of three leaflets and assume brilliant fiery reds for a fortnight in autumn. It is rather slow growing, making a tree 8–15m tall. It will tolerate a wide range of sites, including ones on chalk, and moves satisfactorily.

A. heldreichii **Heldreich maple** Balkans

This species is similar to Sycamore but with more deeply three lobed leaves. The flowers are yellow and quite showy, being carried after the leaves open in May. The fruits have red wings and are quite noticeable. It forms a medium sized tree to 20m, although more often only 15m.

A. japonicum **Fullmoon maple** Japan

Fullmoon maple has nearly orbicular shaped leaves and quite attractive purple flowers in spring. It makes a small tree to 10m. It is usually planted as one of the following forms:

'Aconitifolium' has the leaves deeply cut and lobed; they are a soft green during the summer, assuming a bright ruby-crimson in autumn.

'Aureum' is a slow growing form with the leaves a soft yellow colour.

'Vitifolium' is the commonest form in cultivation and comes fairly true from seed. The leaves are larger than in the species and take on a brilliant red coloration in early autumn.

A. lobelii **Lobel maple** Southern Italy

This species is similar in foliage to Cappadocian maple and also turns yellow-gold in autumn. It has a narrow columnar habit suitable for use in street tree situations. The current year's shoots are covered by a waxy bloom. It is a reasonably fast growing tree to 15–25m.

A. macrophyllum
Oregon maple Western North America

Oregon maple has bold deeply lobed foliage which turns orange or brown in the fall. The fruits are conspicuously coarsely hairy and can be irritant if carelessly handled. It is a fine tall growing tree of good vigour, to 20m.

A. negundo **Box Elder** North America

The Box Elder is unique amongst the maples in having the bright green leaves pinnate with three, five or seven leaflets, giving the tree a light open aspect. It makes a small tree to 15m but of fast initial growth rate. The wood is rather brittle and branches may break in the crown. It is dioecious; the male form is very attractive in spring with the flowers hanging from the previous year's branches like a series of purple tassels, although the female form is commoner in cultivation.

'Auratum' is a small slow growing tree form with bright gold leaves.

'Elegans' has glossy green leaves which are margined by a broad yellow band and bloomed shoots.

'Variegatum' is a plant which has the leaves variously with a broad white border or entirely white. It is a female clone with the variegations persisting on the fruits. It is a slower growing sport of the green form and is inclined to revert.

'Violaceum' is a male form with the young shoots purple with a white bloom.

A. palmatum
Japanese maple Japan, E China

This is a small tree, more often seen as a shrub 3–5m tall but capable of making 10–15m. The leaves are neatly cut and bright green with 5–7 lobes; they assume good colours in autumn. It requires shelter from cold winds. Many attractive cultivars have been named, mainly small shrubs. The following clones will make small trees and embrace the range of variation offered by the species.

'Atropurpureum' is a plant with brilliant purple foliage during the summer, taking on an extra crimson colour in the fall.

'Osakazuki' has green foliage until it develops through various shades to a fiery flame scarlet in autumn, making one of the most brilliant displays.

'Senkaki' ('Sangokaku') is a form which is most renowned for the coral red shoots during the winter; the leaves develop a soft yellow colour in the autumn and are rather smaller than in the above two forms. It is vigorous, making a tree to 15m, although susceptible to dieback during the winter if exposed.

A. platanoides **Norway maple** Europe

This is a very tough tree which is fast growing when young, with a top height of 15–25m. The flowers are quite conspicuous for ten days before the leaves come out in the spring, giving a brief but effective display of greeny yellow. The foliage turns a good yellow in the autumn, rarely becoming reddish. The species will thrive on any freely drained soil and has a likely lifespan of around 150–200 years. It tends to be deeply rooting and will tolerate a degree of shading. It is easily moved at all sizes. It is particularly useful in screens or as a bold tree for amenity purposes. It is not invasive like Sycamore.

'Columnare' is a green foliage form with a narrow columnar habit.

'Crimson King' has the leaves crimson-purple throughout the summer, becoming rather dark and heavy. Like all purple foliaged trees, it should be used sparingly.

'Drummondii' is a cultivar which has the leaves variegated with white. It can be most effective, although any reversion must be culled.

'Emerald Queen' makes an upright tree with rich green foliage.

'Globosum' is slow growing and makes a rounded head on the top of the stem. It is often top-worked.

'Goldsworth Purple' is similar to 'Crimson King' but a duller colour during the summer.

'Lobergii' or the 'Eagle's Claw Maple' has the lobes of the leaves continuing back to the base of the leaf-blade; the segments broaden towards the tip, giving the appearance of an eagle's claw. It makes an interesting tree form.

'Schwedleri' has leaves which flush bright red, slowly turning a dark green. The new growths made during the season are also red, as are the flowers in spring before the new leaves. It is useful for making a splash of colour in spring, without becoming heavy like its seedling 'Crimson King'.

A. pseudoplatanus
Sycamore ('Plane' in Scotland) Europe

This is a very tough tree which will thrive on a wide range of sites and conditions, although not so well suited to waterlogged soils. It is more tolerant of exposure and atmospheric pollution than other species. Its main drawback is that it is not a native tree but behaves like one, regenerating freely on all but the most acid or phosphorus deficient soils. It makes its best growth on fertile soils and in cool moist climates, such as northern Britain, although making a significant contribution to the landscape in many urban areas.

Young trees are rather spiky but as they cease to grow so rapidly and start to fruit freely, the habit becomes more rounded, with large billowing branches. It will grow 20–35m tall and live for 150–400 years. It roots fairly deeply and does not often drop branches until it starts to decay in old age. It produces a good quality but not durable white timber. Sooty bark disease may affect it after hot dry summers (see page 29). The foliage may become spotted by tarspot or blackened by the honeydew excreted by sap sucking aphids.

Its main uses in the landscape are as a pioneer broadleaved tree for rough or barren sites, for the pleasing habit when fully grown, for the timber and as a bold or solid tree in the landscape. It transplants easily at any size.

'Atropurpureum' is a very effective tree and quite different from other purple foliaged trees. The leaves are dark matt green above and a light purple beneath. When this is viewed with the light reflected off the underside, the purple shows up, but when the light is transmitted through the leaves, as when seen from beneath or looking into the sun, the effect is a bright light brown. The wind may cause these changes as it blows the leaves about. Seedlings may exhibit all manner of variations from purple beneath to plain green.

'Brilliantissimum' has the new foliage a brilliant shrimp pink, gradually changing through a bright yellow to green mottled with a rather sickly yellow. In early spring, it is a most effective plant. It is very slow growing and usually top worked. 'Prince Handjery' is similar, although the leaves are purple beneath and persist more of a bronzy gold.

'Erectum' is a clone with a narrow erect habit, suitable for street use or for confined spaces.

'Erythrocarpum' is an effective form in which the wings of the fruits are an attractive flush red.

'Leopoldii' has variegated foliage which begins yellowish pink, passing to green with yellow and pink speckles or splashes.

'Nizetti' makes a large striking tree

whose leaves are marked with yellow, pink and white above and purplish beneath.

'Worleei' has soft golden yellow foliage, gradually becoming green by midsummer.

A. rubrum
Red maple Eastern North America

Red maple is a small to medium tree, up to 15–20m. It has a bright silvery-grey bark and the leaves are silvery beneath. The red flowers are carried before the leaves in spring. Autumn colour can be spectacular on some trees.

'Scanlon' is a narrow crowned clone with a tall habit; it colours well in the autumn. It is suitable as an 'Exclamation' mark but not for a street tree.

'Schlessingeri' is a form whose leaves develop a deep scarlet colour in early autumn.

24 Mature sycamore (Acer pseudoplatanus)

A. saccharinum
Silver maple Eastern North America

Silver maple is similar to Red maple but the leaves are larger and more silvery and deeply lobed. Silver maple is very fast growing as a young tree, growing up to 20–30m tall. The branches are rather brittle and often small ones break, creating disfiguring patches in the crown. It moves well.

'Laciniatum' is a form with more deeply cut leaves and a graceful drooping habit.

'Pyramidale' has an upright growth habit.

A. saccharum
Sugar maple Eastern North America

This tree is the one from which maple syrup is harvested. It makes a small tree, 15–20m, with a leaf similar in outline to that of Norway maple. It develops crimson, orange or gold autumn colours.

'Temple's Upright' is a slow growing and very narrow crowned cultivar which turns orange in autumn.

SNAKEBARK MAPLES

The Snakebark maples are a small group which have the bark striated with wavy white lines or markings, akin to a snake moving along the stem. The background bark colour is usually olive green. They have very attractive habits and make interesting trees. All the species will quickly make trees to around 10m but slow down and scarcely grow much taller. They are susceptible to coral spot fungus (see page 121). They will grow on all reasonable soils and move easily.

A. capillipes
Red snakebark maple Japan

This is one of the commonest of the Snakebark maples, with the petioles a bright red and the leaves slightly lobed. It can be quite an attractive mixture of orange and scarlet in autumn.

A. davidii **David maple** China

This species has usually entire or unlobed leaves which are a shiny blackish green above. The bark can be good but autumn colour is often lacking.

A. hersii **Hers maple** China

This 'snakebark' maple has lobed leaves, good bark and gives yellow, orange and red autumn colours.

A. pensylvanicum
Moosewood Eastern North America

Moosewood has larger leaves than other Snakebark maples, to 20cm long on vigorous shoots, turning pale yellow in autumn.

'Erythrocladum' is an outstanding often shrubby form with the one year twigs conspicuously shrimp-pink in the first winter. Unfortunately, it is not a robust plant and needs a sheltered site, probably on an acid soil, and is only occasionally seen at its best.

A. rufinerve
Grey-bud snakebark maple Japan

This species is similar to Moosewood in having reddish hairy veins but the leaves are smaller and turn orange and red in autumn. The buds are prominent and grey.

AESCULUS

Horse Chestnut Hippocastanaceae

The Horse Chestnuts are a genus of 15–20 species. They all have palmately compound leaves and carry the flowers in erect panicles after the leaves in summer. The fruit is the traditional 'conker'. The species will tolerate all reasonable soils except for waterlogged ones.

Ae. hippocastanum
Horse Chestnut Balkans

This tree is well known to most people and one of the few species generally recognised. It has been an integral part of British folklore for sufficiently long for the fact that it is an introduced species which has only been here since around the beginning of the 17th century to be forgotten. The foliage can be very dense and heavy during late summer, and the mainly white flowers are not appreciated by all, standing erect like candles, but it is one of the most floriferous and solid trees in the landscape; it is the first species of Horse Chestnut into bloom, usually around the end of April to mid May. The fruits can be a nuisance, due to the activities of small (and not so small) boys trying to dislodge them before they are ripe to use the large chestnut-brown seeds in the game of conkers. It should not, therefore, be planted close to roads or in places where these activities may cause problems. The sticky buds can also be an object of wonder and interest, as if a branch is brought inside and put in a vase of water as the buds are just starting to expand, it will produce the furry new growths.

Horse Chestnut is easily established at all practical sizes and will make a tree of 20–30m, rarely to 40m tall. It is only moderately long lived, averaging 100–150 years, although trees over 300 years are reported. It will thrive on all except waterlogged sites but is a better tree where the soil is not too dry or too acidic. It roots moderately deeply and is usually windfirm. The timber is soft, weak and almost useless. The branches are liable to be broken off by strong winds, snow or other events and it is one of the species which may suffer 'summer branch drop' (see page 127).

The main use of Horse Chestnut is as an amenity tree for avenues or as specimen trees.

'Baumannii' is a sterile double flowered form. It is no improvement over the fertile plant except if it is considered essential to plant a Horse Chestnut in a place where it is not safe for youngsters to expedite the falling of the ripe fruit.

A. × *carnea* **Red Horse Chestnut**

This tree is a small growing version of Horse Chestnut. The main difference is in the foliage, which is a darker green, and in the red flowers. The fruit is smoother than in Horse Chestnut and the seed only good from some trees. Red Horse Chestnut is a hybrid between Red Buckeye (*Ae. pavia*) and Horse Chestnut. Red Horse Chestnut will make a tree to 20m but more often is only around 15m tall. It will tolerate similar soils to Horse Chestnut. Some plants develop curious large 'cankers' on the stem, which weaken the bole and reduce the tree's life (see page 129).

Red and ordinary (white) Horse Chestnuts are sometimes seen planted together as alternate plants; this is always an error as the growth rate and habit are very different and not compatible.

'Briottii' is a form with brighter flowers and more glossy foliage, It is an improvement on the normal form of the species and worth specifying.

Ae. indica Indian **Horse Chestnut** Northwest India, Nepal

The Indian Horse Chestnut makes a rounded tree to 20m, usually broader than tall. It has more pointed and neater foliage but its main attribute is in the flowering period. This is late June to early July, some six weeks after Horse Chestnut, whilst still creating a picture with the long erect white, pink and yellow candles. The fruit is larger and also ripens later, rarely attracting the attention of those seeking 'conkers'. The bark is smooth and pinky-grey. It will thrive on all sites except wet ones and deserves much wider planting.

'Sydney Pearce' is a particularly floriferous form which originated at Kew. The panicles are larger and more showy than normal.

Ae. flava **Yellow Buckeye** Eastern USA

The Yellow Buckeye is one of several species of 'Buckeyes' from eastern USA. They differ from Horse Chestnut in the flowers having only four petals, not five, and being more tubular and less showy. The buds are non-sticky. The name comes from the resemblance of the base of the seed to the eye of a deer.

Yellow Buckeye makes a tree to 20m, useful for providing a different colour of flower in the Horse Chestnut stable. Grafted trees with Horse Chestnut as the rootstock should be avoided, as the bark is quite different and therefore the union appears unsightly.

AILANTHUS

Tree of Heaven Simaroubaceae

Ailanthus is a small genus of trees with large pinnate leaves.

A. altissima **Tree of Heaven** China

Tree of Heaven makes a tree with a rounded crown. The leaflets have glandular teeth at the base, which secrete a form of nectar; this is collected by ants, who guard the leaves against marauding caterpillars. The flowers are carried on separate trees (usually) and the female ones are followed by the twisted and winged keys. In some plants these are a showy red colour. The male flowers have a disagreeable odour. The bark is smooth and grey-brown but patterned with vertical wavy white streaks.

Tree of Heaven is late to come into leaf in the spring and is better suited to a hot summer climate. The tree is admirably fitted to urban situations. It will sucker from the roots, producing very large leaves, to 1m in length. The leaves do not take on any autumn coloration, blackening and falling after the first hard frost in autumn. Tree of Heaven will make a tree 15–25m tall, growing better in the warmer south. It is easily moved and initially fast growing. The branches are somewhat brittle.

ALNUS

Alders Betulaceae

The alders are a genus of around thirty species of trees and shrubs tolerant of wet situations. They have the capacity to form nodules with a bacterium which 'fixes' atmospheric nitrogen, turning it into nitrate which can be used by the plant for growth. They will also tolerate drier sites, especially once established. They are very useful for barren situations, such as reclaimed spoil heaps, where there is no topsoil and only a limited nutrient supply. The male catkins are very showy in the spring. Autumn colour is rarely good.

A. cordata **Italian alder** Southern Italy

This is the largest growing of the alders, with heart-shaped deep green leaves, showy yellow catkins in spring and large woody cones, to 2cm. It will make a tree 15–25m, and, despite its southerly origin, is quite hardy. It is fast growing with a narrow columnar habit. It will tolerate a wide range of sites and does much better on shallow chalk soils than other alders.

A. glutinosa
Alder or Common alder Britain & Europe

Common alder is the only species native to Britain where it occurs along the banks and edges of streams, especially in 'Alder carrs', where the soil is swampy and few other plants will flourish. It will grow well on most normal sites, although less well on the poor dry ones on which Grey alder will flourish. It is not so useful on shallow soils over chalk.

Alder makes a tree usually no more than 15m but up to 30m. The growth rate is fairly fast to begin with but soon slows down. The crown varies from broad columnar to broad conic. It is particularly effective in late winter, when the catkins are starting to open, giving a purplish haze to the tree. The leaves are obovate and less attractive than with other species. The seeds are a useful source of food for a number of small birds. Apart from natural history considerations, the species is too dull to be used other than for shelter or to add nitrogen to the soil.

Alder has a lifespan of from 60 to 100 or more years. It coppices easily. Trees will move at most sizes, provided they are not permitted to dry out at the roots. The roots of Alder can exist in water or waterlogged conditions and therefore if they gain entrance to a drain, they may block it.

'Aurea' has the leaves a golden yellow, although not strongly so; it is a small tree.

'Imperalis' has the leaves deeply and pinnately lobed with the lobing reaching halfway to the middle of the blade. It makes a rather feathery tree, usually of narrow habit.

'Laciniata' has the leaves less cut than in 'Imperalis'.

A. incana **Grey alder** Europe

This species is better suited to dry or barren sites than Common alder. It is particularly useful in establishing tree cover on colliery spoil and other reclaimed sites. It will make a tree to 25m, although often much smaller. It is hardier and generally faster growing than Common alder, with more attractive leaves, but its main use is going to be for shelter or soil improvement. It will sucker from the roots.

'Aurea' has yellowish leaves and, more effectively, yellowish red first year winter shoots. 'Ramulis Coccineus' is very similar, but has redder winter shoots. Both make small trees and need a moist site to flourish.

'Pendula' is a delightful small weeping tree, suitable for most sites and smaller growing than Weeping Willow.

AMELANCHIER

Snowy mespilus Rosaceae

Amelanchier is a small genus in the Rose family, related to Apples and Whitebeams. They make small trees or large shrubs and have showy flowers in early spring. Most species also develop colourful tints to the leaves in autumn. The fruits are not showy, being small and ripening mid-summer. The trees thrive on a wide range of sites.

A. lamarckii **Snowy mespilus**

The species makes a small tree to 10m with a wide spreading crown. It is the main one in cultivation and has naturalised on acid sands in parts of Britain.

ARALIA

Devil's Walking Stick Araliaceae

This is a genus of small trees or herbaceous plants belonging to the ivy family. Only the following species is often found as a small tree.

A. elata **Devil's Walking Stick** Japan

This makes a small tree to 10m. It is very valuable for the bold twice pinnate foliage and for the large clusters of small white flowers in August–September; these are followed by small dark purple or black berries. The stems (and leaves near the ground) are richly adorned with small sharp prickles. The tree suckers from the root system. Sucker shoots are densely clothed with thorns and remain unbranched until they are 2–3m tall, which is the origin of the name Devil's Walking Stick. The tree is very useful where the bold foliage and late flowers can be enjoyed but should not be planted where the prickly stems will be a nuisance.

ARAUCARIA

Monkey Puzzle Araucariaceae

This is a genus of conifers from the southern hemisphere. Only the following species is hardy, although Norfolk Island pine (*A. heterophylla*) is often grown as a house plant and is hardy in the Scilly Isles.

A. araucana
Monkey puzzle Chile, W Argentina

This tree is one of the few generally correctly identified. It is totally different from any other tree cultivated in Britain. At its best, it can make a very bold and spectacular tree, retaining the foliage down to ground level. Where conditions do not suit it so well, the lower branches are often lost and an umbrella shaped crown results. It does better in the moister west of Britain, although it grows well in the drier and colder parts of the country. The leaves are large and persist for up to 15 years; they are very sharp. Leaves and branches are often retained on the tree after they have been suppressed and have died.

The male and female cones are carried on separate trees. The male cones are 15cm long; the female cones are globular, eventually to 15cm, and carried at the ends of the branches of the outer crown; they ripen in the second or third autumn and disintegrate to release the very tasty seeds (especially if roasted like chestnuts).

Monkey Puzzle will tolerate exposure, including that from seawinds, but is not well adapted to urban pollution. Single trees can look attractive but the species looks more natural if a cluster is planted. Monkey Puzzle will live for upwards of a century and grow to a maximum of 30m, although more often to 15–20m. It is susceptible to honey fungus, which can kill large trees (see page 118).

ARBUTUS

Strawberry tree Ericaceae

This is a small genus belonging to the Heather family but the species will all tolerate chalk or limestone conditions. They make small evergreen trees but may not be hardy in cold districts.

A. unedo
Strawberry tree Ireland & Europe

This tree is native to the region around Killarney in southern Ireland and to much of Europe around the shores of the Mediterranean. It makes a small tree, with time to 10m. It should be planted out as a small plant, less than 1m tall or from a container. The main attractions are in the evergreen foliage, the attractive bell-shaped white flowers carried in the autumn and in the fruits; these ripen in the autumn and are shaped like a strawberry and edible, although as the Latin name implies ('I eat one!') scarcely a delicacy.

'Rubra' is a form with pink flowers. The flowers alone are quite attractive but they do not provide an agreeable contrast with the previous season's fruits, which ripen at the same time, and the common white form gives an more pleasing effect overall.

A. menziesii
Madroño Western North America

This species is one of several native to Mexico and western North America. It makes a larger tree, to 20m, and has larger leaves. The flowers are carried in larger clusters but, along with the fruits, they are smaller than in the European species. The bark is very smooth and yellowy pink, apart from the base which may be cracked into small square purple plates. The bark on the branchlets is red and peeling. It makes a very attractive tree.

BETULA

Birches Betulaceae

There are about about forty or so species of birch found throughout the northern hemisphere. They range from trees 25m tall down to dwarf shrubs, such as *B. nana*, which are less than a metre in height.

Tree birches are generally fast growing but not long lived. Most have a likely lifespan of 40–80 years. Birches are pioneer species, adapted to colonising bare ground. They are not tolerant of shade; in many sites starting from bare ground there is a natural succession through birch woodland to longterm and more shade tolerant species. Birches cast only a relatively light shade; they can, therefore, be tolerated closer to windows than other species. However, they are surface rooting trees and will dry out the soil surface layers and compete strongly for nutrients in this area. They do not make good companion trees for shrub planting. The shallow root system makes birches susceptible to periods of drought, which if prolonged will lead to early loss of leaves and ultimately death. They are not noticeably afflicted by pests or diseases whilst young; as the tree ages, though, the Birch polypore fungus, *Piptoporus (Polyporus) betulinus*, will decay the soft timber. The fruit bodies can be seen on moribund and dead trees at most times of the year.

Birches readily hybridise and should either be grown from wild collected seed or be vegetatively propagated. Where grafting is used, the scion must be placed as near to ground level as practical, or the bark of the rootstock may look very different from the top variety.

Birches can be tricky to establish at sizes above 1–2m. Naturally, they tend to develop a coarse root system which does not make a good one for transplanting and they are also susceptible to drying out at the roots. However, if trees are carefully handled and well planted, they can be moved as bare root stock at sizes up to 3–4m and at larger sizes with suitable attention to the rootball.

Birches are useful for the outstanding bark of most but not all species. The outer bark of most species consists of a number of layers which successively flake off; the bark can be damaged if these layers are removed prematurely and the resulting damaged area is not attractive, being tight and making a pathetic brown contrast to the surrounding bark. Even with species whose bark is a vivid white colour, that of young trees is brown for upwards of three years. A number of species are notable for the foliage, especially for autumn colour. The habit may also be attractive, in this category none is more delightful than the Silver birch (*B. pendula*). Birches are useful for amenity plantings and for shelter, being tolerant of exposure and good on poor sandy soils. The seeds, or nutlets, are an important winter food for a number of bird species.

Birches often occur naturally in groups or as multi-stemmed individuals (see page 70). Established trees usually withstand cutting but birches will bleed from wounds made over-winter or in early spring; sometimes, heavily pollarded trees will not make new growth.

B. alba

This name was applied to both Silver and Downy or Brown birches. It has been abandoned as of uncertain application and trees offered under this name should be avoided, as it is impossible to be certain whether the attractive Silver birch or the mediocre Brown birch is on offer.

B. albo-sinensis
Chinese red birch West China

This makes an attractive tree with an orange peeling bark which has a creamy glaucous bloom to the underbark. The best forms, such as Wilson 4106, are very attractive trees, developing a spreading crown and a stout bole. It withstands a wide range of sites and makes a tree 10–15m tall.

Var. *septentrionalis* is the commoner form in cultivation, having an orange-brown bark with a thicker waxy pink and grey bloom. The clone cultivated under this name also makes a more upright and narrower crowned tree than some forms of the type species.

B. ermanii
Erman birch Northeast Asia & Japan

This makes a tree with a creamy coloured bark with a pinkish tinge and conspicuous lenticels. The bark flakes off but does not hang in loose strips. The species makes a tree to 12–18m.

B. 'Fetisowii'

This is a hybrid of Polish origin which has a chalky white peeling bark and a graceful narrow habit.

B. nigra — Eastern North America
River or Black birch

Old trees of River birch develop a black bark made up of thick curling scales, although whitish in young trees. The bark of old trees can make a very effective contrast to the common white barks of other birches. It will tolerate wetter sites than most other species and makes a tree 10–15m tall, naturally on several stems.

B. papyrifera — Northern North America
Paper or Canoe birch

This is a very variable tree in the wild and often segregated into several distinct species. It is also variable in the quality of the bark, which at its best is a ghostly white colour; other forms are a duller whitish grey or yellowish white. Generally, a better bark colour is retained than in other species as the tree gets larger. The bark does not flake to the extend of Chinese red birch but was peeled off felled trees in large sheets and used to cover Indian or 'Canadian' canoes. It makes a fast growing tree of 15–20m.

Var. *kenaica* is a form from Alaska with a creamy white bark, with an orange or reddish brown tinge.

B. pendula — Britain & Europe
Silver birch
(Syn. *B. verrucosa* – Warty birch)

This tree is the most graceful of all native species, with a narrow crown with the small branches hanging down vertically. The foliage is small and light, turning a good yellow in autumn. The bark is a silvery white, becoming broken into thick corky fissures at the base in old trees. It is a tree much better suited to light sandy soils and does not do well where the drainage is poor, such as on heavy clays. It will seed profusely, the seeds being an important winter food source for birds such as siskins and redpolls. It tends to be over-planted, which does not mean that it should not be planted but that thought should be given before using too many Silver birch or on the wrong soil types. It is a very attractive tree whilst young but it robs the soil of moisture and nutrients and makes managing the rest of the garden difficult as it gets older. Silver birch makes a tree 15–25m tall.

'Dalecarlica' Swedish or Cutleaf birch makes a narrow tree form with the leaves deeply cut into a number of narrow lobes. Its bark is a good white colour.

'Fastigiata' is a form which lacks the gracefully pendent branchlets of the species. It makes an upright tree with ascending branches, and can be useful for cramped situations or as an 'exclamation mark'.

'Purpurea' is a rather weak tree whose thin or open purple foliage needs a strong background (e.g. *Cupressus macrocarpa* 'Goldcrest') or otherwise it is lost.

'Tristis' is a beautiful form with a narrow crown with strongly weeping branchlets.

'Youngii' is a form which makes a mound of foliage, never making an erect leading shoot. The height of the plant is dependent upon the height to which it is trained or at which it is grafted. It can be used to make a weeping mound on a lawn.

B. pubescens — Britain & Europe
Brown, Downy or White birch

This species is better suited to damp situations than Silver birch and makes a longer lived and larger tree. It has a brownish young bark, slowly giving way to a dull white bark which is retained to the base of the stem, never developing the thick corky basal bark of Silver birch. It is useful for shelter planting on poor damp sites but has little garden value.

B. szechuanica — Western China
Sichuan birch
(Syn. *B. platyphylla* var. *szechuanica*)

This tree is grown for the bark which is a chalky white colour. The whiteness of birch bark is caused by the substance *betulin* which is produced in great quantity by this tree and can be rubbed off in the hand 'like whitewash'.

B. utilis Himalayas from Afghanistan
Himalayan birch to W China

This species has a very wide distribution along the axis of the Himalayan mountains. It is particularly variable in the characters of the bark and is divided into three subspecies and one variety.

Subsp. *jacquemontii* Jacquemont birch (*B. jacquemontii*) is a tree with a very white peeling bark. It comes from northwest India to central Nepal. It is commonly offered in nursery catalogues as *B. jacquemontii*, although some of these plants may be of hybrid origin.

Subsp. *utilis* has a bark without or with only a little betulin; the bark is in various shades of brown, red or mahogany; the best red or coppery coloured forms are as attractive as the white bark of Jacquemont birch, but in a different way. It is found from Nepal eastwards into China.

Subsp. *occidentalis* is found in Kashmir, Afghanistan and the far northwest of India but has only recently been introduced into cultivation. It has a pure white outer bark which peels to reveal a fawn inner bark; the shoots, leaves and buds are strongly resinous.

Var. *prattii* is the form of the species from west China and has a shiny brown or mahogany bark with little betulin. It is very similar to the typical subspecies.

All the forms of Himalayan birch make trees in the range 10-15m, usually of a narrow habit. A number of named cultivars are also in cultivation:

'Grayswood Ghost' and 'Inverleith' are two magnificent white-barked forms which make strong growing trees. They may be hybrids.

'Jermyns' is a bold tree with a creamy white stem. The male catkins create a display in spring when they open to 10–15cm. It develops a good golden-brown autumn colour. It may be a hybrid between subsp. *utilis* and subsp. *jacquemontii*.

'Sauwala White' is a plant collected from central Nepal under Stainton, Sykes and Williams 4382 and raised at Wisley. It makes a small tree with a vividly white bark and belongs to subsp. *jacquemontii*.

CALOCEDRUS

Incense cedars Cupressaceae

This is a small genus of three species, sometimes listed under *Libocedrus*.

C. decurrens
Incense cedar Western North America

An evergreen conifer related to Western red cedar, the crown in cultivated trees is usually very narrow and columnar, with short spreading erect but not fastigiate branches; this makes the tree less liable to wind damage than many others of similar habit, e.g. forms of Lawson cypress (*Chamaecyparis lawsoniana*). In the wild, however, and occasionally with cultivated trees, the habit is broader and the branches horizontal. It is much more tolerant of honey fungus (see pages 118) and also of *Phytophthora*, than is Lawson cypress. It has made a tree almost 40m tall but the range 15–25m is more usual. It a very useful feature tree, both as an individual plant and in groups.

CARPINUS

Hornbeams Corylaceae

This genus of some forty species are excellent foliage plants, mainly making small trees. They thrive on a variety of sites, including shallow chalk soils.

C. betulus
Hornbeam Britain & Europe to Iran

Hornbeam is quite attractive at several different times of the year: when the pendent male catkins open in early spring

25 *Young fastigiate hornbeam* (Carpinus betulus *'Fastigiata'*)

26 *Semi-mature fastigiate hornbeam*

with the new foliage; in the yellow, orange or russet colours of autumn; when the silver-grey fluted bark is shown off to best effect in mid winter. It is generally free from diseases and will make a tree 20–30m tall. It withstands pollarding or clipping and is used for hedges. It is of moderate growth rate and long lived. Trees can be moved at most sizes without difficulty. It makes its best growth on fertile soils, often occurring in the wild on heavy clay ones. In general appearance it looks similar to Beech, especially in the buds and bark, although this is more heavily fluted. The English name derives from the Saxon *beam* meaning tree and *horn* equalling hard, referring to the very tough timber used for wooden cogs, gears and butchers' chopping blocks.

'Fastigiata' is a very commonly planted form. It has a dense crown made up of ascending branches. It looks attractive both in summer and when leafless. It is frequently planted as a street tree, a role for which it is only suitable for a very short period. The habit of young trees is columnar conic but as the top ceases to make additional height growth, the side branches progressively catch up and within 30 years, the tree is a perfect dome, eventually with a radius of around 15m. It is a very formal tree when young and should not be over-planted.

C. japonica **Japanese Hornbeam** Japan

This makes a small tree to 10m with a scaly and furrowed bark. The leaves have 20–25 pairs of veins, giving an attractive appearance.

CASTANEA

Sweet chestnut Fagaceae

This is a small genus mainly of large trees. They have the distinctive saw-toothed leaves and large tasty nuts. A bacterial disease, chestnut blight, casued by *Endothia parasitica*, has devastated the American chestnut (*C. dentata*) and can cause damage on the following species; it is not present in Britain.

C. sativa Southern Europe
Sweet or Spanish chestnut

This makes a large tree of 20–35m with a broad crown. The bark of young trees is smooth and grey becoming in old trees brown with very regular spiral fissures. The flowers are pollinated by wind and create an attractive massed display in July. Usually, ripe fruit is only produced in southern Britain, and then only after good summers.

Sweet chestnut is a fast growing tree which does not thrive on a heavy clay soil or a chalky one. On dry sandy sites it flourishes. It is susceptible to damage from *Phytophthora*, see page 119. It is hardy throughout the country and is extremely vigorous; it is often coppiced for the production of chestnut pale fencing. The timber is similar to oak in appearance but not as strong or so useful. It is only moderately long lived, although making a large tree within a century. It is one of the species which can suffer from summer branch drop (see page 127).

'Albovariegata' has leaves with creamy white variegations, whereas in 'Aureo-variegata' they are golden. Both make strong growing variegated trees.

CATALPA

Bean trees Scrophulariaceae

They make small to medium trees and bear large showy panicles of white or pink flowers in mid to late summer. These are followed by long thin bean-like fruits. The leaves are relatively large but very thin in texture and will not withstand exposure to strong winds. The trees are rather late to come into leaf in the spring and give little autumn colour. They are susceptible to verticilium wilt (see page 120).

C. bignonioides
Indian Bean tree Central Southern USA

This is the commonest Bean tree in cultivation. It makes a low rounded crown, attaining a maximum height of 10–20m on a short bole. The leaves are large and heart shaped, and the flowers, borne in late July or early August, are a showy white with a yellow centre. It is hardy throughout the British Isles but rarely flowers in the north as the summer heat is not sufficient to ripen the wood.

'Aurea' is a form with soft yellow leaves. It will make a small tree but is more commonly seen as a shrub; it is very effective as a yellow foliage plant but must have shelter.

C. × erubescens **Hybrid Catalpa**

This is a hybrid between Indian Bean tree and a Chinese species, *C. ovata*. Its main attraction is the reddish purple colour of the new foliage. The leaves are large and three lobed.

'Purpurea' is the common form of the hybrid in cultivation, with stronger coloured new foliage.

C. fargesii Central & Western China
Farges Catalpa

This species makes a rather columnar upright tree which deserves much wider planting. The flowers are carried in June and are an attractive pink, whilst the leaves are longer pointed. It will make a tree to 12–18m.

C. speciosa Northern Central USA
Northern Catalpa

This species from central USA is much better adapted to the British climate than Indian Bean tree, although far less common. It flowers earlier in June or early July and has neater although similar foliage.

CEDRUS

Cedars Pinaceae

The true cedars are a group of four species of evergreen conifer restricted to the shores of the Mediterranean and the western Himalaya. They include three of the most beautiful conifers. The male cones or catkins are carried in the autumn as a mass of erect yellow 'candle-like' structures on the lower branches.

Cedars will grow on all sites except waterlogged ones, being very suitable for shallow soils over chalk. They can be moved at all sizes, with suitable care. Old trees, particularly of Cedar of Lebanon, develop wide spreading and rather flat branches which, due to the dense development of the evergreen foliage, collect wet snow; this can cause serious damage and it is worth considering bracing the limbs to reduce the danger of this. The timber is naturally resistant to decay.

27 *Young deodar* (Cedrus deodara)

C. atlantica
Atlas cedar Algeria & Morocco

Atlas cedar makes a broad conical tree which will retain live foliage to ground level. It is the most amenable cedar to general cultivation, developing a strong central leader and a silvery bark. Nearly all the trees in cultivation are of the blue form, forma *glauca*, which has the foliage covered with a layer of glaucous wax. It is particularly attractive when the new shoots and leaves develop a silvery cream colour before ageing to blue. Atlas cedar will make a tree 25–40m tall. Young trees are inclined to be rather spiky, but this is lost as the tree fills out.

C. deodara
Deodar West Nepal to Afghanistan

This will also make a tree 25–40m tall but is very much better grown as a tree to 15m; older trees become scraggy with the live crown carried way above ground level, on rather spaced branches, and with a blackish bark. Small trees are very attractive with the green or greenish-blue foliage carried on horizontal branches which are strongly pendulous at the tips. It is not as tolerant as Atlas cedar of drought or pollution.

C. libani Lebanon, SW Turkey
Cedar of Lebanon

This was the first cedar to be introduced and makes a most majestic tree in old age, with a stout bole bearing a number of rising stems which arch out, becoming level at the ends. It will grow into a tree of 40m and live for upwards of 200 years. Old trees can cover up to 1,000 square metres and have a butt diameter greater than 2.5m. It is well suited to large parks where it can be allowed to develop to its full potential but is not appropriate for small gardens, and young trees are inferior to either Atlas or Deodar cedars. It is more susceptible to wind and snow damage than the other species.

CERCIDIPHYLLUM

Katsura Cercidiphyllaceae

This is a genus of two species, of which only the following is commonly grown.

C. japonicum **Katsura** China & Japan

This is a very attractive tree to 15–25m with a narrow habit. The new foliage starts off as shrimp pink, soon changing to green and taking on an assortment of red, orange, yellow or pink in the autumn. The leaves are carried in pairs and are similar in outline to those of the Judas tree (*Cercis siliquastrum*). It tolerates a wide range of soils, including those over chalk or limestone. It can be moved at all normal sizes and is hardy. New growth starts rather early in the spring and the first flush of new leaves may be damaged by spring frosts, although this rarely affects the tree as a second flush is soon produced and usually escapes frosting.

CERCIS

Judas tree Leguminosae

In this small genus of legumes the pea-like flowers are carried on branches one to many years old. The leaves are heart-shaped at the base and simple. The species will grow on all sites, provided the drainage is good. They prefer a hot sunny aspect.

C. canadensis
Redbud Eastern North America

This is a small tree or shrub which bears pale pink flowers. It is not common, nor particularly floriferous, in Britain but worth considering for the following cultivar:

'Forest Pansy' is a small tree form with an appalling name but appealing appearance. The foliage is a deep reddish-purple and, unlike most purple foliaged plants, this colour remains bright and attractive from spring until August when it become a bit duller until revived by the reddish autumn colour. It is one of the few really good purple foliages.

C. siliquastrum — Eastern Mediterranean region
Judas tree

This makes a tree to 15m but is slow growing and long lived. It is very attractive in May when the rosy-pink flowers open on the bare branches. Old specimens develop a gnarled appearance.

'Alba' is a form with white flowers.

'Bodnant' is a cultivar with deep purple flowers.

CHAMAECYPARIS

Cypress — Cupressaceae

This evergreen conifer genus has the foliage in flattened sprays, drooping leading shoots and the small cones. The half dozen species have proved remarkably variable in cultivation and given rise to hundreds of cultivars. They all tolerate a wide range of sites, making attractive trees with narrow crowns and retaining the foliage down to ground level. The growth rate is moderate, usually in the range 30–50cm (12–18 inches), although young trees can exceed this. Trees can be moved at sizes of 2m and up if sufficient attention is paid to the rootball and to post planting maintenance. The species are moderately shade tolerant and survive in city environments; they are not tolerant of salt pollution and trees close to roads are often scorched by the spray thrown up by cars following winter de-icing operations (see page 125). They withstand clipping and make good hedging or screening conifers. The trees may be affected by *Phytophthora*.

C. lawsoniana
Lawson cypress — Western North America

This tree can make 40m in Britain but is usually only 15–20m tall even after a century; this is especially so in the drier regions of the country. Over 200 cultivars have been named, ranging from dwarf conifers to tree forms with gold or blue foliage or distinctive habits; the wild species has grey-green foliage. Most of the tree cultivars have habits with regular conical outlines but some, including the species, develop a less regular crown, with short dense branches splaying out at the top and giving the tree an individual character. The crown is always narrow, never becoming broad, and the main bole is frequently forked, sometimes into innumerable stems which can be subject to storm damage. Lawson cypress is useful as a specimen amenity tree, for shelter or screening and also for cut foliage for wreaths or floral displays. Because of its relatively slow growth rate, it can also be used as a nurse for trees which require shelter. The foliage of Lawson cypress, and other similar cypresses, makes a valuable contribution to wildlife, providing safe nesting sites for the first brood of many songbirds.

The following is a short list of the more prominent cultivars:

'Allumii' makes an upright small tree to 8–15m tall with blue-grey foliage in erect sprays; it develops a 'skirt' of billowing branches at the base.

'Columnaris' is similar in colour to 'Allumii' but more columnar, without the skirt.

'Erecta' has bright dark green foliage in erect plates. The habit is fusiform, with upright branches. It will make a large tree with time but becomes bare at the base. The erect branches are inclined to be blown out in storms.

'Fletcheri' is a small tree, 5–12m, with juvenile greyish-blue foliage.

'Hillieri' is a clone with yellow foliage, becoming greener later in the season. It makes a small columnar tree upwards of 10m.

'Intertexta' is a majestic form with open or spaced grey-green, somewhat pendent foliage and developing a tall crown with character.

'Kilmacurragh' is a green plant which has a narrow habit with short spreading branches. It is an excellent green narrow columnar form.

'Lane' is a columnar tree with feathery sprays of golden-yellow foliage.

'Lutea' has a narrow columnar or conic habit with golden yellow foliage; this is carried in long pendulous sprays in old trees and is quite effective.

'Pembury Blue' is the best blue foliaged form, making a broadly conical tree with pendulous sprays.

'Pottenii' has sea-green feathery foliage held in dense sprays. It will grow to some size but the branches are often displaced by storms when the tree is over 10m tall and then reveal the dull dead inner foliage, at which stage it is better felled and replaced.

'Stewartii' has a conical habit bearing long arching sprays of foliage, golden without and greener within.

'Winston Churchill' develops a narrow conical habit with golden foliage. It can be slow to start growing but when established makes a fine columnar tree.

'Wisselii' has curiously tufted foliage held in spaced radial sprays. It looks as if it is a dwarf clone but has made 25m in fifty years. This clone is particularly striking in April when the massed male cones give the tree a pink tinge; in other forms the male cones are more of a maroon red.

C. nootkatensis **Nootka cypress** Western North America

Nootka cypress makes a tree with an extremely regular conical habit, often forming a perfect cone shape; the shape is increasingly broader the further west the tree is grown. The foliage hangs down on either side of the branches in long flat sprays. It has a moderate growth rate and will form a tree of 15–30m tall. It thrives on a wide range of sites, including both acidic and chalky ones and will tolerate cold conditions.

'Pendula' has an erect leader with the main branches arching down and out; on these, the foliage hangs down in vertical sprays. It makes a very distinctive tree with a gaunt appearance; this has been described as an 'Afghan hound tree'!

C. obtusa **Hinoki cypress** Japan

This cypress has glossy green foliage and a reddish stringy bark. It will make a tree 15–25m tall, with the larger trees growing on moister sites.

'Crippsii' is one of the best of all golden foliaged trees. The habit is broadly conical with dense fern-like sprays of bright golden foliage, which develops the best colour in full sun. It is of moderate growth rate and will make a tree 10–15m tall.

'Tetragona Aurea' has the foliage set in dense four sided sprays; the leaf colour is golden yellow or bronzy yellow in full sun, becoming green in shade. It will make a tree 8–12m.

C. pisifera **Sawara cypress** Japan

This species will make a tree 15–25m tall and grows on a wide range of sites. The wild type of this tree is uncommon in cultivation and rather similar to many Lawson cypress. Much commoner in cultivation are several dwarf cultivars and the following tree forms.

'Filifera' is a small open tree, to 20m, with dark green foliage. The foliage is in whip-like unbranched pendulous shoots; they are carried at erratic intervals but together make a pleasing effect. A number of golden foliaged forms of this cultivar have been raised, of which 'Filifera Aurea' makes a tree to 12m with an attractive weeping habit. 'Golden Spangle' is a sport of 'Filifera Aurea' which has foliage mainly in normal flat sprays (a proportion are whip-like) of a strong yellow colour. It makes a narrow crowned tree to 6m.

'Plumosa' is a form of the species in which the foliage is partly juvenile and thus gives the tree a feathery or plumose aspect. It makes a tree to 20m with a broadly columnar and eventually flat-topped crown. 'Plumosa Aurea' has the foliage a bright golden colour on young trees, becoming less striking with age.

'Squarrosa' has the foliage fully juvenile, with the scale-leaves very soft and 0.5–0.6cm long. It makes a fluffy blue-foliaged tree with an open conic crown, attaining 10–20m in height. 'Boulevard' is a selection with steel-blue foliage which will make a tree with time but is better as a shrub.

CLADRASTIS

Leguminosae

This is a small genus with only the following species in general cultivation. It is suited to most soils.

C. lutea **Yellow-wood** Eastern USA

This makes a round headed tree to 10m. The leaves are pinnate with five to nine large leaflets. In June the flowers are white and slightly fragrant. The autumn colour is a good yellow.

CORNUS

Cornels and Dogwoods Cornaceae

The genus *Cornus* is commonly divided into three genera. Whilst the reasons for this splitting are valid, the old names are more familiar and are used here. The segregate names, which are likely to become more prominent with time, are given in brackets. It includes some very attractive trees. The main beauty is provided by the bracts which subtend the flowers. In the species (*Benthamidia*) where the bracts are large, they are preformed in the autumn and slowly expand as the flowers develop in the summer, changing from green through to white.

They are usually only available at small sizes and are best planted as shrubs and trained up to become trees. They will tolerate all soils, except for *C. nuttallii* which requires an acidic site.

C. controversa Himalayas, China & Japan
Table Dogwood
(*Swida controversa*)

This tree develops a very distinctive habit composed of a series of spaced level tiers. The flowers are carried in June and July and are rather small, making up for it by being in large clusters.

'Variegata' has variegated foliage and an even more tiered habit, making a very imposing small tree, 8–15m tall.

C. florida Eastern North America
Flowering Dogwood
(*Benthamidia florida*)

This makes a small tree notable for the display by the white or pink floral bracts in early summer. It will make a tree to 6m. It is not such a colourful tree in Britain as *C. kousa*.

'Rubra' is the collective name for the forms with red or pinkish bracts.

C. kousa Japan, China & Korea
Japanese Cornel
(*Benthamidia kousa*)

This makes a most floriferous small tree or large shrub. The branches are covered with the large flower clusters which have four creamy-white bracts. It is in bloom in June/July and followed in the autumn by the erect edible strawberry like fruit clusters. Often (but not invariably) the autumn colour of the foliage is good as well.

Var. *chinensis* is a slightly larger and even more floriferous form with more lanceolate bracts. Both this and the species make small trees to 10m. They are better grown in full sunlight.

'Gold Star' has a central gold area within the leaf.

'Silver Boy' is a white variegated selection.

C. mas **Cornelian Cherry** Europe

This makes a small tree to 8m but often less

than 6m. It is most striking in late winter when the flowers open. The bracts are yellow and produced on the bare wood. The fruit is like a cherry and 2cm long.

'Variegata' has leaves with creamy-white variegation, combined with good flowers. 'Aurea Elegantissima' is similar, with yellow or pink variegations.

C. nuttallii Western North America
Pacific Dogwood
(*Benthamidia nuttallii*)

This is the largest growing species, making a tree to 30m in its native habitat. In cultivation it is rarely more than 10m tall. It has a reputation of dying suddenly without reason and appears to need a light sandy soil for optimum development. The flowers are carried for six weeks around May and have four to six large creamy-white bracts. Very often a small flush of flowers is produced in the autumn. It may give good autumn colour, with the foliage dying off a yellow or scarlet colour.

CORYLOPSIS

Hamamelidaceae

This is a genus from eastern Asia of shrubs but some of the larger species, e.g. *C. sinensis* and *C. veitchiana*, may make 6m and are worth considering where a shrubby tree is required. They are useful for the fragrant pale yellow flowers carried in short pendent racemes on the bare branches in late March. They are not suited to chalk soils and need shelter from spring frosts.

CORYLUS

Hazels Corylaceae

Hazels include a number of large shrubs as well as several tall growing tree species. They are widely planted for the edible hazel nuts and in the past were extensively coppiced for the production of faggots and staves for hurdles. They thrive on a wide range of soils, including both damp sites and those over chalk. Their amenity value includes the attractive pendulous catkins in February or March, provision of shelter and habitat for wildlife.

C. avellana **Hazel** Britain & Europe

Hazel occasionally makes a tree on a single stem but is much more often found growing as a large shrub, as which it can make 12m. It can be very attractive in late winter when displaying the lemon yellow catkins, which are a better colour than found in other species.

C. colurna
Turkish hazel Balkans & Asia Minor

Turkish hazel makes a tree with neat conical habit and level twisting branches. It will grow 15–25m tall and can be very attractive when the bare branches are curtained with hanging catkins in late winter. The fruits have a distinctive fleshy husk covered with glandular hairs. The bark is scaly and pale fawn brown, whilst the shoots are corky. It can be moved easily at all normal sizes.

C. maxima
Filbert Southern Europe to Asia Minor

This species is similar to Hazel but has larger leaves and nuts.

'Purpurea' is a form with leaves of a rich purple.

COTONEASTER

Cotoneasters Rosaceae

The Cotoneasters are a diverse group in the Apple subfamily of the Rose family. They are most closely related to the Mays or *Crataegus*. They range from dwarf ground hugging shrublets to trees to 15–20m and most are evergreen. They will thrive on a wide range of sites. Apart from the beauty of their flowers, fruit and foliage, they provide a valuable food source for many bird species, particularly those which ripen the fruits in the later part of the winter. Most of the species are susceptible to fireblight (see page 120).

C. frigidus **Tree Cotoneaster** Himalayas

This is the tallest species, frequently making 10–15m in height. It is semi-evergreen, losing the leaves some time after Christmas except in mild winters. The flowers are white in corymbs and are followed by the red berries. It has large elliptic leaves.

C. glaucophyllus West China

This is an uncommon species which makes a large shrub or small tree to 6–8m. It is fully evergreen and the leaves are glaucous beneath. The main attraction of the plant is that the fruits ripen late, not showing any colour until December and then persisting for several weeks; it, therefore, fills a gap in midwinter.

C. 'Cornubia'

A number of hybrid forms have occurred in cultivation, primarily involving *C. frigidus* and *C. salicifolius*. 'Cornubia' is one of the best. It makes a small tree to 8m and in the autumn is loaded with brilliant red berries. 'Exburyensis' and 'Rothschildianus' have creamy-white or yellow berries.

CRATAEGUS

May or Thorns Rosaceae

The Mays or Thorns are a large group of small trees. They thrive on all sites. Most bear prominent thorns and make small trees wider than tall. The flowers are generally white and carried in dense corymbs, to be followed by the showy, often red, fruits. The species are also useful for autumn colour, provision of food for wildlife and for shelter. They are susceptible to fireblight (see page 120).

C. chlorosarca
Manchurian thorn NE Asia & Japan

This makes a tree with a conical crown and stout shoots which are deep purple-brown over winter, with almost black buds. The haws are unusual, being black.

C. crus-galli
Cockspur thorn Eastern North America

This makes a tree to 9m. The thorns are amongst the longest in the genus, like the spurs of a fighting cock. The leaves assume rich autumnal tints and the fruits persist over much of the winter.

C. × *grignoniensis* **Grignon thorn**

Similar to Hybrid Cockspur thorn, this makes a small spreading tree whose shiny leaves are green until well into winter and set off the large persistent red haws.

C. × *lavallei* **Hybrid Cockspur thorn**

This is a handsome small spreading tree with shiny dark green leaves which turn red in late autumn and persistent orange red fruits.

C. oxycantha Britain & Europe
Midland thorn
(*C. laevigata*, *C. oxycanthoides*)

This is a smaller species than the other native Thorn, making a tree to no more than 8m, with less deeply lobed fruits.

'Paul's Scarlet' is a form with double red flowers.

'Plena' is a selection with double white flowers.

'Rosea Flore Plena' has double pink flowers.

C. monogyna Britain & Europe
May, Thorn or Quickthorn

May is a very common tree in the countryside and is most spectacular in May when covered in the creamy-white flowers. The fruits ripen a dull maroony red and contain but a single seed. It makes a tree to 15m tall and is extremely tough. It is more attractive than the red or pink flowered Mays such as 'Paul's Scarlet' but less readily available as a standard tree.

'Stricta' is a white flowered form with fastigiate branches, developing a narrow upright crown and suitable for street tree use or for confined spaces.

C. phaenopyrum
Washington Thorn Southeast USA

This makes a tree to 10m and has vivid shiny lobed leaves which take on scarlet and gold autumn colours. The fruits are scarlet and persist over winter.

C. × prunifolia
Broadleaf Cockspur Thorn

This makes a small tree to 6m tall with foliage which turns a spectacular orange in autumn. The flowers are showy and the fruits red, although they fall with the leaves in autumn.

CRYPTOMERIA

Taxodiaceae

This is a genus of evergreen conifers from Japan and China, in the Redwood family. They thrive on a wide range of sites, making neat tall trees with columnar conic crowns. They are one of the few conifers which are able to coppice. They are useful as amenity trees, having an attractive reddish fibrous bark in addition to the foliage.

C. japonica **Japanese cedar** Japan

Japanese cedar is the commoner of the two species and hardy throughout the country. It will make a tree 20–40m tall, often with a rather tufted crown. The foliage turns bronze in autumn.

'Elegans' is a vigorous growing plant with soft juvenile foliage which turns a strong reddish colour in the winter. Trees of this clone seem invariably to blow part way over at some stage in their lives, continuing to grow at an angle. It will make a tree 15–20m.

× *CUPRESSOCYPARIS*

Cypress Cupressaceae

This is a hybrid genus, of which three crosses have been recorded but only the following is commonly seen.

× *C. leylandii* **Leyland cypress**

Leyland cypress is a sterile hybrid between Monterey (*Cupressus macrocarpa*) and Nootka cypresses (*Chamaecyparis nootkatensis*). It has only arisen in cultivation in Britain and is propagated by cuttings. It makes a very fast growing tree and has been extensively planted as a hedging conifer. Although it has some merit for this purpose, it is rather formless and very fast growing, requiring much clipping. Left to grow naturally, it will make a columnar tree to 40m, making the first 25–30m of growth in between 25 and 40 years. It will thrive on a wide range of sites. The crown habit is broader in the west and in coastal regions.

'Castlewellan' is a plant with yellow foliage, often taking on a rather unattractive bronzy hue. It is nearly as fast as the green or grey forms.

'Haggerston Grey' is the common form, with grey-green foliage. It is rather open and untidy when young, although filling out later.

'Leighton Green' has green foliage and often carries large numbers of cones.

'Naylor's Blue' has grey foliage which is blue when young. It can be very attractive after light rain, when loaded with sparkling raindrops on the foliage and deserves wider planting.

'Robinson's Gold' is similar to 'Castlewellan' but carries the foliage a better golden yellow.

CUPRESSUS

Cypress Cupressaceae

The true cypresses are a genus of some twenty-five evergreen conifer species found in the northern hemisphere. They come mainly from areas of low rainfall and sunny climates and are very suitable for dry sandy soils or hot situations. They do not move well and are best planted as small container grown plants.

C. glabra SW USA & N Mexico
Smooth cypress

This makes a small tree of 10–15m. It has glaucous blue foliage which is flecked with small white dots of resin. The bark is purplish red and exfoliates in small circular flakes, to leave a smooth shiny surface. It is hardy throughout the country, although growing better in sunny climates. The habit of young trees is conical, but becomes more rounded with age.

C. macrocarpa
Monterey cypress California

Monterey cypress has a fast initial growth rate but then slows down and only makes a tree to 20–35m. It has a narrow crown which broadens considerably as the tree ages, so much so that old trees can be mistaken in Cornwall for Cedar of Lebanon (*Cedrus libani*). The foliage is bright green and the bark shallowly ridged. It will tolerate a wide range of situations, being especially good close to the sea. In the past it was frequently planted as a hedging conifer; however, it is not reliably hardy in cold districts and does not take clipping well, so has been displaced, largely by its hybrid Leyland cypress (× *Cupressocyparis leylandii*). Recently, coryneum canker (see page 121) has killed many trees in southern Britain and may make the planting of this tree impractical.

'Donard Gold' is a clone with rich deep golden yellow foliage.

'Goldcrest' forms a narrow tree with feathery, slightly juvenile foliage of a rich yellow.

'Lutea' is an old clone with foliage at first soft yellow, becoming green later. It is more tolerant of coastal conditions than the type.

C. sempervirens
Italian cypress Southern Europe to Iran

Italian cypress is normally cultivated as a very narrow crowned, spire-like tree, although broader growing forms exist. It makes a tree to 15–25m. Young trees may be killed by cold winters but older ones normally survive.

DAVIDIA

Davidiaceae

This is a genus of one species.

D. involucrata
Dove Tree West & Central China

Dove tree makes a deciduous tree to 15–20m with lime-like foliage. Its beauty lies in the two large but unequal bracts which accompany the flowers in May; the bracts are white or creamy-white and hang down on either side of the flowers. It will grow on both acidic and alkaline sites. It has very fleshy roots and needs careful handling to get it to establish; container grown small trees are more successful than larger bare rooted stock. It also takes some time to flower from planting, possibly a full ten years.

Var. *vilmoriniana* differs from the type in the leaves being glabrous and slightly glaucous beneath, instead of densely and softly hairy. It is equally beautiful.

DIPTERONIA

Aceraceae

This is a genus of two species related to *Acer* but differing in the leaves having seven to eleven leaflets and the seeds being winged on both sides.

D. sinensis **Dipteronia** West China

This makes a small, somewhat shrubby, tree to 10m, with large clusters of green, later reddish, fruits. It will grow on most soils.

DRIMYS

Winteraceae

This is a genus of evergreen plants.

D. winteri **Winter's bark** Southern Chile

This makes a tree to 15m which is only hardy in the open in the milder counties; elsewhere it is better grown against a wall. The leaves are leathery, soft green and silvery beneath. The flowers are ivory white and fragrant, borne in May. It should be planted out as a small plant. It will grow on all soils but ideally needs a moisture retentive one.

EMBOTHRIUM

Proteaceae

This small genus is represented in gardens by the following very flamboyant species.

E. coccinea
Chilean Firebush Southern Chile

This makes an evergreen tree with a narrow crown. The flowers are a brilliant orange scarlet or crimson scarlet (although yellow flowered forms are reported) and carried in profusion from the tips of the branches in May and June. It will make a tree to 15m but needs a moist acidic soil for best development. The roots should not be permitted to dry out during planting.

EUCALYPTUS

Eucalypts Myrtaceae

This is a very large genus of evergreen trees and large shrubs which is native to Australia. The majority of the 500–600 species are too tender for cultivation in Britain but a number of species are hardy, particularly if seed is collected from the higher altitude or colder parts of their ranges, or from thriving trees already growing in cultivation. The trees grown here all coppice readily when cut back, either by man or the weather. Eucalypts are more severely damaged by long cold spells and those accompanied by cold drying winds than by sharp overnight frosts.

Eucalypts have several different types of leaves. The juvenile leaves are in pairs and clasp the stem, without a petiole; often they are glaucous blue and differently shaped from adult leaves. Juvenile leaves are produced as a stage in the sequence of leaves from the seed leaves to the mature leaves but also as the first type of leaves formed when the tree is cut back. Adult leaves are longer and narrower, with a distinct petiole or stalk; they may be glaucous but are often green. The leaves are the same on both sides, without an upper or lower surface.

The flowers of eucalypts are showy due to the massed stamens. The petals are fused together into a cap which covers the flower in bud and is lost when the flowers open. In the hardy species the flowers are creamy white, opening in late summer.

Eucalypts are useful for the very attractive bark; in some species this is a waxy white colour, in others it is shed in attractive scales like a Plane's bark (*Platanus*).

Eucalypts are very fast growing, some species capable of growing 3m in the first twelve months from seed. They must have a position in full sunlight, being very intolerant of shading. They are useful as amenity trees. The species with strongly glaucous juvenile foliage can be cut back to encourage juvenile foliage, giving either a garden display or material for floral arrangements.

Eucalypts are very intolerant of root disturbance. They must be planted out whilst small, preferably when less than 50cm tall. Using larger plants is a sure recipe for slow growth and trees which blow over. They tend to make rather lanky young trees in cultivation. They can be encouraged to make a thick stem by cutting them back in the spring to about half the height, repeating the process later if needed; this method is much more effective than trying to stake the tree. They will grow on most sites, including over chalk or limestone.

E. dalrympleana
Mountain gum Tasmania & SE Australia

This makes a fast growing tall tree with long hanging leaves. When young it has a very attractive bark, initially pale cream, fading through salmon pink to light brown. It is a most attractive species, not, unfortunately, particularly hardy and only reliable for more than a few average winters in milder areas.

E. globulus **Blue gum** South Australia

This attractive tree with glaucous juvenile foliage is widely used in summer bedding schemes. It is not hardy, except in very mild areas or for mild winters. In southern Britain, trees may survive for 3–4 winters before being killed; by this time, they may be 10m tall.

E. gunnii **Cider gum** Tasmania

This is the commonest eucalypt in cultivation and is hardy throughout the country. It will make a tree to 20–30m, and live for over a century. The bark is shed in large flakes, revealing pale green or creamy white beneath. The leaves are grey green and the juvenile ones glaucous blue.

E. niphophila
Alpine Snow gum SE Australia

In many ways the most attractive Eucalypt, it develops a chalky white bark, which sheds the outer bark erratically. It makes a small tree 6–10m tall. It is closely related to *E. pauciflora* and is usually considered a subspecies of it.

E. pauciflora
Snow gum Tasmania & SE Australia

This is similar to Alpine Snow gum but generally less attractive. It makes a taller tree, to 15m.

EUCRYPHIA

Eucryphiaceae

This is a small genus of normally evergreen trees and shrubs from Chile and Australia. They are most valuable for the massed white flowers, with a large central boss of stamens, which are carried in July and August. The only reliably hardy and tree-like ones are the following two, which differ from the other species in that they will grow on chalky soils.

E. cordifolia **Ulmo** Chile

This tree has simple leaves and makes a narrow crowned specimen to 20m. It has a reputation for tenderness but some forms, at least, seem hardy.

E. × nymansensis **Nymans Eucryphia**

This magnificent evergreen tree has a columnar habit and carries both simple and pinnate leaves. It will grow on a wide range of sites, including chalk sites.

'Nymansay' is the clone in general cultivation. It makes a tree 10–20m tall, flowering well when over 3–4m in height.

EUODIA

Rutaceae

This is a large genus of warm temperate trees with pinnate leaves. The following two are most useful for flowering in September. They will not tolerate the roots drying out and should be moved as small plants.

E. daniellii
Korean Euodia Korea & North China

This makes a tree 15–20m. The white flowers are followed by purplish fruits.

E. hupehensis
Hubei Euodia Central China

Closely related to Korean Euodia, this is of similar garden value and makes a spreading tree to 18m.

EUONYMUS

Spindle Celastraceae

This large genus includes a few small trees. They are characterised by the four or six parted fruit, each segment having a single seed with a bright scarlet aril. They are suited to a wide range of sites, and are especially good on shallow chalk soils.

E. europaeus
Spindle Britain & Europe

This makes a small tree 10–12m tall with a upright rounded crown. It often grows on several stems. The autumn foliage is attractive.

'Red Cascade' is a particularly good fruiting form which in autumn is loaded with rosy red fruiting capsules.

E. bungeanus
Bunge Spindle North China

This makes a small tree 10m or so tall. The leaves may partly persist, especially in mild winters. It has a rounded crown and makes a neat foliage tree.

FAGUS

Beech Fagaceae

There are about ten species of Beech found in temperate woodland in the northern hemisphere. They are rather uniform in foliage characters whilst the fruit is a woody cupule containing two triangular nuts. The bark is remarkable; it is smooth, thin and somewhat silvery grey. The individual cells in the bark may remain alive for up to a century. In a number of respects, this thin bark is a weakness of beech, as it is vulnerable to sun scorch, vandals engraving their names and diseases or insects. Beech trees are attacked by a scale insect, beech coccus, which feeds on the sap through the thin bark and can cause the entry of decay organisms (see page 118). Beech timber, despite its excellent properties as a wood, is not naturally resistant to decay and once this has started, or a tree begun to fall apart from wind damage or as the ravages of time catch up with it, the final destruction of the tree is not far off.

F. engleriana
Engler beech Central & West China

This Chinese species makes a small tree to 10–16m with leaves of an attractive sea-green. It makes a useful variant on the Beech line.

F. orientalis
Oriental beech Balkans, Asia Minor, Caucasus

Oriental beech makes a tree to 10–18m in cultivation. It has larger leaves with more veins than in *sylvatica* and the cupule is covered with leafy, not spiny, appendages.

F. sylvatica **Beech** Britain & Europe

Beech is the native and generally cultivated species. It will grow to a height of 20–40m and old specimens may eventually cover more than 1,000 square metres. It is slow growing and is not long lived, 150–200 years being about the maximum. It is commonly planted as a hedging plant as it withstands clipping and young or clipped trees retain the dead leaves giving winter protection, in forestry as a timber tree or as an amenity tree. The new foliage in spring is a particularly refreshing light green and is followed by the russet colours of autumn. Beech casts a dense shade and competes strongly for moisture and nutrients in the soil, consequentially few other trees or shrubs can grow beneath a thick beech plantation. Young beech are tolerant of some shade. Beech can tolerate exposure, although creating very one-sided crowns where the wind effect is strong.

Beech will thrive on both very acidic and alkaline soils such as thin soils over chalk; it can, however, show signs of nutrient deficiency on the latter sites if they have been ploughed. The pH of the soil is of less concern than the standard of drainage; Beech do not tolerate poor drainage or waterlogged conditions.

Beech do not like being moved bare rooted above standard sizes and larger stock should be rootballed to prevent the roots drying out. The root system is naturally close to the surface and is easily damaged by machinery or simply by people trampling over the roots. It is a species more prone to windblow from the roots than many others, and it is also more susceptible to drought conditions.

'Dawyck' is a tall plant with a narrow fastigiate habit, similar to a Lombardy poplar (*Populus nigra* 'Italica'). It is very useful as an exclamation mark and, although slower in growth, is a much longer lived tree than the poplar. 'Dawyck Gold' is a seedling which has pale golden leaves, soon pale green and the habit of 'Dawyck'. 'Dawyck Purple' is a similar form with purple foliage.

Forma *heterophylla* Cut-leaved beech (Fern-Leaved beech) has the leaves narrower and variously lobed and cut.

'Pendula' develops a majestic habit, with the leader and branches arching down and out. There are probably several clones in cultivation under this name, as some form a more pronounced upright bole than others. Weeping beech have made trees to 30m tall.

Forma *purpurea* Copper beech is the name which covers all the plants which have purple foliage. These usually open a good coppery red but become darker, almost black, after a while from outside and greener within the tree where shaded, again turning a brighter colour in autumn. These plants are very strong in the landscape and are generally much over planted. They are useful for creating an effect, but if over used become tedious and dull. 'Atropurpurea' and 'Riversii' are two named purple clones. 'Rohanii' is the Cutleaved Copper beech. 'Purpurea Pendula' is a mound forming purple leafed form.

'Prince George of Crete' is a selection with very large green leaves, up to 18cm by 13cm on young trees.

'Zlatia' Golden beech has the flushing foliage soft yellow. It is very effective at this time, but a few weeks later indistinguishable from normal green leafed forms.

FICUS

Fig Moraceae

This is a large genus of mainly tropical trees, shrubs and climbers.

F. carica **Fig** E Mediterranean

The fig makes a small sprawling deciduous tree 6–8m tall, with large, deeply lobed leaves. The fruit, developed at the ends of the twigs, will only ripen satisfactorily in southern Britain when given the shelter of a wall, although the tree is hardy.

FRAXINUS

Ash Oleaceae

The ashes are a large northern hemisphere genus of small to large deciduous trees. They have pinnate leaves and cast a light open shade. Some species are showy in their flowers, and all thrive on a wide range of sites, including calcareous ones. They can be planted in a wide range of sizes.

F. americana E North America
White or American ash

This tree makes a tall domed crown and will grow to 20–25m. It has bold foliage and often gives a good golden yellow autumn colour.

'Autumn Purple' is a selection which develops good purple autumn colour.

F. angustifolia S Europe, N Africa & W Asia
Narrow leaved ash

This makes a tree to 15–25m with a tall domed crown. The leaves are narrow and give a dense leafy appearance to the tree.

'Veltheimii' is a cultivar with the leaves reduced to a single leaflet.

F. excelsior Britain, Europe & Asia Minor
Ash or Common ash

Ash is very tolerant of site and conditions, although for good growth and timber production it should be grown on base rich moist soils. It is attractive for the rounded domed crown, and light shade produced but has no floral beauty. The leaves are often lost with no hint of autumn colour. It has a very fibrous root system and establishes well, soon making rapid growth. It is a 'hungry' feeder and does not associate well with surface rooting plants, such as *Rhododendron*, or near vegetable plots. It is rarely damaged by squirrels, or affected by aphids, but the branches of old trees become brittle and are frequently broken by strong winds in trees over 60–70 years old. It has a maximum life of 120–200 years, but a probable safe life of less than 80–100 years in urban areas. It will make a tree 20–35m tall; its uses are as a timber tree (on the best sites), as a component in mixed woodland or as an amenity tree. It can be damaged by late spring frosts, despite being one of the last native trees to flush.

'Altena' makes a medium width conical tree with vigorous foliage, turning yellow in autumn.

'Atlas' makes a slender crowned conical tree with deep green leaves which flush late. It does not produce seeds.

'Diversifolia' has the leaves reduced to a single leaflet.

'Jaspidea' or 'Golden ash' is an excellent form. The leaves emerge yellow in late spring, turning green and then becoming a good yellow in the autumn. The shoots are also yellow, giving a strong effect over winter. It can make a tree to 20m.

'Pendula' is a form with weeping shoots. It makes a tree as high as it is trained or grafted.

'Pendula Wentworthii' is a taller growing version of 'Pendula' and can make a large tree. The leading shoots are erect, with very pendulous branchlets.

'Westhof's Glorie' is a selection which develops into a strong growing upright tree with glossy dark green leaves.

F. latifolia
Oregon ash W North America

This makes a tree 20–25m tall, with stout hairy shoots and a good autumn colour from the large leaves.

F. ornus
Manna ash S Europe & W Asia

Manna ash is one of the species with showy flowers; these are white and carried in late May. It can make a tree 15–20m tall with a rounded domed crown and can be very attractive when in flower. The leaves turn a purplish colour in autumn. The bark is smooth; where trees have been grafted above ground level onto common ash rootstocks, the comparision between the barks can be unsightly.

F. oxycarpa S Europe & W Asia
Caucasian or Raywood ash

'Raywood' is the main cultivated clone and makes a very attractive tree to 15m, of rapid growth and dense small narrow leaflets, turning plum purple in autumn.

F. pennsylvanica
Red ash E North America

The normal form in cultivation is the variety *lanceolata*. This makes a tree to 20m. It has a leafy and attractive crown, turning a good yellow colour in early autumn.

'Summit' is a selection of good growth, form and vigour.

F. velutina
Velvet ash SW USA & N Mexico

Velvet ash is a small growing tree, to 12m. It comes from a hot dry region and does better in the drier and sunnier eastern half of Britain, than in the west. It will grow on sandy soils better than other ashes. The shoots and leaves are usually softly hairy, with three to seven leaflets.

GENISTA

Leguminosae

Only the following species commonly makes a small tree.

G. aetnensis
Mount Etna Broom Sicily & Sardinia

This is a large shrub or a small tree to 10m. It scarcely has any leaves, but photosynthesis is carried out by the green shoots. These are pendulous when young, and give the tree an open light evergreen appearance. It is most attractive when copiously bearing its yellow pea-like fragrant flowers in July and early August. It needs a sunny site and will tolerate dry light soils. It needs to be planted out as a shrub and trained to make a tree.

GINKGO

Ginkgoaceae

This genus contains only the following species.

G. biloba **Ginkgo** Southern China

This makes a long lived and very distinctive tree to 30m. The habit is narrow in young trees, only broadening after the tree is a century or so old. Young trees have strong apical dominance, making long erect shoots with short side branches, but every now and then a side branch grows away, forming a broader crown with an interesting, if erratic, outline. The fan-shaped foliage has an oily texture; it turns a brilliant gold in autumn. In China and Japan dated trees are known which were planted 500–600 years ago, whilst the original tree at Kew, planted 1762, is still in the best of health.

Ginkgo is useful as a specimen tree of character habit and neat attractive foliage. It will thrive on a very wide range of soils, tolerating urban sites and pollution and is rarely affected by any pest or disease. Both long and short shoots are produced, but if the tree is not happy, it may only make short shoots for a period.

'Fastigiata' is a selection which as a young tree has a narrow columnar habit with semi-erect branches.

'Pendula' is recorded as a form with a pendulous habit.

'Tremonia' has made a very narrow crowned tree so far; after 40 years, the original plant was 12m tall and only 0.8m wide.

GLEDITSIA

Honey locusts Leguminosae

This is a small genus characterised by the pinnate or bipinnate foliage and usually bearing prominent simple or branched spines which may grow directly out of the bole. They are useful foliage and shade trees, being much better suited to regions with hot sunny summers. The following species is the commonest in cultivation. It is hardy, although young trees may suffer dieback due to growing too late into the autumn and getting caught by autumn frosts.

28 Ginkgo (Ginkgo biloba) *mature (200 year) crown shape, young trees are much more upright*

G. triacanthos
Honey locust Eastern USA

Honey locust has foliage which turns a clear bright yellow in autumn, whilst being an attractive feathery bright green during the summer. It will thrive on any well drained soil, and is good for urban sites. The trunk bears clusters of stout, usually three pronged thorns, making the normal wild form inappropriate for street tree planting. It will attain a maximum height of around 25m.

'Bujoti' makes a pendulous tree of elegant habit. The shoots are very fine, with leaves narrower than normal, and often mottled white.

Forma *inermis* is the botanical name for all plants which do not develop spines on the bole. For street tree plantings these are preferable, as the spines on the bole can be a problem adjacent to paths, but away from crowded streets, the spines can be an object of interest and quaint beauty.

'Sunburst' is a magnificent small tree or large shrub. The foliage starts off a bright golden yellow, becoming greener but retaining a very bright green or yellow-green colour. It belongs to forma *inermis*.

GYMNOCLADUS

Leguminosae

This is a small genus, only represented in cultivation by the following species.

G. dioica
Kentucky Coffee-tree Eastern USA

Kentucky Coffee-tree will slowly make a tree to 15m with a domed open crown. The foliage is very bold and bipinnate, with individual leaves to a metre in length. The shoots are stout, to match the huge foliage, and covered with a white waxy bloom. It will thrive on a range of soils, preferring a rich moist one.

HALESIA

Styracaceae

This small genus contains five deciduous species. They belong to the Storax family and make very floriferous plants.

H. monticola
Snowdrop tree South East USA

This makes a tree to 15m with a broadly conic crown, with rather spreading branches. The main attraction is the large showy snowdrop flowers. These are carried hanging down on the previous season's wood in May with the newly flushing leaves and can be very striking. Snowdrop tree will grow best on moist well drained soils; it prefers an open sunny but sheltered site.

HIPPOPHAE

Rhamnaceae

This is a genus of three shrubs, but the following species can make a tree to 10, or even 15m tall.

H. rhamnoides
Sea Buckthorn Britain, Europe & Asia

This native plant is useful for the silvery-grey foliage and the orange ,coloured berries. It is tough and will thrive on most sites, especially dry sandy ones or windswept seaside locations. Sea Buckthorn is dioecious and either one male and to four or five female plants should be used or a range of seedlings planted to ensure pollination of the female flowers. It suckers from the roots.

HOHERIA

Malvaceae

This genus comes from New Zealand. There are five species which make small deciduous or evergreen shrubs or small trees. They need some form of shelter and a sunny open situation.

H. glabrata — Western South Island, New Zealand

This makes a small deciduous tree of fast growth, bearing masses of fragrant white flowers in June/July. It is not long-lived.

H. sexstylosa — North & South Islands, New Zealand

This is the commonest evergreen species in cultivation, where it makes a fast growing tree to 8–10m. Outside of mild areas, it may need the protection of a wall. The white flowers are produced in July and August.

H. 'Glory of Amlwich'

This makes a very narrow crowned small evergreen tree to 8m, which freely flowers. It is believed to be a hybrid between *glabrata* and *sexstylosa*. Like the latter, it will lose its leaves in severe winters.

ILEX

Holly — Aquifoliaceae

The Hollies are a large genus of trees and shrubs found almost throughout the world. The species are both evergreen and deciduous, but only evergreen species are commonly grown as trees in Britain. The berries can make a valuable display, sometimes lasting until well into the New Year. The cultivated hollies are dioecious, with the male and female flowers on separate trees. Trees which are male can be determined when in flower by the 4–6 stamens and rudimentary ovary, whilst female flowers have 2–4 styles and only rudimentary stamens.

Hollies will thrive on all soils, including chalk or limestone. They do not transplant easily and should either be moved with a ball or be container grown.

I. × *altaclerensi* **Highclere holly**

This is a hybrid between *I. perado*, from Madeira, the Canary Islands and the Azores, and common holly. It has broader leaves than common holly, and makes a vigorous small evergreen tree to 20m. It is tolerant of exposure and poor but well drained soils.

'Camelliifolia' makes a conical tree with dark green, generally spineless leaves and rather large dark berries.

'Golden King' is a female form! The leaves have a rich gold margin. It makes a very effective variegated plant.

'Hodginsii' has leaves a deep sea-green, variously spined. It is a male form, and will withstand salty winds and atmospheric pollution.

'Lawsoniana' has the dull green leaves with a central variegated zone of gold and bright green. It is female. Both 'Lawsoniana' and 'Golden King' are sports from a green leafed clone, 'Hendersonii'.

I. aquifolium — Britain,
Common holly — Europe & W Asia

Holly is a common large evergreen shrub or small tree. It is very useful in wildlife or shelter plantings as it retains the foliage to the forest floor, therefore providing shelter and screening. It is capable of growing in quite shady conditions, and will regenerate into old woodland. It is a tough tree, suitable for all sites except boggy ones. It is rather slow in growth, but steady, eventually making a maximum of 15–25m. The leaves on seedling plants and regrowths from cutting back are very spiny, as an adaption against browsing. Some clones are consistently spiny, e.g. 'Ferox'.

'Amber' is a form with bronze-yellow fruits.

'Bacciflava' produces abundant bright yellow berries.

'Golden Queen' is a male form! It is one of several clones with variegated foliage, in this case margined with yellow. It makes a suitable companion to *I.* × *altaclerensis* 'Golden King'.

'J. C. van Tol' is a female form producing masses of large bright red berries, and has almost spineless leaves.

JUGLANS

Walnuts Juglandaceae

The walnuts are a group of deciduous trees from Europe, Asia and America, south into the Argentine. They make large bold trees, with large pinnate leaves. They will grow on most sites but do far better on deep fertile and sheltered ones. The fruit is the walnut, whose fleshy covering contains a persistent yellow stain.

Walnuts can be difficult to move and are better planted as small trees, but, with care, large trees can be successfully transplanted.

J. nigra **Black walnut** E & C USA

Black walnut makes a very large, impressive tree, to 30m, with bold leaves 30–60cm long and from 11–23 leaflets. Young trees have a conical habit, becoming rounded in old ones. The nut is large, around 4cm, but does not have any culinary value, requiring a sledge hammer to open them. Black walnut has a very valuable timber and thrives throughout Britain.

J. regia
Common walnut SE Europe & Asia

This is the commonest walnut and differs from the other species in the obovate leaves with fewer untoothed, or rarely slightly toothed, leaflets. The bark is pale grey and deeply fissured. It will grow throughout Britain, doing best on fertile lowland sites; it is hardy, but can be damaged by spring frosts.

Walnut makes a tree 15–25m tall with a low, rather spreading rounded crown. It has a maximum life of around 200 years, but usually less. Sound large butt lengths of timber with the stump are very valuable, and it is worth pruning the tree to give a clean stem of 2–3m from an early age. Walnuts can bleed profusely from pruning wounds, occasionally seriously weakening the tree, and all branch removals should be carried out during the summer period.

JUNIPERUS

Junipers Cupressaceae

The junipers are a large genus of evergreen conifers, ranging from mat forming species to trees 20–30m tall. They are rather slow growing, but will tolerate a wide range of well drained sites, including chalk. They are usually only available as small plants.

J. chinensis
Chinese juniper China, Korea & Japan

This makes a narrow crowned tree to 20m. Adult scale leaves and juvenile needle shaped leaves are usually found on the same shoot.

'Aurea' is an excellent small tree form, with an ovoid or ovoid-conic habit. The foliage is golden-yellow, and the massed male cones can enhance the display in the autumn.

'Kaizuka' makes a small tree, to 10m; it has an erratic habit, often forming several divergent trunks, and is useful where a character small evergreen tree is needed. The foliage is a vivid green colour. This is a female clone, profusely carrying the glaucous berries.

'Keteleerii' is a columnar free-fruited clone with pointed scale-like leaves.

'Obelisk' has juvenile bluish-green foliage and makes a dense small columnar tree.

'Pyramidalis' is a form with juvenile bluish foliage; it makes a slow growing conical bush, ultimately a small tree.

J. communis Britain &
Common juniper Northern Hemiphere

This native plant is usually a shrub but small tree forms are common in parts of its range. They will make a maximum of 8m with a narrow columnar crown. It is very tough, growing on very poor sites, of both acidic and alkaline reaction.

J. drupacea — Asia Minor, Syria & Greece
Syrian juniper

This makes a narrow columnar tree to 20m, with large needle leaves set in whorls of three.

J. recurva — Himalayas to W China
Himalayan Weeping juniper

This makes a tree to 20m tall, with a conical habit and the foliage in slender nodding sprays. The leaves are usually bluish-grey, and the bark flaky, becoming fibrous in old trees.

Var. *coxii* is a form with longer needle-shaped leaves which are grey-green.

J. scopulorum
Rocky Mountain juniper — Western USA

This makes a tree with a columnar or broad columnar crown.

'Skyrocket' is the commonest form in cultivation and has a very narrow upright habit, making a maximum of around 8m, and useful as a formal feature plant.

'Springbank' is one of a number of clones with silvery blue-grey foliage and broader habits, to 10–15m.

J. virginiana
Pencil cedar — Eastern North America

This makes a broad columnar crowned tree of open aspect. It is rather slow, but will make 15–18m. It is similar to Chinese juniper, but differs in the much smaller fruit which ripens in the first year.

'Skyrocket' see *J. scopulorum* 'Skyrocket'.

J. wallichiana
Wallich juniper — Himalaya

This is a narrow conic tree to 13m in cultivation, but broader and taller in the wild, with shaggy orange fissured bark.

KALOPANAX

Araliaceae

This genus contains only the following species.

K. pictus — Japan, China & NE Asia
Prickly Castor-Oil Tree

This makes a deciduous tree of upright and rather open habit with large leaves, often to 35cm. The one year shoots are stout and bear short soft-pointed spines. It is useful and interesting as a hardy arboreal representative of the large ivy family.

KOELREUTERIA

Sapindaceae

This genus is native to eastern Asia south to Fiji.

K. paniculata
Pride of India — China, Korea & Japan

This makes a tree to 15m with a rounded crown. It has pinnate, usually bi-pinnate, leaves which can measure 45cm; they turn yellow in autumn. The flowers are very showy, in conical erect panicles 30–40cm tall containing many bright yellow 1cm flowers which are held above the level of the foliage. They are followed by bladder-like fruits. Pride of India makes a very colourful sight in July and August. It likes a good loamy soil, although it will grow on a wide range of soils. It is well suited to hot dry situations, but is not long lived.

LABURNUM

Leguminosae

This genus contains three species, of which the following two are small trees. They have trifoliate leaves which remain functional until turning yellow in autumn, and the long racemes of yellow flowers. All laburnums will tolerate a wide range of sites, being especially good on dry limestone or chalk. They can make very useful floriferous trees for urban parks, and have been grown over pergolas, with the flowers hanging down through the structure. They can be planted at a variety of sizes. The seeds are very toxic, although there are few records of people suffering actual harm.

L. alpinum
Scotch laburnum Southern Europe

This makes a small tree to 6m, rarely to 8m. The flowers are in long pendent racemes 25–35cm long. It will grow on damper soils than the following species.

L. anagryoides
Common laburnum C & S Europe

This tends to make a larger tree than Scotch laburnum, rarely to 10m. The flowers are in much shorter racemes, from 15–25cm.

L. × *watereri* **'Vossii'**

This hybrid between the above two species has flower racemes which can be up to 60cm long and, important for some sites, only a few of them develop seeds.

LARIX

Larches Pinaceae

The larches are a group of 15 deciduous conifers. They all develop good autumn colour, whilst in spring they are often one of the first trees into leaf, with bright green new foliage. They are pioneer species, making fast early growth on a wide range of sites, often averaging 70–120cm a year soon after planting. On sites which suit them, such as deep moist soils, they are very long lived, for upwards of 250 years. Here old trees eschew the narrow columnar-conic habit, developing broad crowns set on large spreading branches. Larches will not take shade, and larch plantings should be regularly thinned out to keep space between the trees. The shadow cast by the trees is open, permitting light to reach the forest floor, thereby a larch plantation can contain a rich shrub or herb layer. However, the roots are aggressive and surface rooting plants like ornamental *Rhododendrons* do not thrive under larch. Larches are best planted out as small transplants, 30–45cm tall; at these sizes they will quickly grow away. Larger plants can be moved with care.

L. decidua
European larch Central Europe

European larch is the commonest species and makes a tree to 40m. The one year old twigs are a bright pale yellow, giving a distinctive haze to larch plantations in winter. The seeds provide food for birds and squirrels. It does not take kindly to atmospheric pollution, exposed sites or frost pockets. Apart from planting it as a timber or nurse tree, European larch can make an interesting specimen tree, with its narrow habit, fast initial growth rate and good foliage.

L. kaempferi
Japanese larch Honshu, Japan

This tree is closely related to European larch, making a faster growing tree to 35m. It is more tolerant of acidic or other poor soils, such as clays, although not as good on limey soils. It is better for exposed sites. The crown is broader, with denser, slightly bluish foliage. The one year old shoots are purplish-red, covered with a waxy bloom, and in winter give a reddish, not yellow, haze to a plantation.

'Pendula' is a form with horizontal branches bearing weeping branchlets. It can be very effective, provided it does not form an erect leader. Usually top grafted.

L. × *marchlinsii* **Hybrid larch**

This is the hybrid between European and

Japanese larches. First generation crosses exhibit hybrid vigour (heterosis) and are faster growing than either parent, and tolerant of a wider range of sites. It is intermediate between the parents in characters, such as twig colour. Second and later generations of the cross lose some of the distinctions, becoming more like one or t'other parent. Hybrid larch arose at Dunkeld, Scotland and in Switzerland and is usually known as *L.* × *eurolepis*.

LAURUS

True Laurels Lauraceae

There are two species in this evergreen genus.

L. nobilis Eastern Mediterranean
Bay or Poet's laurel

This makes a tree to 20m with a rounded crown, often on several stems. It is reliably hardy along the south coast and in warm gardens elsewhere, but inland and further north it can be cut back to ground level in hard winters, although sprouting from the base. The leaves are the fragrant herb 'Bay', used in cooking. Bay laurel will move satisfactorily at small sizes. Its use is mainly as a garden herb or small evergreen tree.

LIGUSTRUM

Privets Oleaceae

The privets are a rather neglected genus. Often they are thought suitable for hedging but little else. However, they include some excellent trees, appropriate to many urban sites. They will tolerate chalk and are useful for their fragrant late summer flowers.

L. compactum Himalayas to W China

This species is deciduous or nearly so, with leaves to 15cm long. The flowers are carried in numerous large terminal panicles in July. These are followed by the purplish-black fruits which remain on the branches until spring. It can make a tree to 15m with a rounded crown. *L. chenaultii* is very similar, and of equal merit, but with longer leaves, to 25cm.

L. lucidum **Chinese privet** China

This evergreen species has leaves to 15cm long, and glossy green above. The habit is ovoid, or hemispherical, making a tree up to 15m. The flowers are produced in September, when few other large trees are in bloom, making it especially useful. It will tolerate a wide range of soils, including urban streets, and atmospheric pollution. It is usually only available as small plants, but will move as a standard tree size with a rootball.

'Excelsum Superbum' is a splendid variegated small tree, with the 'evergreen' leaves margined and mottled deep yellow and creamy white.

'Tricolor' also is variegated, the leaves having a border of white; they are pinkish when young.

LIQUIDAMBAR

Sweet gums Hamamelidaceae

This small genus has one species in western Asia, one in North America and two or three in China. They give excellent autumn colour and prefer a moist acidic or neutral soil, not performing well on chalk or dry sites.

L. styraciflua
Sweet gum North America to Guatemala

This tree will make a tree 20–30m tall. The twigs are rather curiously winged with corky flanges in the second year. Sweet gum is one of the best trees for autumn colour, slowly changing over several weeks and holding the coloured leaves well. It is best suited to the warmer parts of Britain, but thrives at least as far north as Edinburgh.

'Aurea' has the leaves blotched and striped yellow and makes a medium sized tree.

'Golden Treasure' makes a medium tree with the leaves margined golden yellow.

'Lane Roberts' is a selection noted for its good autumn colour.

LIRIODENDRON

Tulip trees Magnoliaceae

The Tulip trees are a genus of two deciduous species. They are unique in the truncate apex to the leaves; they also have two side lobes. Tulip trees are related to Magnolias, and like them have fleshy roots which do not take kindly to moving. They are best planted out as small trees, or from containers.

L. tulipiferum Eastern North America
Tulip tree or Yellow poplar

The Tulip tree has yellowy green flowers, carried in early summer. The leaves are yellow-green to bright green and have only shallow side lobes and a shallow truncate apex. They assume brilliant golds and rich browns in autumn. Young trees do not carry the flowers, but have a very neat columnar conic habit which broadens in old trees. It does best in a rich moist fertile soil, but will grow well on clays and on chalk or limestone. It is fairly fast.

'Aureomarginatum' has the leaves margined yellow or greenish yellow. It is slower growing.

'Fastigiatum' has erect or fastigiate branches. At first rather narrow, it broadens with age. It needs a sheltered site, as the erect stems are liable to wind damage. It is not well suited to street tree planting, and is no narrower than most young trees.

MAGNOLIA

Magnolias Magnoliaceae

The magnolias are a genus of large shrubs and trees from North America and Asia. They generally have large regular flowers with very similar sepals and petals, called tepals. These may be carried before the leaves or later on the current year's shoots, and are often fragrant. They are generally trees for sheltered situations on good rich soils; they will tolerate heavy clay, and also urban atmospheres. They should be planted out when young, preferably in early autumn or late spring, as the roots are thick and fleshy and likely to rot if damaged when not actively growing. Larger sizes can only be moved with great care. They resent disturbance to the roots.

M. campbellii E Himalayas to W China
Campbell magnolia

This makes one of the most striking of all hardy flowering trees. The white, pink or purplish flowers, up to 25cm across, are carried on the bare branches before the leaves in February to early April. It is hardy throughout most of Britain but the flowers are easily damaged by spring frosts. Seed raised plants of the Himalayan form are slow to flower, taking around 25 years, but vegetatively propagated plants are much quicker, often taking only three or four years. Campbell magnolia needs a well sheltered site, avoiding frost pockets. It does less well on chalk or limestone than some other species.

Subspecies *mollicomata* usually has purplish pink flowers, but produces them after only 10–15 years from seed.

'Alba' is a white flowered form.

'Charles Raffil' is one of many excellent named clones.

M. grandiflora SE USA
Bull Bay or Evergreen magnolia

This is an evergreen species. The fragrant

flowers are carried from July through to October or November. It is hardy in sheltered locations, although often grown as a wall plant. The leaves are large, glossy dark green above and thickly red-brown felted beneath.

M. hypoleuca
Japanese big-leaf magnolia N Japan

This species is very attractive for the very large leaves, to 50cm. The flowers are strongly scented and creamy white, but buried amongst the leaves in June. It is hardy throughout the country.

M. kobus
Northern Japanese magnolia N Japan

This is a very vigorous tree to 15–20m. It has white flowers carried on the bare branches before the leaves in April. Young trees are slow to flower, but large old ones regularly carry many hundreds. A number of different forms have been raised from crosses with Star magnolia (*Magnolia kobus* var. *stellata*). These are small trees, flowering at a younger age, such as 'Leonard Messel' and 'Merrill'.

M. salicifolia
Willow-leaf magnolia S & C Japan

This makes a narrow crowned deciduous tree with willowy leaves. The white flowers are carried in April on bare shoots; they are much more frost hardy than in other precocious flowering species. The bark has a pleasant fragrance when crushed.

MALUS

Apples or Crab apples Rosaceae

This is a genus of deciduous trees, most making small trees 6–10m tall, with rather spreading dense low crowns. They thrive on a wide variety of sites, and are mainly useful in urban and amenity plantings. Some can be used as street trees, especially where the verges are wide. They are usually propagated by budding onto a rootstock and may form a thin wand-like stem in the nursery; if this happens, some form of stem support will be needed (see page 80).

*29 Tulip tree (*Liriodendron tulipiferum*) approximately 30 years old*

M. baccata N Asia,
Siberian crab south to the Himalayas

This makes a vigorous small spreading tree with a low rounded crown, occasionally attaining 15m. The flowers are pure white in May, followed by the abundant small 0.8cm apples which ripen to bright red.

M. floribunda **Japanese crab** Japan

This small tree to 10m has a spreading crown. It is very floriferous, creating a vivid display in early May with the flowers red in bud, opening pink and fading to white. The fruits are yellow or red in autumn.

M. hupehensis **Hubei crab** C & W China

This vigorous species has large flowers, 3–4cm across and up to 5–6cm when fully open; they are pink in bud but open pure white. The fruits are around 1–1.5cm across. It is an excellent small tree to 15–18m.

M. sylvestris **Crab apple** Britain & Europe

This makes a small tree to 10m. It is of little interest except as a native tree for sites where nature conservation is important.

M. transitoria **Gansu crab** NW China

This makes a small spreading tree to 8m. It is very attractive when covered with masses of small white flowers in late May, again in late autumn when the leaves change to bright yellow-gold and after the leaves have fallen when the many small yellow crabs are prominent.

M. trilobata
Syrian crab Asia Minor, Syria, Balkans

This makes a narrow crowned erect growing tree, to 15m. The leaves are maple-like, with three main lobes. The white flowers come in June, after the leaves have fully developed, and it has good autumn tints. It is useful as a street tree.

M. tschonoskii **Chonosuki crab** Japan

This tree has an narrow upright habit making it an excellent street tree. It does not flower or fruit freely but develops a wonderful mixture of colours to the foliage in the autumn, bronze, crimson, orange, purple and yellow.

M. yunnanensis **Yunnan crab** W China

This is mainly planted as the variety *veitchii*. This makes an erect tree with white flowers followed by bright red fruits and lobed leaves which give scarlet and orange autumn colours.

MALUS hybrids

A large number of hybrid Crabs have been raised, of which the following is a selection of the more useful ones.

M. 'Echtermeyer' has a wide-spreading habit with pendulous branches. The new leaves emerge bronze-purple, later green. It has carmine-red flowers, followed by reddish-purple fruits 2.5cm across.

M. 'Golden Hornet' is a small upright tree with white flowers followed by deep yellow crabs, 2–2.5cm across and persist long on the branches in autumn. 'Butterball' is similar.

M. 'John Downie' has flowers which are pink in bud but open white in late May. The conical fruits are 3cm long by 2cm wide and bright orange and scarlet. Apart from their obvious attractions, they make an excellent crabapple jelly.

M. 'Liset' is an improvement on the old clone 'Profusion'. The leaves flush purple, before becoming bronzy-green. The flowers are deep purplish red, followed by blood-red 1cm crabs. It makes a small vigorous tree and is resistent to apple scab.

M. 'Red Jade' makes a mound shaped tree with cascading weeping branches. The red or white flowers are followed by small, dark red fruits.

M. 'Red Sentinel' makes a small spreading tree with white flowers in early May and large clusters of deep red fruits, sometimes persisting through the winter.

M. 'Royalty' has reddish-purple leaves and bears crimson flowers followed by dark red fruits. It makes a small spreading tree.

MAYTENUS

Celastraceae

This is a large mainly tropical genus.

M. boaria **Maiten** South America

This makes a small evergreen tree to 10m with a shapely erect crown. The leaves are glossy and willow-like. It will thrive on any well drained soil but is only available as small plants.

METASEQUOIA

Taxodiaceae

A monotypic genus of deciduous conifer.

M. glyptostroboides
Dawn redwood C China

This forms a fast growing tree, so far to 20m since its introduction in 1948 but probably to 30m. On dry sites, growth appears to slow down after about 10m, only continuing fast on damp soils. It will grow on most soils. The feathery foliage is yellow-green or blue-green in colour, changing to brick red in autumn. Large trees can be moved with care, although normally only small plants are available.

MESPILUS

Medlar Rosaceae

This is a monotypic genus related to *Crataegus*.

M. germanica **Medlar** Central Europe

This makes a small spreading tree, to a maximum of 9m. The flowers are large, single, and white, followed by the medlar fruit with its long persistent styles. The fruit is palatable after it has been 'bletted' or frosted.

MORUS

Mulberry Moraceae

A genus of small trees from Asia and North America.

M. nigra **Black mulberry** China

This is the common species in cultivation, making a tree to 15m with a spreading, billowing dense crown, usually on a short stout bole. The fruit is very palatable in late July or August. It will grow on a wide range of sites but is not long lived, perhaps to a maximum of 100.

M. alba **White mulberry** China

This tree is the principal one fed to silkworms in silk production but is less satisfactory in Britain than Black mulberry; also the fruit is rather insipid. It makes a tree 10–15m tall.

NOTHOFAGUS

Southern beech Fagaceae

The Southern beeches are generally similar to the northern hemisphere beeches. They do not, however, grow well on chalk or limestone soils and are much more sensitive to transplanting. Trees should be planted out when small and the roots must not be permitted to dry out. Several species have potential for planting as forestry trees, combining very fast growth with a canopy which encourages a ground flora similar to that found under English or Sessile oaks (*Quercus robur*, *Q. petraea*), although not supporting as many insect species. All the hardy ones make interesting amenity trees. They do not tolerate shading.

N. antarctica
Antarctic beech S Chile & S Argentina

This small tree is the hardiest species, coming from the southern tip of South America. It makes a small deciduous tree to 15m with small dark green leaves; when young, these are delightfully balsam-scented.

N. dombeyi
Coigue C & S Chile & S Argentina

Coigue is an evergreen species, developing a domed crown 20–35m tall. The foliage is rather dense, letting little light penetrate to the ground. It is hardy but it is not suitable for cold districts where cold dry winds can cause damage. It does not transplant easily.

N. fusca **Red beech** New Zealand

This makes a more open tree to 25m. The evergreen leaves are rather sparse and yellow green. It is only suitable for milder sheltered areas.

N. obliqua
Roble beech C & S Chile & S Argentina

Roble beech is one of the promising species for forestry conditions. It is hardy, being recorded as far north as Aberdeen. It will quickly make a tree with an attractive mature-looking habit, with a likely top height of 25–35m.

N. procera
Rauli C & S Chile & S Argentina

Rauli is the best timber species, with very

fast growth, to 30m, and attractive in the oblong or narrowly oval leaves with 15–18 pairs of impressed veins; in autumn the leaves turn reddish gold. It thrives best in the milder and wetter parts of Britain, occurring as far north as Ullapool on the west coast of Scotland. It can be damaged, at least as a young tree, by severe winters, and more research is needed into the best provenances for British conditions. As with other species, it does not take kindly to urban pollution.

NYSSA

Tupelo Nyssaceae

This small genus of about ten species occurs in southern Asia and North America. Only the following species and *N. sinensis*, which has brilliant autumn colour but is only a shrubby tree, are common.

N. sylvatica **Tupelo** SE USA

This makes a small tree with a broad columnar conic habit, to 20m. The foliage is glossy dark or yellow-green and in autumn turns brilliant red and yellow. It does best on a rich acid or neutral soil.

OSTRYA

Hop hornbeam Corylaceae

The Hop hornbeams are closely related to hornbeam (*Carpinus*) but differ in the hop or bladder-like husk around the nutlets and the male catkins being exposed overwinter. They tolerate a wide range of sites and make interesting foliage trees; the hanging male catkins can be attractive in early spring, with the pale green emerging leaves.

O. carpinifolia
Hop hornbeam SE Europe

This is the commonest species in cultivation and makes a deciduous tree to 20m.

OXYDENDRUM

Ericaceae

This is a monotypic genus.

O. arboreum **Sorrel tree** SE USA

This makes an evergreen erect tree to 18m. It is useful in bearing white racemes of flowers from July to October, followed by rich autumn colours. It must have an acidic soil.

PARROTIA

Hamamelidaceae

This is a monotypic genus.

P. persica
Persian Ironwood N Iran & the Caucasus

This makes a small deciduous tree to 12m with a flaking bark similar to London plane (*Platanus* × *hispanica*). It has dark red flowers before the leaves in spring and in autumn the foliage turns yellow then red. It thrives on a wide range of site conditions.

PAULOWNIA

Paulownia or Empress trees Scrophulariaceae

This is a small genus of trees from China. They bear large foxglove-like flowers in spring before the leaves, but as these are overwintered as exposed buds, spring frosts often mar the effect. The leaves are large and palmately lobed, to 40cm across, although on coppiced plants they can be 90cm. They make rather lush annual growths which are usually cut back by autumn frosts in young plants. They thrive on a wide range of sites, preferring deep loams.

P. tomentosa **Paulownia** N China

This makes a tree to 25m and makes an excellent foliage tree with an open aspect.

PHELLODENDRON

Cork-bark trees Rutaceae

This is a genus of trees from eastern Asia with pinnate leaves.

P. amurense
Amur cork-bark tree NE Asia

This is the commonest species in cultivation and attractive for the thick corky bark. It forms a tree to 17m, tolerant of urban situations.

PHILLYREA

Phillyrea Oleaceae

This is a small genus of evergreen trees and shrubs from the Mediterranean region.

P. latifolia
Phillyrea Mediterranean region

This makes a small elegant tree to 10m with a rounded domed crown and glossy dark green leaves.

PHOTINIA

Photinia Rosaceae

This is a large genus of mainly evergreen trees and shrubs, native to California and eastern Asia. They tolerate all soils, including chalk.

P. beauverdiana
Beauverd photinia W China

This makes a small tree to 10m with large deciduous foliage which give good autumn colours.

P. davidiana W China
David photinia (*Stranvaesia davidiana*)

Previously included in a segregate genus, *Stranvaesia*, it makes a small evergreen tree with willowy leaves, a proportion of which turn red in autumn and spring. The flowers are white, followed by the red fruits. It makes a tree to 10m.

P. serrulata **Photinia** China & Taiwan

This makes a domed evergreen tree to 18m. The new leaves emerge wine-coloured, but less strongly so than in some of the shrubby species, and need protecting from spring frosts.

PICEA

Spruces Pinaceae

The Spruces are a genus of 30 evergreen conifers. They have narrrow columnar-conic crowns and short branches; as young trees, they can be spikey. Some have very silvery or glaucous blue foliage, others attractive cones or habits. They tolerate most soils and situations, although are not good in polluted areas. They are best planted as small trees. They are useful as amenity trees, for timber or as nurse trees for establishing oak (*Quercus*).

P. abies **Norway spruce** Europe

Norway spruce makes a columnar tree to 40m. It is the tree usually used as a Christmas tree in Britain but is inferior as an amenity tree compared to the following spruces. It does not like dry sites.

P. breweriana
Brewer spruce Oregon & California

A very popular spruce, with a crown composed of short spreading branches with the lateral twigs hanging vertically down as a curtain. Seedlings are very slow to adopt the mature habit and the tree is usually propagated by grafting. It can make 15–20m.

P. omorika **Serbian spruce** Yugoslavia

This tree has a very narrow spire-like crown. It is virtually indifferent to soil conditions, growing at the same steady rate on good loams, acidic sands and on limestone sites, eventually attaining 20–30m. It is the best spruce for urban locations, but should be planted as a small tree.

P. orientalis
Caucasian spruce Caucasus & E Turkey

Caucasian spruce has very short neat dark green needles and makes a dense columnar tree. The male flowers are brick-red in April, creating a strong effect in old trees. It will grow to 20–35m tall.

'Aurea' is an attractive form; the new foliage flushes golden yellow for the month of June, then maturing to normal green.

P. pungens
Colorado Blue spruce W USA

This is normally grown as the forma *glauca* which has blue foliage. It makes a slow growing tree to 20m and can be very striking for the strong blue colour of the one year old foliage; as the needles age, they become greener, and in slow growing trees can contrast badly with the new foliage. The older foliage can be attacked by the green spruce aphid, which causes the loss of the older needles; it can be controlled on small trees by spraying with malathion or primicarb. 'Hoopsii', 'Koster' and 'Spek' are three clones selected for their very bright, glamorous blue foliage.

P. sitchensis
Sitka spruce W North America

This tree is planted extensively in western and northern areas in forestry, where it can produce a usable timber crop on otherwise inhospitable soils. In small doses it can be a very attractive fast growing tree, and is useful for shelter in exposed locations. It does not grow well in the drier eastern regions of Britain. In cool moist glens, it has made 60m.

PINUS

Pines Pinaceae

This genus contains about 120 species of evergreen conifers, ranging from shrubs 1–2m tall to 60–80m tall trees from throughout the northern hemisphere. In Britain the tallest pine is only to 46m. They are all tolerant of drought and most grow well on dry sandy soils. They are also suitable for hot dry situations, and some grow well in towns. Pines need full daylight for satisfactory growth. Most are hardy and will withstand a degree of exposure, several being good for seaside plantings. The needles are in bundles, or fascicles, of 2, 3 or 5. The cones ripen over two, occasionally three, years. The male cones are carried at the base of the current year's shoots, and can make an effective display. The shoots of pines expand rapidly early in the summer; at this stage, they are all erect, and known as candles, only subsequently do the needles extend and the lateral shoots point out sideways.

Pines are generally planted out when small, but larger plants can be moved reasonably safely with a suitable rootball either in late spring or early autumn.

P. aristata **Bristlecone pine** SW USA

This is a small five needled pine which, unusually for pines, retains its needles for 10–15 years, thereby making a dense plant with the shoots appearing bushy like a fox's brush. It is hardy and slow growing to 12m, and suitable for a small site. Ancient pine (*P. longaeva*) is similar, living to a maximum of nearly 5,000 years in the wild.

P. contorta NW North America
Lodgepole or Shore pine

This very tough tree is used in forestry on the most barren sites, such as wet peats but is of only limited value elsewhere. The foliage turns yellow-green overwinter. Lodgepole pine will make a tree 20–30m tall, and can be showy for the massed male flowers in early summer.

30 Mature black pine (Pinus nigra *subsp.* pallasiana)

P. coulteri California & N Baja California
Coulter pine

This is a magnificent tree with massive cones bearing sharp forward pointing prickles; these are only borne on older trees and can weight over 2kg. The foliage is stout, 20–30cm long and grey-green or bluish grey-green, in fascicles of three needles. It makes a relatively fast growing bold tree, to 15–25m, and it thrives on a wide range of sites, including heavy clay soils.

P. leucodermis Balkans & S Italy
Bosnian pine

This species has dense short dark green needles in bundles of two and cones which are a beautiful cobalt blue during the summer before ripening. In the wild it grows on alkaline sites and should be worth trying on shallow chalk soils.

P. muricata **Bishop pine** California

This species with needles in pairs occurs in two forms, a northern blue form and a southern dark green one. The blue form grows extremely fast on very poor sandy soils, and reasonably fast elsewhere. It has potential as a timber tree for barren sites.

P. nigra
Black pine C & S Europe & W Asia

Black pine occurs in a number of different forms in its range. The two principal ones in cultivation are Austrian pine (var. or subsp. *nigra*) and Corsican pine (var. *maritima* or subsp. *laricio*). Austrian pine has a dense crown of dark green foliage, whereas Corsican pine is more open, making a faster growing tree but needs a high summer temperature to grow well (see page 29). They will make trees to over 40m, but 25–35m is more usual.

Planting should only take place when the roots can make new growth, i.e. in early autumn or late spring. Generally small transplants are used, but with care larger sizes, up to several metres, can be moved satisfactorily. Early losses sometimes are heavy but once established growth is fast. They will grow on most sites, being especially useful on chalk and clay sites.

P. parviflora
Japanese white pine Japan

This makes a small tree with short five needled bluish foliage. Usually it is only 10–15m tall, but occasionally to 25m.

P. pinaster
Maritime pine W Europe & N Africa

This pine has long needles in pairs and large bright brown cones. It regenerates naturally on sandy soils in the New Forest, and is hardy as far north as Edinburgh. It will make 20–30m.

P. ponderosa
Ponderosa pine W North America

Ponderosa pine makes a bold three needled tree 20–40m tall with a distinctive bark, which has deep fissures and broad smooth plates, of yellow-brown, red-brown and pink-grey. The needles are stout, to 25cm, and the young cones purplish. It will grow on most soils, including heavy clays.

P. radiata **Monterey pine** California

This makes a fast growing tree to 30–45m. It has the needles three to a bundle and bright grass green, although the crown appears black on the skyline. The cones persist unopened on the tree for 20 years or more. Monterey pine is hardy throughout Britain, except in upland and cool northern parts. It is especially useful for maritime plantings, but will grow on a range of soils. It is not long lived, usually going into decline after 100 years.

31 *Mature Monterey pine* (Pinus radiata)

32 *Mature Scots pine* (Pinus sylvestris)

P. sylvestris Scotland, Europe
Scots pine & N Asia

Scots pine is Britain's largest native conifer and one of the most attractive native trees. The foliage is blue-green and as the tree matures, it develops a rounded crown. The bark of the upper bole is orange and flaky, that nearer the ground is purple-grey and fissured. It supports a wider range of insects, birds and animals than most conifers, and many broadleaved trees. It usually makes a tree 25–35m tall and may live for up to 300 years. It withstands a moderate degree of exposure and will grow on most soils, although like many other pines, it may only last 20–30 years on shallow soils over chalk. Its main uses are as a timber tree, a nurse for broadleaved plantings, for wildlife, to introduce an evergreen element into deciduous woodland, and as an amenity or specimen tree.

'Aurea' is a form which turns gold overwinter, from December to April. The colder the season, the better the colour. During the summer, it is the same colour as normal Scots pine.

P. thunbergii
Japanese black pine S Japan & S Korea

This uncommon tree is similar to Austrian and Bosnian pines. It is more tolerant than most trees of sea spray or de-icing salt and will make a tree 20–30m tall.

P. wallichiana **Blue pine** Himalayas

Blue pine is a five-needled species which has a broad conic crown 20–30m tall and soft blue, or less often dull green, hanging foliage. It will grow on a wide range of sites, including chalk and limestone.

PLATANUS

Plane Platanaceae

The planes have bold palmately lobed leaves. The outer bark is shed in large plates, giving a mottled effect of whitish-yellow patches on a darker olive or brown background. They will grow on a wide range of soils and are very tolerant of pruning and urban situations.

P. × *hispanica* **London plane**

This is the hybrid between Oriental and American (*P. occidentalis*) planes and is also called *P.* × *acerifolia*. It shows hybrid vigour, or heterosis, and makes a very large long-lived tree, of 30–50m. Trees 300 years old are still in good health. The leaves are large and slow to decompose. It requires a climate with sufficient summer heat. It is very tolerant of poor soils, growing surprisingly fast in builder's rubble, and smokey or polluted atmospheres. Too often it has been planted in locations where there is insufficient space for it to develop to its full potential. Frequent planting, large size and ability to grow on clay subsoils have resulted in a number of claims of damage caused to houses by its roots, particularly in the London area. It is a very stable tree, rarely blowing down or even losing live branches in strong winds. It can suffer from anthracnose (see page 121) and the hairs on the leaves and seeds can be an irritant, especially to people working on the tree.

'Augustine Henry' is the best form, making a large open crowned tree of great vigour, with large leaves.

'Pyramidalis' is a rather uninteresting form, with a more conical habit and a poor, more fissured bark.

'Suttneri' is a variegated form.

P. orientalis
Oriental plane SE Europe & W Asia

This tree is similar to London plane. It has the leaves more deeply lobed, and is more resistant to anthracnose. Oriental plane makes a slightly smaller tree, to around 25m, and is very long lived.

'Digitata' is a tall growing form with leaves deeply divided into three to five coarsely toothed finger-like lobes.

PLATYCLADUS

Biota Cupressaceae

A monotypic genus of evergreen conifer often placed in *Thuja* but differing in the cones and non-fragrant foliage.

P. orientalis **Biota** N & W China

This makes a small slow-growing tree to 15m. The foliage is green and held in flat vertical sprays. It is very tolerant of hot dry or polluted atmospheres and grows on most soils.

PODOCARPUS

Podocarps Podocarpaceae

This is a large mainly tropical genus of evergreen conifers.

P. salignus **Willow leaf podocarp** S Chile

This makes an interesting tree to 20m with a columnar crown. The foliage is up to 12cm long and the bark is shaggy, orange to red-brown. It grows best in moist mild areas but is hardy with shelter elsewhere. It is only available as small plants.

POPULUS

Poplars Salicaceae

The poplars are a genus of large deciduous trees. They make their best growth in damp soils, and are gross users of water, but will grow in most soils. They have a reputation for causing damage with their roots and should not be planted near buildings on shrinkable clay soils, or near to drains. The wood is soft and old trees regularly lose branches in strong winds, particularly if they have been pollarded in the past, or there is decay in the bole. They are dioecious, the female trees releasing the cottony seeds in midsummer, sometimes to the annoyance of neighbours when it sticks to washing. They are unusual in producing larger leaves at the top of the tree and in later flushes of growth. They establish easily at any size.

P. alba Europe, N Africa &
White poplar or Abele W & C Asia

This makes a tree to 20m, with a rather low rounded crown. The leaves are palmate and very white beneath. It suckers freely from the roots. It withstands coastal conditions.

P. × candicans **Balm of Gilead**

This has large deltoid leaves which are glaucous beneath and smell strongly of balsam. It is very susceptible to poplar canker (see page 123).

'Aurora' is a very attractive clone in which the foliage produced in summer is green with white flushed pink.

P. × canescens **Grey poplar**

This tree is a natural hybrid between Aspen

and White poplar. The leaf outline is similar to Aspen, being rounded and toothed, with the white felt beneath of White poplar. It suckers and makes a vigorous tree 20–35m.

P. lasiocarpa
Chinese Necklace poplar C & W China

This species has large leaves, to 30cm even on mature trees. It makes a broad conic crown, to 25m, and is unique in having both male and female flowers on the same catkin. It is hardy throughout the country, north to Aberdeen.

P. nigra
Black poplar Europe, W & C Asia

Black poplar has rhombic or deltoid leaves and makes a dense tree with a rounded domed crown, 25–40m tall. It has largely been supplanted by hybrids with an American species.

Var. *betulifolia* or Manchester poplar tolerates polluted atmospheres and has been planted in cities.

'Italica' is the Lombardy poplar, with a narrow crown of ascending branches. It is male, but 'Gigantea', with a slightly broader crown, is female. Lombardy poplars are useful as exclamation marks but are not ideal for belts or lines, as they are too fragile.

A number of Hybrid Black poplars are cultivated. They have more open crowns, with spaced branches and larger leaves, with faster growth rates. 'Serotina' is one of the commoner forms. 'Serotina Aurea' is a mutation with very yellow new leaves, changing to yellowish green. It is slower, but will make a tree to 30m.

P. tremula Britain, Europe,
Aspen N Africa & N Asia

Aspen makes a tree 15–20m tall with a columnar crown. It suckers. The leaves are grey-green and rounded, soon glabrous. The petiole is flattened in cross-section, allowing the leaf to flutter in the slightest breeze, hence 'quaking aspen'.

P. trichocarpa
Black cottonwood W North America

This makes a columnar tree 25–40m tall with a dense crown. The new foliage smells strongly of balsam, scenting the air around the trees, and turns a good yellow in autumn. It may sucker and can be susceptible to poplar canker (see page 123). Sometimes grown as a timber tree are hybrids between Black cottonwood and *P. balsamifera*, such as 'TT32' and 'TT37'.

PRUNUS

Cherries and Plums Rosaceae

This genus contains a large number of species, and more cultivars and hybrids. They are very important horticulturally, including many floriferous trees. Some are rather dull when not in flower, others also have interesting habits, or good autumn colour. Although in the Rose family, they do not suffer from fireblight (see page 120). Cherries are susceptible to silver leaf disease (see page 121) and pruning (if essential) should take place in early summer to reduce the likelihood of this disease occurring.

Cherries are not long lived; Gean may live for 150 years, but most others will last only a quarter to half as long, particularly on unfavourable soils, such as on chalk or acidic sands.

Many of the species are grafted onto rootstocks. Cherries are usually grafted onto Gean but sometimes Sour cherry (*P. cerasus*) is used; similarly Myrobalan plum (*P. cerasifera*) rootstock is used for plums, almond and some other species. These rootstocks may sucker.

They can be moved and planted at most sizes and times, except for the evergreen species which should be planted in early autumn or late spring for best results.

P. × *amygdalo-persica*

This hybrid between the almond and the

peach is mainly represented by the following clone.

'Pollardii' makes a small spreading tree with bright pink flowers. It is similar to almond, but slightly earlier flowering and much less affected by peach leafcurl.

P. avium
Gean or Wild cherry Britain & Europe

This is fast growing and can make a tree to 30m, although usually smaller. It is very attractive in April when bearing the white flowers and again in the autumn when the leaves turn. The branches tend to be in pronounced whorls. Gean thrives on a wide range of sites, including heavy clays. It is a useful tree to scatter through broadleaved woods, adding an extra element of colour and variety.

'Plena' is a very attractive form with double flowers, which last for nearly three weeks in spring.

P. cerasifera **Myrobalan or Cherry plum**

This makes a small tree to 8–12m. It has pure white flowers before the leaves in early spring, varying upon season between January and April, and sometimes ripens yellow or red Cherry plums.

'Pissardii' is one of several purple foliaged forms with pink flowers.

P. dulcis
Almond SW Asia, Balkans & N Africa

This makes a small tree to 8m, renowned for the early pink flowers. It can be badly affected by peach leafcurl. It is not a long-lived tree, usually lasting for only 20 or so years.

P. laurocerasus Balkans, Asia Minor
Cherry laurel & Caucasus

This is an evergreen species with large shiny leaves. Although usually planted as a shrub, it can make a tree to 15m.

P. lusitanica
Portuguese laurel Iberian peninsula

This makes a small evergreen tree or large shrub, to 15m.

P. maackii **Maack cherry** NE Asia

This is a magnificent but grossly under planted tree which has a striking shiny brownish yellow trunk and small racemes of fragrant white flowers in April. It makes a small tree to 10m.

'Amber Beauty' is a selection for the rich bark colour.

P. padus
Bird cherry Britain, Europe & N Asia

Bird cherry is a showy small tree, to 20m. The flowers are in racemes carried after the leaves. In Britain, it is native mainly to the cooler and moister regions. It will grow at altitude and in some exposure.

'Watereri' is a selected form with longer (to 20cm) and brighter white racemes of flowers, making a display in May.

P. sargentii **Sargent cherry** N Japan

This species has pink flowers in spring and gives brilliant early autumn colour, usually in late September or early October. It makes a tree to 15m.

'Rancho' has upswept branches, making a narrow crowned tree suitable for confined locations or streets.

P. × schmittii **Schmitt cherry**

This hybrid of Gean makes an open tree with a very distinct vase-shaped upright whorled habit and is appropriate for many street plantings. The bark is shiny mahogany coloured, the flowers pale pink.

P. serrula **Tibetan cherry** W China

This species with willowy leaves and delicate small white flowers has an outstanding

33 Prunus x schmittii *makes a good medium-sized street tree*

bark which is shiny mahogany coloured and has been likened to Sheraton furniture. It makes a small tree, to 10–15m, but displays the best bark effect when young.

P. serrulata Japan, C China & Korea

Many of the Japanese cherries contain genes from this species in their hybrid make-up and in the past have been treated as cultivars of it; they are best treated as cultivars of the genus. The wild species is attractive for the pink flowers in spring and brilliant autumn colour, and makes a small rather spreading tree.

P. subhirtella Japan

This small tree is usually cultivated as the Autumn cherry, 'Autumnalis'; it flowers intermittently over the late autumn/winter period. 'Pendula Rosea' and 'Pendula Rubra' are two mound-forming, small tree forms which flower in spring.

P. × *yedoensis* **Yoshino cherry**

This makes a very floriferous small tree of low spreading habit. Flowers are white or pink, borne in late March or early April.

P. virginiana
Pin cherry E North America

This is mainly grown as the cultivar 'Schubert', which is unique in the foliage starting off green and *then* ageing to purple; it makes a small tree.

PRUNUS Cultivars

The many cherry cultivars can be divided into two groups: species crosses and the Japanese cherries or Sato Zakura.

Cherry species hybrids

P. 'Accolade' makes a low spreading tree, loaded in early spring with masses of semi-double pink flowers.

P. 'Hillieri Spire' combines a narrow erect or spire-like habit with profuse blush-pink flowers and good autumn colour.

P. 'Pink Shell' is a wide spreading tree which carries many shell-pink flowers in mid April.

P. 'Snow Goose' and 'Umineko' both have snow-white flowers in early spring, contrasting with the bright green new leaves. As young trees they are very erect, broadening with age but suitable for restricted locations.

Japanese cherries

P. 'Amanogawa' makes a very fastigiate young tree, less than 1m wide when 6m tall, but broadens out to 2–3m as it attains 8m tall. The pink, semi-double, fragrant flowers are carried in early May and it makes an attractive companion tree to beds of tulips. It is not long lived, as the erect branches are liable to storm damage in trees 20 or so years old.

P. 'Cheal's Weeping' and 'Kiku-shidare' are two very similar weeping cherries with strongly pendulous branches. They are only as tall as the stem on which they are trained or grafted (they are usually top-worked) and will form cascading mounds of pink double blossom in late April.

P. 'Kanzan' is the ubiquitous Japanese cherry, bearing masses of double pink flowers in May. Young trees have stiffly ascending branches but older trees become wide spreading and somewhat weeping. It is a striking tree when in flower, but rather too frequently planted at the expense of the other cultivars discussed here.

P. 'Pink Perfection' is a small spreading tree which has bright rosy-pink double flowers in long hanging clusters in late April.

P. 'Shimidsu' has an almost flat habit, scarcely taller than the stem is trained. In late April or early May, the spreading branches are wreathed with drooping clusters of pure white flowers.

P. 'Shirofugen' flowers in early May, when the spreading branches are covered with large double white flowers, which are pink in bud, and by the dark red new foliage, which matures green.

P. 'Shirotae' has large single or semi-double snow-white flowers in late April or early May, contrasting with the fresh green of the young leaves. The habit is wide spreading.

P. 'Tai Haku' makes a spreading tree with large leaves. In April, it carries the largest of all cherry flowers, single, to 6cm in diameter and a dazzling white.

P. 'Ukon' has flowers which are pale yellow with a distinct greenish tinge. Makes a large tree with a spreading habit.

PSEUDOLARIX

Pinaceae

This is a monotypic genus.

P. amabilis **Golden larch** E China

This deciduous conifer is similar to the larches (*Larix*) but differs in the cones. It is very beautiful in autumn with the bright, almost Spanish, gold autumn colour. It will make a tree 15–20m but is very slow to get started.

PSEUDOTSUGA

Douglas firs Pinaceae

This is a small genus of evergreen conifers.

P. menziesii
Douglas fir W North America

This is a fast growing tall tree, so far to 60m in Britain. It is used in forestry and has a valuable timber. The bark of old trees is very thick, rugged and corky, with reddish fissures. Douglas fir grows best in deep, fertile soils but will tolerate other site conditions. It can be susceptible to late spring frost when young. It is not suitable for exposed conditions, and only tolerates a degree of shading.

Var. *glauca* is a geographical form with very blue foliage. It makes a smaller tree but suffers from a needle disease, caused by the fungus *Rhabdocline pseudotsugae*, which restricts its use.

PTELEA

Hop trees Rutaceae

A small genus of deciduous trees or shrubs from North America.

P. trifoliata **Hop tree** E North America

This makes a small tree to 8m with a rounded crown and trifoliate leaves which turn yellow in autumn. The whole plant emits a strong aromatic scent when bruised. The fruits, similar to those of elm, are a small nutlet surrounded by a circular wing. It will grow on a wide range of sites.

PTEROCARYA

Wingnuts Juglandaceae

This is a small genus of deciduous trees allied to Walnuts (*Juglans*), but differing in the naked buds and small winged fruits which hang down in long racemes. They make fast growing trees, especially on damp sites.

P. fraxinifolia
Wingnut Caucasus & N Iran

This is the commonest species in cultivation, making a tree with a rounded domed crown, 20–35m tall, often on several stems. The long pale yellow green fruiting clusters and yellow autumn foliage are attractive. It suckers from the root system, frequently forming a small grove.

PTEROSTYRAX

Styracaceae

A small genus of deciduous trees from China and Japan.

P. hispida
Winged Storax China & Japan

This makes a small tree to 12m, with a narrow crown. The flowers are white, fragrant and carried in large panicles in June and July. It will grow on most soils, including on chalk or limestone.

PYRUS

Pears Rosaceae

The pears are a genus of small trees related to the apples (*Malus*). They will grow on most soils and have showy white flowers in spring, appearing with or soon after the leaves. They tolerate urban conditions.

P. betulifolia **Birch-leaf pear** N China

This makes a narrow crowned tree of fast growth rate; the leaves are grey-green, maturing glossy green.

P. calleryana **Callery pear** C & S China

This upright tree to 12m is semi-evergreen, keeping the leaves until late in autumn when they turn rich claret and purple, although a few hang on into the New Year. The white flowers are carried early in spring.

'Chanticleer' is normally cultivated as the clone and is suitable for use in narrow streets, although eventually making a medium sized tree.

P. communis
Common pear Britain & Europe

Common pear makes a large, long lived tree to 15m. It can look very attractive in spring when covered by the pure white flowers, but is less impressive later.

'Beech Hill' is a form with good autumn colour and a narrow upright habit.

P. salicifolia Caucasus,
Willow-leafed pear Asia Minor & N Iran

This small tree is represented in gardens by the cultivar 'Pendula', which makes a rounded tree with weeping branches, ultimately attaining 12m, but slow growing and suitable for gardens with limited space. The leaves are willow-like and silvery grey when new. The flowers are pure white in April, but lost amongst the new leaves.

QUERCUS

Oaks Fagaceae

The oaks are a very large genus of woody plants. Most of these are evergreen. Oaks generally come from warm, dry climates and the two British native species are amongst the last native trees to come into leaf. Oaks range from shrubs 1m tall to trees of 40–50m. They are only of moderate growth rate but generally very long lived. They thrive on a wide range of soils, and can be planted out at most sizes.

Q. canariensis — N Africa & Iberian Peninsula
Mirbeck oak

This tree is semi-evergreen, only losing the leaves sometime after Christmas. It makes a tree to 20–30m with a domed crown. It is a very attractive tree, unfortunately only available at relatively small sizes.

Q. castaneifolia
Chestnut-leaf oak — Caucasus & N Iran

This tree is related to Turkey oak but has a leaf similar to a chestnut (*Castanea*). It has made a tree to 30m.

'Green Spire' is a vigorous upright selection with a broad columnar crown.

Q. cerris
Turkey oak — S & C Europe & Asia Minor

Turkey oak makes one of the largest and grandest of trees, with a broad and tall domed crown, to 25–40m. Young trees are very conical in outline. The leaves are variously indented. It will grow on a wide range of soils, being especially good on chalk and light soils. It is faster growing than the native oaks, but has an inferior timber.

Q. coccinea
Scarlet oak — E North America

This tree has glossy leaves which can turn a brilliant scarlet in autumn, although sometimes don't. It makes a tree to 25m. It is often cultivated as the clone 'Splendens'.

Q. frainetto **Hungarian oak** — S Europe

This tree makes a very large specimen with a broad domed crown, to 25–35m. It is one of the faster growing oaks. The leaves are large and obovate, with deep double indentations, giving a very characteristic outline; they turn russet colours in autumn. It makes an excellent specimen tree.

Q. × hispanica **Lucombe oak**

This hybrid between the Turkey and Cork oaks makes a large vigorous tree to 25–35m with nearly evergreen leaves (usually lost at the beginning of March) and a corky bark. Several slightly different forms exist, such as 'Lucombeana' and 'Ambrozyana'.

Q. ilex
Holm oak — Mediterranean Region

Holm oak is a fully evergreen species. It makes a rounded tree to 20–25m. It is especially suited to coastal conditions and will tolerate salt laden gales better than nearly all other trees. Away from such testing sites, it is dismally dull, except in June when the male flowers and yellow new foliage are produced.

Q. palustris **Pin oak** — E North America

This tree will grow well on damp sites and on dry sandy ones. The crown is narrowly domed, to 20–30m, with the lower branches becoming pendulous. The leaves are deeply lobed; they turn crimson and dark red in autumn.

Q. petraea — Britain, Europe, Asia Minor & Caucasus
Sessile oak

This makes a taller more erect growing tree (25–45m) than English oak; it has a neater leaf, less subject to galls and insect herbivores. It prefers a moister site than English oak and is commoner in the western parts of Britain. It does better on sandy soils than on heavy clays. Its uses are as a forestry tree and as a parkland specimen.

Q. robur — Europe, Asia Minor & Caucasus
English oak

34 *Stagshorn sumach* (Rhus typhina)

English oak makes a broad domed crown on a tree 20–40m tall. It supports a richer number of insect and other species than any other British tree. Like most other oaks, it can be planted out at a range of sizes, although trees 2–3m tall can be harder to establish than either smaller or larger ones (they are too small to have an effective rootball, yet too large to be easily moved bare-rooted). It is one of the species showing the best enhancement of growth using individual tree shelters (see page 92). It does best on a heavy soil, such as clay or silty loams, and roots very deeply. The roots are not tolerant of heavy compaction of the soil, close excavations or deep cultivation, especially those affecting the watertable; such shocks often cause the tree to go into a slow decline, and over a period of years it may become stagheaded.

Oak requires full sunlight to grow well, and open space around the crown. It makes long lived trees, with a likely maximum of 500–1,000 years, although only for squat trees which have been regularly pollarded; for general plantings, a likely maximum lifespan is 200–300 years. Oak is a very good overstorey tree for a woodland garden, with plants such as *Rhododendron*.

'Fastigiata' is a clone with a narrow erect habit of growth, to 15–30m.

Q. rubra **Red oak** E North America

Red oak will make a fast growing large tree, especially good for poor sandy soils. It is less suited to heavy clay soils. The mature crown is a rounded dome, 25–35m tall. The leaves emerge pale yellow in the spring, assuming good red and russet colours in the autumn. It is only likely to live for around 150–200 years, but quickly makes a large tree.

'Aurea' is a form in which the new foliage flushes a bright yellow colour.

RHUS

Sumach Anacardiaceae

The species are deciduous with pinnate leaves which give autumn colours. They grow on a wide range of soils, and usually

sucker from the roots. The sap of some species is very poisonous and can cause injury to people sensitive to it.

R. typhina
Staghorn Sumach E North America

This small tree may attain 8m, with a broad rounded crown.

ROBINIA

Robinia or False acacia Leguminosae

This is a small genus of deciduous trees with pinnate leaves.

R. × ambigua

This hybrid is mainly represented in cultivation by the following clone.

'Decaisneana' makes a vigorous medium sized tree which bears long racemes of pale pink flowers in June. It flowers better on hot sunny sites.

R. pseudacacia
Robinia E North America

Robinia makes a fast growing tree, to a maximum of 20–30m and quickly will look 'mature'. It has bright green leaves, white flowers in racemes in June and a rugged fissured bark. The shoots often bear two stout spines beside the buds. It is not long lived. Robinia is sensitive to transplanting and the roots must not be allowed to dry out. It is much better planted as a tree 2m tall or less. The wood is very brittle, and branches are often broken by strong winds, especially when laden with foliage. It suckers and will grow on most soils, especially on sandy ones.

'Bessoniana' forms an ovoid tree with a strong central bole. It makes a suitable street tree, although rather shy of flowering.

35 Robinia pseudacacia *'Frisia' – golden yellow foliage to enliven dark locations*

'Fastigiata' has upright branches which give a narrow crowned tree. It needs a sheltered location, else the branches are too badly damaged by strong winds.

'Frisia' has the new leaves golden yellow, paling to a bright yellow-green during summer and becoming bright yellow in autumn. It is a very effective foliage plant, to 15m.

'Inermis' or Mopheaded robinia is a thornless form, making a rounded domed crown on top of the stem when top grafted.

R. 'Hillieri'

This makes a small tree with a rounded crown and carries slightly fragrant lilac-pink flowers in June, even as young plants.

SALIX

Willows Salicaceae

The willows are a large group of woody plants, ranging in size from subshrubs less than 5cm tall to trees upwards of 30m. The tree species are all fast growing, tolerant of a wide range of soils but much happier in moist or even wet ones. Their ability to grow in waterlogged conditions, or in water, leads to problems when the roots gain access to a drain. They are rather short lived, with a brittle and easy decayed timber. Willows are very easy to move at any size, due to the ease with which almost all species can root from hardwood cuttings. They are mainly planted for amenity, and one clone for cricket bat manufacture. The catkins can be very attractive in early spring and, in some species, the one year shoots in winter.

S. alba **White willow** Britain & Europe

White willow makes a very vigorous tree on fertile moist sites to 25–30m tall; the branches are ascending, with pendulous branchlets. The leaves are blue-grey, silky beneath.

'Caerulea' is the Cricket bat willow and is

36 Weeping willow (Salix *'Chrysocoma'*), *ideal beside water given sufficient space*

grown for its timber. It may be of hybrid origin.

'Chermesina' has the one-year twigs orange scarlet. The colour develops best after Christmas, and a tree in the distance can look very effective in winter sunshine. It will grow to 30m, although is often coppiced to produce longer and brighter one-year shoots.

'Sericea' is the Silver willow, with very silvery white leaves. It makes a smaller tree.

'Vitellina' has yellow or orange-yellow winter twigs. It will make a tall tree, or can be coppiced to maximise the production of colourful one year wood. It is probably a parent of *S. chrysocoma*.

S. caprea **Goat willow** Britain & Europe

Goat willow makes a small tree, occasionally to 20m. It is very attractive in March when carrying the silver (female) and yellow (male) 'pussy willow' catkins. Grey willow (*S. cinerea*) is similar.

S. × chrysocoma **Weeping willow**

This species is the common Weeping willow and makes a very fast growing large tree, to 25m, and is totally unsuited to most gardens. It can look very attractive set beside large bodies of water. The winter twigs are golden yellow and strongly pendulous.

S. daphnoides
Violet willow S Europe, C & W Asia

This makes a tree to 10m but is mainly grown for the attraction of the glaucous waxy coating on the one year old shoots.

S. fragilis
Crack willow Britain, Europe & N Asia

Crack willow makes a similar tree to White willow but differs in the glossy green upper surface to the leaves and the way that two year old shoots break off the joints. It will make 20–25m.

S. matsudana **Peking willow** N China

This is mainly grown as the clone 'Tortuosa', which has contorted one-year shoots. It is very vigorous, and most effective in winter, when the tracery of the twigs is evident. It will make 15m.

S. pentandra
Bay willow Britain, S Europe & W Asia

Bay willow is unusual in having the flowers on short leafy shoots in June; they are bright yellow and attractively displayed, along with the glossy deep green leaves. It makes a tree to 15–20m.

SEQUOIA

Redwood Taxodiaceae

This monotypic genus includes the tallest trees in the world, to 112m (367 feet).

S. sempervirens
Coastal redwood California

Redwood is very fast growing in mild sheltered sites, to 20–40m. In exposed areas the foliage may be cut back in winter. It has a very thick and soft fibrous bark and is one of the few conifers to coppice. It makes a very impressive tree for a grove, or as a single tree.

'Adpressa' is a form with broad needles. The new shoots are creamy white.

SEQUOIADENDRON

Wellingtonia Taxodiaceae

Related to *Sequoia*, this genus contains the largest living thing, 'General Sherman', estimated to weigh 6,000 tonnes and 83m tall.

S. giganteum California
Wellingtonia or Sierra redwood

Wellingtonia makes a fast growing tree, to 30–50m. It is much hardier than Coastal redwood, and undamaged by winter cold in Britain. It will also put up with polluted and dry atmospheres. It quickly forms a stout tree. It needs a rich deep soil for best growth. Regularly the tallest tree wherever it is planted, it is frequently damaged by lightning. It is also rather susceptible to honey fungus (see page 118), which can kill established trees. Its main use is to make a substantial tree in amenity or

37 *Wellingtonia* (Sequoiadendron giganteum)

landscape plantings. Groves of a number of trees can be very effective features.

SOPHORA

Leguminosae

This is a large genus of legumes with pinnate leaves.

S. japonica
Pagoda tree Japan, China & Korea

This makes a deciduous tree to 20–25m. It has dark shiny green leaves which flush pale yellow or nearly white. The flowers are white and carried in large erect panicles from August to September, especially in hot summers. It is long lived, with 150-200 years as a general maximum, and tolerates a wide range of soils.

'Pendula' makes a mound shaped weeping tree; the winter silhouette is of a mass of contorted and pendulous branches.

SORBUS

Rowans and Whitebeams Rosaceae

This is a very useful genus of small trees and large shrubs. They are tolerant of a wide range of growing conditions, and make excellent trees for poor sites, or as street trees. They have white flowers in May followed by red, white or russet fruits. They can be planted out at all normal sizes. The species are all susceptible to fireblight to some extent (see page 120), except possibly *Sorbus intermedia*.

The genus divides into two major groups. The whitebeams have entire leaves which are usually silver hairy below, and often more so above when young, turning russet colours in autumn; the rowans have pinnate foliage, giving good autumn colour. These have hybridised to give a range of 'microspecies', with various extra sets of chromosomes.

S. aria **Whitebeam** Britain & Europe

This native tree is usually seen as a tree 10–15m tall, but can make over 20m. The new leaves are very silvery white. The berries ripen bright red in September. It is very often found growing on chalk or limestone sites, and tolerates both industrial pollution and sea winds.

'Chrysophylla' has the leaves yellowish throughout the summer, turning a richer yellow in autumn.

'Decaisnea' makes a tree to 20m with a broad columnar crown and has large leaves to 15cm.

'Lutescens' is the best form for spring foliage. It makes a tree with small leaves and a dense ovoid crown.

S. × *arnoldiana*

Mainly cultivated as 'Schouten', which makes a small erect tree with bright green foliage and golden yellow fruits.

S. aucuparia
Rowan Britain, Europe & N Asia

This is a common native tree, growing from sea level to 600m (2,000 feet) in Scotland. It will grow on most soils, although the rowan does not like shallow soils over chalk. It can make a tree to over 20m tall but is usually only half this. The berries ripen around the beginning of August but are often stripped from the trees by birds before the leaves turn yellow or red in the autumn. Rowan is not long lived, to a maximum of less than 100 years.

'Asplenifolia' is a plant with the leaflets fern-like and deeply divided.

'Beissneri' is a beautiful form. The leaflets are deeply cut and yellowish green, whilst the bark is a coppery red which is particularly effective after rain. The crown is rather open and upright.

'Cardinal Royal' is a vigorous selection with dark green leaves, an upright habit and large bright red berries.

'Fastigiata' is very slow growing with stout and stiff shoots and large bunches of red berries.

'Fructu Luteo' ('Xanthocarpa') has amber yellow fruits.

'Shearwater Seedling' is a selected form with a narrow upright crown, very well suited to use in confined spaces.

S. cashmiriana
Kashmir rowan Kashmir

This makes a small spreading tree to 5m. It has pink flowers which are followed by large (2cm) glistening white fruits which last into winter.

S. commixta
Japanese rowan Japan & Korea

This is a narrow crowned rowan with orange-red berries and glossy green leaves which turn brilliant deep purple and scarlet in autumn. It makes a tree to 15m.

'Embley' has an upright habit and scarlet autumn colour.

S. cuspidata
Himalayan whitebeam W & C Himalaya

This is a vigorous whitebeam 15–23m tall with bold elliptic leaves bright silvery white beneath. The fruits are large and russet coloured.

S. domestica
Service tree S Europe, N Africa & W Asia

This has pinnate foliage and makes a large tree often 15–20m tall. The bark is fissured and scaly.

S. 'Eastern Promise'

This is a rowan with an upright habit. The leaves turn purple, then flame in autumn, whilst the berries are rose-pink.

S. hupehensis **Hubei rowan** C China

This tree has attractive white flushed pink fruits which are usually not eaten by birds until after Christmas. The leaves are bluish-green, and develop good autumn colours in late October or early November. Several different microspecies are in cultivation. *S. glabrescens* has pure white berries, whilst *S. forrestii* has larger glistening white fruits; both have good autumn colour but rather stout and spaced twigs.

S. hybrida
Hybrid service tree Scandinavia

'Gibbsii' is the normal form in cultivation, making a small tree. It has lobed and partly pinnate leaves which are white tomentose beneath. The fruits are deep scarlet crimson.

S. 'Golden Wonder'

This is a rowan with a fastigiate habit, bearing pure orange-yellow fruits.

S. intermedia
Swedish whitebeam Scandinavia

This is a hybrid species with the leaves deeply lobed but not pinnate and grey-green beneath. It makes a very tough tree to 15m with a dense domed crown and is particularly good for coastal or street plantings.

'Brouwers' is a selection made in Holland with a dense upright habit.

S. latifolia
Service tree of Fontainebleau France

This makes a tough, medium sized tree which has broad leaves with coarse triangular teeth. The flowers are carried in large corymbs, followed by reddish brown or yellow-brown berries.

S. 'Mitchellii' see *S. thibetica* 'John Mitchell'.

S. rehderiana **Rehder rowan** W China

This small tree is mainly cultivated as the following two clones.

'Pearly King' makes a small spreading tree with rose-pink fruits which fade to white, flushed pink, and has good autumn colour. It makes a more vigorous but otherwise similar tree to *S. vilmorinii*.

'Joseph Rock' makes an upright tree of narrow habit and is suitable for streets and restricted sites. It has amber coloured berries contrasting with the crimson and purple autumn colour, and then persisting on the bare branches for several weeks.

S. sargentiana **Sargent rowan** W China

This makes a tree to 12m with a broad domed crown. The leaves are large and turn bright scarlet and gold in autumn, whilst the fruits are in very large clusters. The buds are rounded, red and very sticky.

S. scalaris **Ladder rowan** W China

This is a small tree with a very spreading habit, suitable for parks and gardens where there is space. The leaves are ladder-like, with 21–33 leaflets, flushing bronze or brownish crimson, then become glossy green; they make an attractive foil for the white flowers in late May and the red fruits in October, before turning orange-yellow or scarlet.

S. 'Sunshine'

This is a seedling of 'Joseph Rock' and makes an erect tree with large lax clusters of golden yellow berries.

S. thibetica E Himalayas
Tibetan whitebeam SE Tibet & N Burma

'John Mitchell' (-'Mitchellii'-) is the main form in cultivation of this vigorous white-beam which makes a tree to 15–20m tall. It has large round leaves up to 15cm long which are silver beneath and dark glossy green above. It is most attractive in a parkland setting where the leaves can be left lying beneath the tree over winter; they turn russet colours on the top surface, whilst the lower face remains silver and in February sun, the combination of silver and russet leaves on the ground beneath the tree is impressive.

S. thibetica KW21127 see *S. wardii*.

S. × *thuringiaca*
Bastard service tree Germany

'Fastigiata' is the principal clone. This has erect or fastigiate branching. At first it makes an erect tree, becoming ovoid with time. The leaves are partly pinnate and greyish white beneath. The fruits are red. It is a tough tree, suitable for exposed sites and poor soils.

S. torminalis Britain, Europe
Wild service tree & W Asia

This tree has leaves with deep triangular lobes and russet autumn colours. It makes a tree to 15–25m.

S. vilmorinii **Vilmorin rowan** W China

This makes a small spreading tree, rarely more than 5m tall. The fruits ripen maroon and fade through pink to almost white. The leaves are composed of many small leaflets and turn red and purple in autumn. It thrives better on a moist sheltered site.

S. wardii **Ward whitebeam** N Burma

This is a small narrow crowned tree to 6m. It has amber fruits and ribbed grey-green leaves which are silvery when young. It has been confused with *S. thibetica* and is in cultivation from seeds collected by Kingdon-Ward in Burma in 1953, under KW21127. It is very useful where a small upright whitebeam is needed.

STUARTIA

Stuartia Theaceae

This genus is related to *Camellia*. The species have large white flowers in July and August. They need a lime-free soil and resent root disturbance. They are best suited to woodland conditions.

S. pseudocamellia
Stuartia Japan & Korea

This is the commonest species in cultivation and makes a tree to 15m with good yellow to red autumn colours. The bark is orange-brown.

STYRAX

Storax Styracaceae

This is a large genus of deciduous shrubs and trees with showy white flowers hanging down from the branches in early summer. They need a moist loamy and lime-free soil, either in full sun or light shade.

S. hemsleyana
Hemsley storax C & W China

This makes a small tree 10–15m tall. The flowers are in lax erect racemes 15cm long in June.

S. japonica
Snowbell tree Japan, Korea & C China

This is a tree to 15m with a graceful upright habit with spreading branches. The snow-white flowers are carried *en masse* in clusters of 3–6 and hang below the branches in June. It is better planted in a site sheltered from spring frosts.

S. obassia
Big-leaf storax Japan, Korea & N China

This has the large (2.5cm) flowers in fragrant drooping racemes to 20m. It makes a tree 10–17m tall, needing sheltered woodland conditions for best effect.

SYRINGA

Lilacs Oleaceae

The lilacs are normally grown as shrubs but some, such as *S. yunnanensis*, will make small trees to 8m. Lilacs need well drained soils, growing very well on chalk, but need shelter from spring frosts.

TAXODIUM

Swamp cypresses Taxodiaceae

This is a genus of three deciduous conifers.

T. ascendens **Pond cypress** SE USA

This makes a tree to 20m with a narrow crown. It is similar to Swamp cypress, but does not produce any knees and has the leaves arranged radially on the shoots.

'Nutans' has the shoots erect at first, becoming nodding.

T. distichum
Swamp cypress or Bald cypress SE USA

Swamp cypress makes a tree to 20–35m. The bright green foliage does not emerge until June and turns brick red in November. It will coppice. The wood is very brittle and old trees suffer from storm damage. It is useful for its ability to grow on damp sites, and it will grow, albeit very slowly, when standing permanently in water; it does better on more normal soils. When beside water, the roots develop special structures ('knees') to enable them to exchange gases with the air; these may be 90cm tall.

TAXUS

Yews Taxaceae

The yews are a genus of evergreen conifers, capable of withstanding very dry and shady conditions when established, growing on a wide range of sites. They are of moderate growth rate and can be planted at a range of sizes.

T. baccata Britain, Europe,
Yew N Africa & W Asia

Yew, one of only three native conifers, will

make a tree 15–20m tall, with a spreading crown. The foliage, seeds and bark are poisonous. There are a number of records of animals eating yew foliage and dying, although few of people accidentally harming themselves. It will grow on very chalky sites, as well as on more acidic soils and is very long lived, possibly to over 1,000 years. It can be used as a hedging tree, for shelter or as a backcloth to other plants.

'Adpressa' is a curious clone with short broad leaves. It can make a tree to 15m.

'Dovastoniana' is a form with pendent branch tips. It has made 17m. 'Dovastonii Aurea' has yellow margined leaves.

'Fastigiata' is the Irish yew and makes a tree with an upright crown, to 20m.

Tetracentron

Tetracentronaceae

This is a monotypic genus.

T. sinense C & W China
Tetracentron & E Himalayas

This tree to 15m has ovate or heart shaped leaves and hanging yellowish catkins. It will grow on most soils, doing best in acidic or neutral woodland conditions.

Thuja

Thujas Cupressaceae

This is a small genus of evergreen conifers.

T. koraiensis **Korean thuja** Korea

This makes a small slow growing attractive tree, to 5–13m, with the foliage vividly silver glaucous beneath and having a rich fruity aroma.

T. orientalis see *Platycladus orientalis*.

T. plicata
Western red cedar W North America

This species is very fast growing and will make a tree to 25–45m. It has a narrow columnar conic crown. It will grow on a wide range of sites, and is especially tolerant of, although slow growing on, very wet or heavy sites. It will take a degree of shade and is comparatively easy to transplant. It has a rich bronzy green foliage which smells of pineapple. The stem is invariably straight. It withstands clipping very well, and can make an effective hedge or screen.

'Aurea' makes a tree which has the foliage a rich old gold colour.

'Zebrina' is a form with the foliage banded with whitish yellow. It makes an interesting light foliaged tree to 25m.

Thujopsis

Cupressaceae

This genus of evergreen conifers contains but a single species. It is close to *Thuja* but differs in the cones and the much stouter foliage which is silvery beneath.

T. dolabrata **Hiba** Japan

Hiba makes a tree to 15–23m with a dense habit. It usually grows on several stems. It will grow on a wide range of soils, including shallow ones over chalk.

Tilia

Limes or Lindens Tiliaceae

The limes are a genus of large trees from Europe, Asia and eastern North America. They make large and fast growing trees with a white timber. The flowers are fragrant and provide a good source of nectar for bees. They are easy to move and establish at any reasonable size and will grow on a wide range of soils, preferring moist and base rich ones.

*38 Mature Common lime (*Tilia x europaea*)*

T. cordata Britain, Europe & W Asia
Small leaved lime

This species was formerly much more abundant as a native tree, but repeated clearance and woodland management has restricted it to scattered old trees in woods on base-rich soils. It regenerates well from coppicing but only occasionally sets viable seed, due to the vagaries of the British climate. It will make a tree 30–40m tall and live for several centuries. It is suitable for planting as an amenity tree in parks and in rural areas, for formal plantings, as a street tree where sufficient space is available and as a component of 'natural' woodland. It can suffer from aphids and honeydew but not as seriously as Common lime.

'Green Spire' makes a broadly conical tree.

'Swedish Upright' forms a slender erect crown with horizontal and slightly pendent branches.

T. × euchlora **Caucasian lime**

This tree, to 20m, has glossy green leaves, which turn light yellow in autumn. It does not suffer from aphids and honeydew, and consequently has been widely planted in recent years. It is fine as a young tree, but older ones are scarcely attractive with their winter tracery of a tangled mass of large downswept lower branches.

T. × europaea **Common lime**
(T. × vulgaris)

This is the commonest lime in cultivation but a very inferior tree, to 25–45m. The leaves are heavily affected by aphids, creating a honeydew problem. Often they are lost prematurely in early autumn due to a rust fungus.

'Pallida' forms a broadly conical tree, with the leaves yellowish green beneath.

'Wratislaviensis' has the new leaves yellow, changing to yellow-green.

T. mongolica Mongolia, N China & Pacific Russia
Mongolian lime

This makes a small tree, usually only 10m but capable of 20m when drawn up in woodland. The leaves are lobed and bear large triangular teeth.

T. 'mongolica × insularis' is a hybrid of Mongolian lime. It promises to make a vigorous small to medium sized tree with strongly toothed leaves.

T. oliveri **Oliver lime** C China

This makes a tree 10–25m tall with the foliage bright silver on the under side.

T. platyphyllos
Large leaved lime Britain & Europe

Large leaved lime is an uncommon native to Britain. It differs from Small leaved lime in the taller habit and larger leaves, and has been reported to 50m tall, although usually 25–30m.

'Aurea' has the one year old twigs golden yellow over winter.

'Fastigiata' makes a narrow crowned tree with the branches steeply ascending, suitable for situations where a tall narrow tree is appropriate.

'Rubra' is a form with reddish twigs in winter, giving a colourful display on a mature tree.

T. tomentosa
Silver lime SE Europe & Asia Minor

This tree has the leaves silver beneath and develops a dense rounded domed crown. A proportion of the leaves are carried so that the silvery white underside is visible in the distance. It makes a tree 20–35m tall. In certain conditions, the flowers contain a sugar which some bumble bees are not able to digest, and the bees can be found dead around the flowering tree. This condition is not unique to this species, as dead bumble bees can be found beneath common lime when there has been a prolonged dry spell prior to the flowering time.

'Petiolaris' or Pendent silver lime is very close to this species and best considered as a cultivar. It has longer petioles and the leaves and branches are carried hanging down. It makes a vigorous tree to 20–35m. The leaves of old trees are silvery beneath, but in young vigorous trees, the underside is much paler.

TRACHYCARPUS

Palmae

This is a small genus of palms.

T. fortunei **Chusan palm** C & S China

Chusan palm is the only palm which can be grown out of doors in southern England. It makes a tree eventually attaining 10m and has large palmate leaves, 1–1.5m across, and a fibrous covering to the stem (this appears to be the bark but is the basal part of the petiole). Young plants are more tender than the mature tree and should be protected for the first few winters. Its use is as a specimen tree or as a focal plant.

TSUGA

Hemlocks Pinaceae

This is a group of attractive evergreen conifers. They do not grow well in urban localities or where very exposed, and should be planted out whilst small.

T. canadensis
Eastern hemlock E North America

This is a bushy tree to 20–30m, often on several stems. It makes a broad dark green foliage plant.

T. heterophylla
Western hemlock W North America

This tree is one of the most beautiful of all evergreen trees when growing well, with an upright habit bearing pendulous foliage on horizontally spreading branches. It can remain attractive into old age, particularly in moist areas, and will make a tree 25–30m tall (to 50m). It is fast growing and has a single stem. It is well suited to acidic sandy soils, although will grow on chalky ones at the expense of becoming slightly yellow. It is also extremely tolerant of shade. Its uses are as an amenity tree, for underplanting or as a novel hedge.

T. mertensiana
Mountain hemlock W North America

This species has bluish or grey foliage and makes a narrow crowned tree, usually only 10–15m tall but up to 35m in cool moist conditions.

ULMUS

Elm Ulmaceae

The elms have been severely depleted by the ravages of Dutch elm disease (see page 121). Research and breeding is continuing into finding disease tolerant elms and there are a number which can be planted with some chance of success. It is sensible to make *small scale* plantings of these resistant forms, as only by trying the trees on a wide range of sites and conditions will future tree planters be able realistically to assess their value. Where there are existing trees, good sanitation practice and injecting with 'Ceratotect' fungicide can reduce the loss of trees. Elms are very good for seaside plantings, tolerating salt spray. They also make interesting amenity trees.

U. carpinifolia
Smooth leaved elm Europe

This tree has attractive foliage but is not resistant to Dutch elm disease.

39 *Young Western hemlock* (Tsuga heterophylla)

U. glabra **Wych elm** Britain & Europe

This is the only genuinely native British elm. It makes a tree with a domed crown.

U. procera **English elm**

This majestic hybrid tree is sterile, reproducing by suckers; it is not resistant to Dutch elm disease.

U. japonica
Japanese elm Japan & NE Asia

This makes a tree to 10–20m. Some forms, at least, are very resistant to the disease and worthy of trial. It will make a tree similar to Wych elm.

U. **'Sapporo Autumn Gold'**

This is a hybrid of Siberian elm (*U. pumila*) and Japanese elm which shows promise as a resistant tree.

ZELKOVA

Ulmaceae

This is a small genus of deciduous trees, related to the elms. They tolerate urban conditions and can be planted satisfactorily at normal sizes.

Z. carpinifolia
Caucasian elm Caucasus & N Iran

This is the best species for planting in Britain, where it makes a tree to 20–40m. The bark is smooth and grey, scaling to reveal orange patches. The crown is an upright ovoid dome, with many erect stems. It will grow on a wide range of soils, including over chalk or limestone. It is long lived, although of slow growth, and suitable as a specimen tree.

Z. serrata **Keaki** Japan

This tree makes a lower tree 15–20m, with a more spreading branch system. The leaves often turn a good red or orange in autumn. It is suitable as an amenity tree for parks and large gardens.

Trees for Specific Sites

The following lists give genera suitable for specific sites. More information is given in the Gazetteer section, to which reference should be made. In some genera, not all the species have the listed characteristic.

List 1 · Tree Genera NOT Suitable for Chalk Soils

Most genera of trees have species which will grow satisfactorily on chalk soils, although not all will thrive, especially if the soil over the chalk is thin. The following is a list of the principal genera which will not grow, or will not grow well, on these soils. See also Chapter 2, pages 30–2.

Castanea
Embothrium
Halesia
Liquidambar
Nothofagus
Nyssa
Stuartia
Styrax
Taxodium

List 2 · Tree Genera with Species Suitable for Heavy Clay Soils

Most trees will be very slow to establish on heavy soils. Drainage will speed up establishment or young trees can be mound planted.

Abies
Acer
Aesculus
Alnus
Amelanchier
Araucaria
Calocedrus
Carpinus
Chamaecyparis
Cornus
Corylus
Crataegus
Cupressocyparis
Eucalyptus
Fraxinus
Ginkgo
Ilex
Juniperus
Laburnum
Larix
Liquidambar
Magnolia
Malus
Metasequoia
Picea
Pinus
Platanus
Populus
Prunus
Pseudotsuga
Pterocarya
Pyrus
Quercus
Salix
Sequoia
Sequoiadendron
Sorbus (Whitebeams)
Taxodium
Taxus
Thuja
Thujopsis
Tilia
Tsuga

List 3 · Tree Genera with Species Suitable for Wet/Boggy Soils

As the soil changes from wet to boggy, the number of species which will thrive will be reduced and only the genera marked with a ⋆ contain species capable of growing in extremely wet situations where there is free water on the soil surface.

⋆*Alnus*
Amelanchier
Betula
Carpinus
Cryptomeria
Crataegus
Eucalyptus
Metasequoia
Nyssa
Picea
Pinus
Populus
⋆*Pterocarya*
Pyrus
Quercus
⋆*Salix*
⋆*Taxodium*
⋆*Thuja (slow on very wet sites)*

List 4 · Tree Genera with Species Suitable for Dry/Sandy Soils

The rate of growth of most trees will be much slower on these soils than on 'normal' loams. The genera marked with a ⋆ contain species which will grow as or nearly as fast on these dry soils.

Acer	⋆*Gleditsia*
Alnus	*Ilex*
Ailanthus	⋆*Juniperus*
⋆*Betula*	*Koelreuteria*
⋆*Castanea*	*Larix*
Cercidiphyllum	⋆*Pinus*
⋆*Cercis*	*Populus*
Chamaecyparis	⋆*Robinia*
Cupressocyparis	*Taxus*
⋆*Cupressus*	*Thuja*
Fraxinus	*Thujopsis*
Ginkgo	⋆*Tsuga*

List 5 · Trees Suitable for Narrow Upright Situations, e.g. as Street Trees for Confined Sites

Those marked with a ⋆ may or will eventually grow more than 15m tall.

⋆*Acer lobelii*
⋆*A. platanoides* 'Columnare'
⋆*Alnus cordata*
⋆*Betula pendula* 'Fastigiata'
⋆*Chamaecyparis* – most
⋆*Corylus colurna*
Crataegus chlorosarca
C. monogyna 'Stricta'
⋆*Fagus sylvatica* 'Dawyck'
⋆*Ginkgo biloba*
Juniperus chinensis 'Obelisk'
Malus trilobata
M. tschonoskii
M. yunnanensis veitchii
⋆*Picea omorika*
⋆*Populus nigra* 'Italica'
Prunus 'Hillieri Spire'
P. sargentii 'Rancho'
P. × *schmittii*
P. 'Snow Goose'
P. 'Umineko'
Pyrus betulifolius
P. calleryana 'Chanticleer'
P. communis 'Beech Hill'
Sorbus – many

List 6 · Tree Genera with Species with Attractive Flowers

Genus	Month of the Year
Abies	5/6
Acacia	3
Acer	4
Amelanchier	4
Arbutus	10
Castanea	7
Catalpa	6/8
Cercis	5
Cladrastis	6/7
Cornus	3, 6/7
Corylus	4
Cotoneaster	6
Crataegus	5
Davidia	5
Embothrium	5/6
Eucryphia	7/9
Euodia	9
Fraxinus	5/6
Halesia	5
Koelreuteria	7/8
Laburnum	6
Ligustrum	7/10
Magnolia	3/10
Parrotia	3/4
Paulownia	5
Picea	5
Pinus	6
Prunus	2/12
Pyrus	4
Robinia	6
Salix	3, 6
Sophora	7/8
Sorbus	5/6
Stuartia	7/8
Styrax	6
Tilia	7/9

List 7 · Tree Genera with Species with Attractive Fruits

Abies	*Arbutus*
Acer	*Cedrus*

Cornus
Cotoneaster
Crataegus
Ilex
Malus
Morus
Picea
Pinus
Prunus
Pterocarya
Sorbus
Taxus

List 8 · Tree Genera with Species with Bold/Architectural Foliage

Aesculus
Ailanthus
Aralia
Catalpa
Gymnocladus
Idesia
Juglans
Liriodendron
Paulownia
Populus
Pterocarya
Trachycarpus

List 9 · Tree Genera with Species with Fast Growth Rates

Abies
Alnus
Betula
Cryptomeria
Cupressocyparis
Eucalyptus
Fraxinus
Larix
Nothofagus
Picea
Pinus
Platanus
Pseudotsuga
Pterocarya
Salix
Sequoia
Sequoiadendron
Thuja
Tsuga

List 10 · Tree Genera needing Extra Care on Planting

Apart from a general requirement that evergreens need extra care, the information in the Gazetteer section should be consulted concerning the following genera.

Davidia
Embothrium
Eucalyptus
Euodia
Liriodendron
Magnolia
Nothofagus

List 11 · Tree Genera with Species with Evergreen Foliage

Abies
Acacia
Araucaria
Arbutus
Calocedrus
Cedrus
Chamaecyparis
Cotoneaster
Cryptomeria
Cupressus
Embothrium
Eucalyptus
Genista
Ilex
Juniperus
Ligustrum
Maytenus
Nothofagus
Phillyrea
Photinia
Picea
Pinus
Platycladus
Podocarpus
Pseudotsuga
Prunus
Quercus
Sequoia
Sequoiadendron
Taxus
Thuja
Thujopsis
Trachycarpus
Tsuga

List 12 · Tree Genera with Species with Attractive Bark/Twigs

A ⋆ indicates that the tree has an attractive winter twig, rather than an outstanding bark.

Acer griseum and 'Snakebark maples'
Arbutus unedo
A. menziesii
Betula most
Corylus colurna
Eucalyptus most
⋆*Fraxinus excelsior* 'Jaspidea'
⋆*Larix decidua*
⋆*L. kaempferi*
Phellodendron amurense
Pinus sylvestris
Platanus × *hispanica*
Quercus × *hispanica*
⋆*Salix* several
Sequoia sempervirens
Sequoiadendron giganteum
Stuartia pseudocamellia
⋆*Tilia platyphyllos* cultivars

List 13 · Tree Genera with Species with Outstanding Autumn Colour

Acer several
Amelanchier lamarkii
Betula most
Cercidiphyllum japonicum
Crataegus × *prunifolia*
Fagus sylvatica

Fraxinus most
Ginkgo biloba
Larix all
Liquidambar styraciflua
Liriodendron tulipifera
Malus transitoria
M. trilobata
M. tschonoskii
M. yunnanensis veitchii
Metasequoia glyptostroboides
Nyssa sylvatica
Parrotia persica
Populus several
Prunus several
Pseudolarix amabilis
Pyrus calleryana 'Chanticleer'
Quercus coccinea
Q. palustris
Q. rubra
Rhus typhina
Sorbus many Rowans
Taxodium distichum

List 14 · Tree Cultivars with Variegated Foliage

Acer negundo 'Elegans', 'Variegatum'
A. platanoides 'Drummondii'
A. pseudoplatanus 'Leopoldii', 'Nizetti'
Castanea sativa 'Albomarginatum', 'Aureomarginatum'
Chamaecyparis several
Cornus controversa 'Variegata'
C. kousa 'Gold Star', 'Snow Boy'
C. mas 'Aurea Elegantissima', 'Variegata'
Ilex × *altaclerensis* 'Golden King', 'Lawsoniana'
I. aquifolium 'Golden Queen'
Ligustrum lucidum 'Excelsum Suberbum', 'Tricolor'
Liquidambar styraciflua 'Aurea', 'Golden Treasure'
Liriodendron tulipiferum 'Aureomarginatum'
Platanus × *hispanica* 'Suttneri'
Populus × *candicans* 'Aurora'
Taxus baccata 'Dovastonii Aurea'
Thuja plicata 'Zebrina'

List 15 · Tree Genera with Species with Purple Foliage

Acer campestre 'Schwerinii'
A. palmatum 'Atropurpureum' and forms
A. platanoides 'Crimson King', 'Goldsworth Purple', 'Schwedleri'
A. pseudoplatanus 'Atropurpureum'
Betula pendula 'Purpurea'
Catalpa × *erubescens* 'Purpurea'
Cercis canadensis 'Forest Pansy'
Corylus maxima 'Purpurea'
Fagus several
Prunus cerasifera 'Pissardii'

List 16 · Tree Genera with Species with Gold/Yellow Foliage

Acer campestre 'Postelense'
A. cappadocicum 'Aureum'
A. japonicum 'Aureum'
A. negundo 'Auratum'
A. pseudoplatanus 'Worleei'
Alnus glutinosa 'Aureum'
A. incana 'Aureum', 'Ramulis Coccineus'
Chamaecyparis lawsoniana several
C. obtusa 'Crippsii'
Cupressocyparis leylandii 'Castlewellan', 'Robinson's Gold'
Cupressus macrocarpa 'Donard Gold', 'Goldcrest', 'Lutea'
Fagus sylvatica 'Dawyck Gold', 'Zlatia'
Fraxinus excelsior 'Jaspidea'
Gleditsia triacanthos 'Sunburst'
Juniperus chinensis 'Aurea'
Picea orientalis 'Aurea'
Pinus sylvestris 'Aurea'
Populus 'Serotina Aurea'
Quercus rubra 'Aurea'
Robinia pseudacacia 'Frisia'
Sorbus aria 'Chrysophylla'
Thuja plicata 'Aurea'
Tilia × *europaea* 'Wratislaviensis'

List 17 · Tree Genera with Species with Grey/Silver/Blue Foliage

Abies several (leaf underside)
Cedrus atlantica glauca
Chamaecyparis several
Cupressocyparis leylandii 'Naylor's Blue'

Cupressus glabra
Eucalyptus several
Hippophae rhamnoides
Juniperus several
Picea pungens glauca several
Pinus several
Populus several (leaf underside)
Pseudotsuga menziesii glauca
Pyrus salicifolia
Salix alba 'Sericea'
Sorbus (Whitebeams)
Thuja koraiensis (leaf underside)
Tilia tomentosa and 'Petiolaris'
Tsuga mertensiana

List 18 · Tree Genera with Species with Attractive Non-Green New Foliage

Acer cappodocicum 'Rubrum'
A. pseudoplatanus 'Brilliantissimum'
Kalopanax pictus
Prunus several
Quercus several, especially *Q. rubra* 'Aurea'
Sequoia sempervirens 'Adpressa'
Sorbus several

List 19 · Trees with Aromatic Foliage or Shoots

In some of these species, the aroma is only released when the leaf is crushed or the bark scraped off a shoot.

Abies several
Cercidiphyllum japonicum
Cupressus several
Eucalyptus several
Euodia daniellii
E. hupehensis
Laurus nobilis
Magnolia salicifolia
Nothofagus antarctica
Phellodendron amurense
Pinus several
Populus × *candicans*
P. trichocarpa
Ptelea trifoliata
Thuja koraiensis
T. plicata

List 20 · Tree Genera with Species with Fragrant Flowers

Aesculus
Cercis
Cladrastis
Crataegus
Eucryphia
Laburnum
Ligustrum
Malus
Paulownia
Phillyrea
Prunus
Robinia
Sorbus
Styrax
Tilia

List 21 · Tree Genera with Wildlife Value

This includes plants which have value for either food or shelter. Food can be in the form of seeds or nuts, or by supporting a rich variety of insects. This list is not exhaustive!

Acer
Alnus
Amelanchier
Betula
Chamaecyparis
Corylus
Cotoneaster
Crataegus
Fagus
Fraxinus
Ilex
Juniperus
Larix
Malus
Picea
Pinus
Prunus
Quercus
Salix
Sequoia
Sequoiadendron
Sorbus
Taxus
Tilia

List 22 · Tree Species Suitable for use in exposed locations

Most of these species are appropriate for use in Shelterbelts. Those marked with a ⋆ will tolerate exposure to sea winds.

⋆*Acer pseudoplatanus*
Alnus all
Betula pendula
Carpinus betulus
⋆*Crataegus monogyna*
⋆*Cupressocyparis leylandii*
⋆*Eucalyptus gunnii*
Fagus sylvatica
⋆*Fraxinus excelsior*
⋆*Ilex* × *altaclerensis* 'Hodginsii'
I. aquifolium (understorey)

**Picea sitchensis*
**Pinus nigra* and others
**Quercus ilex*
**Q. robur*
**Salix alba*
**Sorbus aria*
Thuja plicata
Tilia several
**Ulmus* (not recommended for large scale planting)

List 23 · Tree Genera with Species Suitable for Longterm Avenues

Many tree species will make good avenues for beside a drive or other small-scale and short-term feature; the following genera contain species useful for the creation of avenues which are likely to last upwards of 70 years.

Acer several
Aesculus several
Araucaria araucana
Carpinus betulus
Castanea sativa
Cedrus several
Chamaecyparis lawsoniana
Corylus colurna
Cryptomeria japonica
Fagus sylvatica
Fraxinus several
Ginkgo biloba
Juglans regia
Liriodendron tulipiferum
Pinus several
Platanus several
Pyrus calleryana 'Chanticleer'
Pterocarya fraxinifolia
Quercus several
Sequoia sempervirens
Sequoiadendron giganteum
Thuja plicata
Tilia several

List 24 · Tree Genera Suitable for use on Land Reclamation sites

Species which can fix atmospheric nitrogen are marked with a ⋆.

Acer
**Alnus*
Carpinus
Crataegus
Cupressocyparis
Larix
Picea
Pinus
Populus
Quercus
**Robinia*
Salix
Sorbus
Thuja

Bibliography

The following is a short list of other books which provide more information on trees.

1. W. J. Bean, *Trees and Shrubs hardy in the British Isles*, 8th edition, 1970-80, 4 vols, John Murray, London. Reference tome to plants in general cultivation in the UK.

2. *European Garden Flora*, 1984–, vols 1-5, Cambridge University Press, Cambridge.

3. G. Krusmann, *Manual of Cultivated Conifers*, 1985, Batsford, London. Comprehensive with respect to named cultivars. Originally published in German, 1972.

4. G. Krusmann, *Manual of Cultivated Broadleaved Trees and Shrubs*, 1985, Batsford, London. Comprehensive with respect to named cultivars. Originally published in German, 1972.

5. H. G. Hillier, *Hillier's Manual of Trees and Shrubs*, 1972, David & Charles, Newton Abbot, Devon.

6. *Hillier Colour Dictionary of Trees and Shrubs*, 1981, David & Charles, Newton Abbot, Devon.

7. K. D. Rushforth, *Conifers*, 1987, Christopher Helm, London.

8. K. D. Rushforth, *Mitchell Beazley Pocket Guide to Trees*, 1980, Mitchell Beazley, London.

9. A. F. Mitchell, *A Field Guide to Trees of Britain and Northern Europe*, 1974, Collins, London.

10. A. F. Mitchell & J. Jobling, *Decorative Trees for Country, Town and Garden*, 1984, HMSO, London.

Index